Quinton Brandon
"The Marshal Who Tamed Zwolle"

by
Robert Roy Gentry
and
Patricia Brandon Martinez

Edited by
Catherine Vines Davis

Published by
Sweet Dreams Publishing Company
P. O. Box 850 ~ Many, La. 71449
Ph. (318) 256-3495 FAX (318) 256-9151
PRINTED IN THE UNITED STATES OF AMERICA

Quinton Brandon
"The Marshal Who Tamed Zwolle"

ABOUT THE COVER

The items used for the cover photo are authentic from Quinton Brandon. They include his Smith and Wesson .357 Magnum, which he started out using in 1946 when he began his law enforcement career. At left are his white Stetson hat and his shirt, with the American flag sewn on the sleeve. Two of his patches are shown, one with the word "Chief," the other with "Chief of Police." Also shown are some of his U.S. Army badges and medals, his boots, his slapjack, his handcuffs and several other items. Photo of Marshal Brandon courtesy of his daughter, Becky Loupe.

ABOUT THE PHOTOGRAPHER

JOHN CURTIS GUILLET of Natchitoches, Louisiana took the photo for the cover. Mr. Guillet has operated Guillet Photography for many years and is renown as one of the country's most outstanding photographers. He has taken cover photos for many books during his long and distinguished career.

ABOUT THE GRAPHICS COMPOSITER

PRINCE SEAN JOHNSON was the graphics compositor for this edition. He has been employed at *The Sabine Index,* a Many, Louisiana newspaper, for two years. He has a long-time interest in art, computer programming and computer composition.

ISBN 1-893693-00-7
Copyright © 1999
Library of Congress Catalog Card Number: 98-091132

Printed 1999 in the United States of America

Zwolle Marshal
Quinton Brandon

An Introduction

When Quinton Brandon died, he took with him a kind of law enforcement that will probably never been seen in these parts of Louisiana again. He was an officer who came along at the right time to fulfill a mission, a duty and a calling. He was Matt Dillon, Wyatt Earp, Buford Pusser and John Wayne all rolled into one. He was definitely one of a kind. He was 'Walking Tall' long before it was popular to do so.

Like many country folk of that long ago era, he was born into poverty. But back then country folk didn't know they were poor because everyone around them was in the same boat. They didn't know how things were outside their boundary and just accepted being poor as a way of life. This gave him a compassion for people that would stay with him the rest of his life.

Brandon lived through the Great Depression doing the best he and his family could. When World War II came along, being the Great American that he was, Brandon volunteered for the U.S. Army. He rose quickly in rank and distinguished himself as a serviceman.

He came back to Zwolle in 1946 looking for work. He was hired as marshal and then left that job for work as an investigator with the Louisiana Forestry Commission, then with the Louisiana State Police and finally back home to stay as marshal.

Zwolle was a lawless and mean place back in the l940's and early 1950's from all accounts. Drunkenness, fights, cuttings, shootings, murders and urinating in the streets were a way of life. As a young man, Brandon had seen all these things. It worried him that a woman or a black couldn't walk down the street without being harassed. He vowed to do something about it.

In order to clean up the town and survive, Brandon had to be fearless. He had to look death in the face, again over and over, and smirk. Folks who knew him said there wasn't a scared bone in his body. He was fearless.

Brandon had a strong belief in doing his duty. He never shirked from duty, regardless of the circumstances or possible outcome.

During his career, his reputation as "one tough nut" spread far and wide, among both law-abiding citizens and criminals. Word had it that he had killed at least a half dozen men. The fact is he only killed one, but did have to shoot a few others along the way. He used his .357 magnum pistol as a club when the need arose and used his fists to fight countless times if he had to.

In his lifetime, he underwent many trials and tribulations including bootlegging, integration and an attempted by the mayor and city council to remove him from office. He withstood these and many other storms of life.

He could handle almost any hand life delt him, but the loss of a son and grandson almost caused him to loose the will to live. He overcame these tragic events and then he was felled by a stroke.

By sheer hard work, determination and the will to live, he came back strong from the disabling stroke. But it would be about fifteen years later before he would feel the cold hand of death.

His is the story of one of the last of the old "Wild West" marshals. He was a man who came along at the right time and made a difference in life for so many people. His life was worth living and now is worth reading about.

Foreword

First of all, I want to thank my cousin, Lanty H. Wyle of Tyler, Texas who, beginning a couple of years ago, encouraged me to start writing again. Without his kind words, this book might not have come about.

Now, let's turn back the pages of time to the summer of 1960. I was a journalism student at Northwestern State University in Natchitoches, Louisiana and had been lucky enough to land a job as Public Relations Man for the late-great Earl Kemp Long, in his last race. He had served as governor twice, but this time he was seeking election as congressman from Louisiana's Eighth District.

It was Saturday afternoon, June 18, as Earl's driver and bodyguard, the late Dick Davis, pulled the big white Buick into Zwolle. As we stopped, Uncle Earl looked at me in the back seat and pointed to a law officer who was coming toward the car.

"That's Quinton Brandon," Uncle Earl said, "and if you want to carry Zwolle, you've got to have him with you. And he's with me." That was the first time I met the "Marshal Who Tamed Zwolle."

I never saw him again until 1965 when I came to Many as editor of *The Sabine Index*. Quinton and I did not readily become hard, fast friends. I found he was cautious about who his friends were and that you had to prove yourself to him.

Through the years, I think I did that and we became good friends. In doing research for this book, I looked through back issues of *The Index* from 1940 to date. I refreshed my memory that *The Index* always supported Quinton and spoke well of him.

I have spent many hours doing research and writing this book and have enjoyed every one of them. I told Mrs. Nannie Brandon that doing the research made it seem as if I had gotten to know Quinton all over again. That alone made the project worthwhile.

Robert Roy Gentry
Many, Louisiana
January 5, 1999

6

Foreword II

"Big" is the word I always think of when I remember my Uncle Quinton. From the time I first saw him, when I was a little girl, I could see that big hat he wore and that big gun he carried. I can hear that big, gruff voice. As we began doing research for this book, I was astonished to discover he was actually only six foot, one inch tall. He always seemed so much larger than that to me.

His oldest son, Jerry, and I were the same age. Sometimes other kids could be difficult about Uncle Quinton being a "lawman" and would voice their opinions about him. One time I felt it necessary to get into an argument with a girl after such an out-burst. When Jerry heard about it he told me, "Pat, you don't have to take up for Daddy. He doesn't need or want us defending him." Jerry was right. He knew his daddy well. Uncle Quinton had his own code of honor. He always did what he thought was the right thing to do at the time and he never second-guessed himself. He lived by his decisions and never worried about what other people thought. He was true to himself and his convictions. He was the most self-assured person I have ever known.

When I was in elementary school, Uncle Quinton came to talk to us about "Being Good Citizens." All the other kids were just a little bit afraid of him. After all, he was a "lawman" and he had a gun. If you were bad, he could put you in jail. I wanted all the kids to know he was my uncle. My heart swelled with pride when he saw me and said, "Pat, come over here and give your 'ole Uncle a hug." I couldn't get there fast enough.

Throughout the years, no matter how old I was, or where I was, each time I saw him he said the same thing to me again. And each time I felt the same way I had in grade school—so very proud he was my uncle.

Patricia Brandon Martinez
Zwolle, Louisiana
January 14, 1999

Acknowledgements

No undertaking of this magnitude could be possible without the help of a lot of people. There were many who helped and without them this endeavor would not have been possible.

First of all, thanks to Linda Procell of Baton Rouge, Louisiana, the person who proposed the book. She is a native of Noble, Louisiana and had known and admired Quinton Brandon all her life.

Second, thanks go to Mrs. Nannie Brandon and members of the Brandon family for their help, encouragement, and support thoughout this project. When this project was just a seed, the first thing we did was contact Mrs. Brandon for her support, assistance and cooperation. She gladly gave all three.

Mrs. Catherine Vines Davis assisted us greatly in being editor for the book. The many contributions she made greatly improved the book. We could never thank her enough. Mrs. Josephine Barbee Gibson, the great niece of the Reverend Sam Holladay, ably and gladly assisted her. We appreciate this very much.

Next, our thanks go to the Sabine Parish Library for a lot of assistance from Librarian Becky Morris, Branch Manager Mary Wedgeworth and the entire staff. We researched the files of *The Sabine Index* from 1940 to date, plus a lot of other items. Tedd Dumas with KWLV and KWLA radio stations and the Illini Cable Television in Many, Louisiana assisted with promotion. We thank him for that.

Dr. George Douglas Brandon of Leesville, Louisiana graciously assisted in every way possible. Others we need to single out are Kenneth Edwards of Alexandria, Louisiana, Keith Brandon of Hemphill, Texas, and Sergeant William Davis with the Louisiana State Police in Baton Rouge, Louisiana.

Also going above and beyond the call of duty to assist were Mrs. Evelyn Hopkins of Zwolle, Louisiana, and Mrs. Wanda Heflin and Sean Johnson of *The Sabine Index* staff.

To all those who shared information with us, to those who took time to assist, and to those who just said a kind word of encouragement along the way, we say thank you.

Robert Roy Gentry
Patricia Brandon Martinez

Contents

Chapter 1

Johnnie McComic

"Greater love hath no man than this,
that he lay down his life for his friends."
—from the book of St. John

Zwolle's first marshal lost his life in the line of duty in 1898. The Louisiana town was rough and rowdy even back then. Johnnie H. McComic was appointed marshal even before the town was officially incorporated. The town was rough from the beginning and for many years thereafter it remained the same. This was the frontier remnants of a no-man's land until a marshal came along named Quinton Brandon, popularly referred to as "The Marshal Who Tamed Zwolle."

But first, one must turn back the pages of time to Saturday afternoon, March 19, 1898, at about 5:30. McComic was in his first year as marshal on that fateful day.

Everyone who knew him said that he was a good man; well almost everyone. He was born at nearby Clyde on August 15, 1871. He married Miss Bettie Parrott. They later had two adorable young sons. The young couple loved Zwolle. He built his family a house just across the street from the Methodist Church. In fact, he helped build the Methodist Church.

Zwolle had been established in 1896. During the first year of Zwolle's existence, there had been no marshal; it was every man for himself. Then they hired McComic to bring law and order to the new town. The job was big, but he felt he could handle the town's law enforcement. He fought some battles, but felt he had made progress also, even though he still had a long way to go.

Johnnie McComic, Zwolle's first marshal, died in a street shoot-out at the age of twenty-eight years in 1896. He is buried at Parrott Cemetery and his wife wrote on his stone: "Sleep darling sleep; Many tears I have shed since you went to sleep."

However all that was not on his mind as that March day was coming to a close. The end of winter was in sight and spring was just around the corner. The day had been beautiful. He looked upward to the skies and the sun had begun to set in the West streaking the sky with glorious reds, yellows, and golds. It was one of his favorite times of day. A few birds were still singing and he could smell the fragrance of yellow jasmine. He was glad to be alive.

From the beginning, folks said that Zwolle was a tough town. Although it was Saturday, the day that folks from the outlying areas usually came to town, the day had been relatively uneventful. McComic's thoughts were of going home soon and seeing his family and of going to church the next day. He always went to church.

The marshal thought that he would make one more round through town before going home for supper. He usually came back and kept watch around town on Saturday night, because there were always those who got drunk and sometimes fought and cut and shot.

McComic was a handsome man. He was well thought of by those around Zwolle. Everyone liked him and spoke well of him; that is except those he either had to arrest or to send home.

He always wore a hat. He thought lawmen should be dressed well. They should be distinguished looking and they should always wear a hat, he believed. That afternoon was somewhat on the chilly side, so he had put on his long black leather coat. He had his badge on. He always wore that badge. He was proud of the symbol and wanted everyone else to be as proud of the law insignia as he was. Unfortunately, that was not the case.

As he started down the street, he suddenly heard a commotion and rushed across the alley to see what the problem was. On his way there, he found several other people already running in the same direction.

When he got there, he found Nick Sepulvado, a

man who lived not far from Zwolle. He knew Nick well. He was one of those who came to town on occasion to drink and to have a good time and most of those good times for Nick meant trouble for Johnnie. Nick was a man of about thirty-five years with a quarrelsome disposition. He was always having problems with somebody. He liked to drink and he would fight, or cut or shoot at the drop of a hat, anybody's hat.

When he was drinking, he was mean and this was one of those days. The first thing McComic did was to tell the gathering crowd to get back.

"Move back," he ordered. "I'm afraid there's going to be trouble. I don't want anybody to get hurt. Get back and do it now." When he first arrived on the scene, he noticed the image of a pistol bulging from Sepulvado's back pocket.

McComic tried at first to reason with Sepulvado, but did not have any success. He had had to arrest Sepulvado many times in the past and he did not look forward to doing it again. Sepulvado was a big, strong, husky man—much bigger and stronger than McComic. But McComic held his position of trust as Zwolle Marshal very highly and he always did his duty. He liked the words of Confederate General Robert E. Lee, "You can never do more than your duty. You should never do less." Those thoughts were what he tried to live by.

"Come on Nick," McComic said patiently. "You have no reason to try to start a fight with Joe over there. He doesn't want to fight you. All he wants is for you to go home. Now come on Nick, let's go down to the jail and let you cool off a bit and then I'll turn you loose and you can go home and so can I."

"Hell no!" Sepulvado yelled back quickly as he staggered on the board sidewalk. "I ain't going home. I'm gonna fight. I can fight Joe or I can fight you. It just don't matter to me."

McComic had always bent over backward to be fair. Most of the time when he had problems with Sepulvado, he would let him cool off or sober up in jail and then send him home. That was all he wanted this night.

Sepulvado started walking toward McComic with his hand toward his back, although he did not appear to have it on his pistol. Sepulvado was wearing an old jacket that hung past his waist, so McComic could not see whether he was drawing his gun or not.

McComic had seen Sepulvado in action too many times during the last year. When he was drinking, not only was he mean, but he was also stubborn and hard to handle. A person just could not reason with him and nothing made McComic think things would be any different this time. He knew that he had to move and move fast. First he had to get the gathering crowd back once again and then he had to make his play. And he had to do it all very quickly. He did not want an innocent person to get hurt.

"Get back all of you!" McComic yelled. He glanced around and saw people looking from behind doors, from windows and around the corners of buildings.

McComic, who was about fifteen feet away, made a running leap to try and knock Sepulvado to the ground in order to disarm him, but the man was too fast. Sepulvado had already pulled his pistol from his back pocket and had kept the weapon hidden under his coat. At a range of just a few feet, he shot McComic. The bullet pierced his stomach and he could immediately feel the warm flow of blood running down his belly and legs. He knew it was serious; he did not have to have a doctor look at it to tell him that. However, he also knew he had something else to do.

With all the strength he could garner, McComic rolled over and at the same time drew his .38 revolver from its leather holster. Sepulvado felt good about shooting McComic and was looking around with a grin on his face. He was not paying any attention to what McComic was doing. From the ground, McComic bravely fired three shots into Sepulvado. Two of them entered his body and the third penetrated his heart, killing him instantly.

McComic dropped his pistol and put his hand on his stomach. The wound was big and deep and blood continued to flow. Folks came running from all around to help the downed marshal. He was immediately brought to Dr. N.C. Stone's office, where he was cleaned up and the wound bandaged.

Dr. Stone tried to find the bullet but could not. He had probed for it all he could; McComic just could not stand any more of the agonizing pain. He had lost a lot of blood and Dr. Stone was also afraid that infection would set in.

McComic wanted to go home and Dr. Stone said that he could. Some of the town's men put a mattress in the back of a wagon bed. They carefully put McComic on the mattress and headed for his home.

As the wagon approached, Mrs. McComic came running out of the house. Their two sons followed her, even though she had told them to stay inside. She had heard the commotion downtown earlier and had feared what it might be. Johnnie would not allow her to come near him when he was on duty. This was not a rule she liked, but she obeyed his wishes.

She lived with the fear of something happening to him ever since he had taken the job. But this evening, when she heard the gunshots, in her heart she knew. She did not want to know, but she did. She put it off as long as possible, but when the wagon pulled into their yard, she had to go out and face the facts.

Her heart was pounding as she saw Johnnie in the back of the wagon, the crimson blood all over his pants. His face was ashen and his voice was weak. She looked at him and remembered that he was only twenty-eight years old—much too young to die and leave her to raise two young boys alone.

They took Johnnie into the house and put him in bed. Brother Sam Holladay, the parson at the Methodist Church, and a group of women arrived to pray and keep a vigil and help in any way they could. One by one, others from around town arrived.

16

Bettie sat on Johnnie's bed and held his hand and cried. He did not need that, but she could not restrain herself. She felt so helpless. It seemed that was all she could do. She kept cool cloths on his brow to try to bring him some comfort. He held her hand and told Bettie he loved her and that he was going to be all right. She knew differently. She had known from the first moment when she saw him in the wagon.

As the night wore on, they could see his condition deteriorate by the hour. Dr. Stone had come, but he told them there was nothing more he could do; that it was in God's hands. This made Brother Holladay and the women of the church pray longer and louder. McComic now had a high fever and the debilitation was getting worse. The cool, wet cloths on his brow helped some, but not enough.

By midnight, McComic's voice was almost inaudible and he was continually getting weaker. The fever was running higher and he was in and out of consciousness. He was talking, but it was rambling and delirious. At 3:00 a.m. that Sunday, he lost all consciousness. At 10:00 a.m., he died.

His funeral was held the next day at the Methodist Church that he had helped build and loved so much. Folks from all around Zwolle filled the church to capacity and many mourners stood outside by the window trying to hear Brother Holladay's message.

Brother Holladay said that those who knew Johnnie held him in highest esteem for his sterling qualities of both head and heart. The parson said that McComic was honorable and upright in all his dealings and stood high in the community in the defense of peace and order, for which he lost his life.

The folks in Zwolle remembered the fine family to which he had been a member. They remembered him as cool, nervy, and a fearless man, as demonstrated by the affray in which he killed his assailant after being mortally wounded.

After the service, family and friends viewed the

17

marshal's body one last time. Tears filled their eyes as memories flooded their minds and sadness and hurt filled their hearts. Marshal Johnnie McComic was taken on his last ride and was buried beneath the red clay of Sabine Parish in the nearby Parrott Cemetery. He was gone, but he would never be forgotten. On his headstone, his wife wrote those words: "Sleep darling sleep; Many tears I have shed since you went to sleep."

The tragedy caused intense excitement in Zwolle and the death of the courageous officer was deeply deplored by the citizens.

Dr. Stone was so moved by the death that he was motivated to write a piece in *The Shreveport Times*, a newspaper published in Shreveport, Louisiana, which was carried in the March 31, 1898, edition, as follows:

"Once more the grim monster, death, has visited one of our happy homes and true to the adage, 'Death leaves a shining mock,' has robbed that home of its founder and protector, Johnnie H. McComic, while faithfully performing his duties as town marshal of Zwolle March 19, received a wound from which he died on Sunday, March 20, 1898, at 10:00 o'clock. He leaves a young wife and two lovely little boys and a great many friends and relatives to mourn his untimely death. Johnnie was a young man whom to know was to love. He was honest, brave and true, a model husband, and above all, he was a Christian, having professed religion and joined the Methodist church and died triumphant. Oh, what a comfort to those of us who knew and loved him, to know that while we can not call him back from that great beyond we can one day go to him in that beautiful home above where no sad parting ever comes and where sickness, sorrow, pain nor death are felt or feared no more in this beautiful city of gold where no marshals are needed to enforce the one and only law, the supreme law of love. May the great loving Father protect and guide the sorrowing wife and help her raise up her boys in His nurture and admonition and at last may they be gathered an unbroken family around His great white throne are the wishes of one who loved him."

The die was cast. Zwolle had been born a rough and rowdy town. The first marshal had given his all for law and order, but it was not enough. And in doing so, he left a wife and two young boys. He had crossed over that river much too early, but he left a legacy behind. It would be many more years—more than fifty—before the tamer of Zwolle would finally come along.

Chapter 2

The Birth of Zwolle

"Zwolle was born out of necessity."
—A thought

Quinton Brandon once said that Zwolle had the reputation of being the roughest town on the Kansas City Southern (KCS) line.

The KCS Railroad many years earlier had led to the birth of Zwolle. In 1895 the KCS completed its railroad from Kansas City, Missouri to Shreveport. Soon a committee of Dutch stockholders arrived in America for a first hand look at the project. After the committee reported favorably, the stockholders decided to extend the line from Shreveport to a point twelve miles north of Beaumont, Texas, in order to connect between Kansas City and the Gulf of Mexico.

With this news, the folks along the proposed route became excited about vantage points for KCS depots. In the beginning Clyde, located about a mile northwest of Zwolle, had tentatively been selected as one site.

However, at this time William Pott, a one-time engineer and one of the largest landowners in the area, and Teofilo Laroux, another landowner, made plans for getting the new depot built in what would become Zwolle. They were successful and each man donated twenty acres to the Kansas Terminal Construction Company. That became a forty acre square around the soon to be constructed depot.

In 1896 the Arkansas Townsite Company laid off lots and Louis B. Gay, Sr., as the local agent, sold practically all the plots in a short time.

By September 19, 1896, the railroad was extended to Zwolle and on September 11, 1897, the last

21

spike was driven and the line was complete from Kansas City to the gulf.

Zwolle was named in 1896 by Jan DeGoeijen (the name is pronounced DeQueen, and DeQueen, Arkansas was named after him), a KCS stockholder, for his birthplace, Zwolle, the capital of the Province of Overijssel, Netherlands. He has been referred to as "Zwolle's Godfather." There have been erroneous historical reports through the years that the town was named after DeGoeijen's daughter.

The story has been told that upon his first visit to the area, DeGoeijen was impressed by the inhabitants and the land area; and because he was Catholic, he esteemed and revered the St. Joseph's Catholic Church. The church was a product of the early Spanish missionaries. The church stood silhouetted against the pines on a hill overlooking the townsite and the peaceful valley below. He also gave financial aid to Zwolle's founding.

Arriving by train, DeGoeijen took pictures of the town and mailed letters from there to his friends back home. After he went back to Holland, DeGoeijen kept a relationship with the people in Zwolle until his death in 1944.

The first inhabitants of the bowl-shaped area of land, which later became Zwolle, were possibly the Mound Builders. Historians have surmised that these early people were lured to the area for protection from severe weather, because "the bowl" afforded them some measure of safety. Some have said that the prehistoric people built the dome-shaped mounds that once lined the banks of Bayou Scie and Bayou San Miguel, forming the bowl-like impression around the townsite. However, there are those who say these same mounds are natural. These first inhabitants are believed to be ancestors of The Caddo Indians found occupying the territory when the Europeans arrived.

The Europeans probably handed down to the Indians the belief that no storms hit "the bowl" because it lies nestled within a circle where Bayou

Scie and Bayou San Miguel merge, fork, and merge again in the southwestern flow to the Sabine River, now Toledo Bend Lake.

Early pioneers of the Zwolle area found the Indian tribes friendly and there were numerous intermarriages. That is why among the people living within the vicinity today there may be found many of French and Indian or Spanish and Indian descent.

Dr. Hiram F. (Pete) Gregory, professor of Anthropology at Northwestern State University in Natchitoches, Louisiana, said, "The Apache connection at Zwolle was through the Spanish and French, maybe some Adaes or Caddo. Choctaw blood was claimed by lots of people and came in by the late eighteenth century."

In closing his remarks, the professor stated, "The Indian 'connection' at Ebarb-Zwolle is pretty much 'Connechi' or Lipan Apache and/or Choctaw. Some now say Adaes, too. The mixture was at Los Adaes, then Nacogdoches, then after the Americans took over Texas, they did get chased back."

What was to become Sabine Parish began to experience a steady influx of English speaking white settlers by 1824. At that time, Sabine was a part of Natchitoches Parish. These pioneers came chiefly from Mississippi, Alabama, Georgia, and the Carolinas. Some reports say the first of these settlers to reach the Zwolle area settled at Bayou Scie where as early as 1795 Spanish priests established a Roman Catholic mission called Vallecillo, where Bayou Scie and Bayou San Miguel merge.

In March, 1843, Sabine Parish was created by Legislative Act, with Many designated as the Parish Seat. The first census was enumerated for Sabine in 1850 and registered four thousand five hundred and fifteen residents. After 1871 many more settlers moved in acquiring land under the Homestead Act. Between that time and 1890, moderate but steady settlement occurred, as the population grew to nine thousand three hundred ninety by 1890.

In 1717, the Catholic Priest, Father Antonio Margil, a Franciscan Spanish missionary, visited the area that is now Sabine. He helped found Los Adais, about twenty-five miles to the east, which served as the capital of the Spanish Republic of Texas for more than fifty years. Los Adais was located about twelve miles from the French capital of Louisiana at Natchitoches. Father Margil and Friar Manuel worked among the Indians between Los Adais and west to the Sabine River.

The first settlement in the Zwolle area was made in about 1797 by Vicente Meshell.

The Spanish government pulled back west and the Sabine River was accepted as the boundary between the Spanish and French areas in 1819.

The first church in the area was built at Bayou Scie, which means heavenly sky of blue, as meaning the bayou waters of blue, in 1746. Bayou Scie is located about four and one-half miles northeast of Zwolle. It was originally named Bayou Cielo, which in due time became Bayou Scie. In 1836 a Catholic church was built about one mile south of present-day Zwolle and another church building was erected in 1856 near the same spot. St. Joseph's was erected at its present location on the western edge of Zwolle in 1836. A Catholic school was started in 1881. The First Methodist Church was established in 1897 and the First Baptist Church in 1900.

In those early days of Sabine history, freighting was done chiefly by wagons and oxen, which joined the trains that moved from Hamilton's Ferry on the Sabine River to Natchitoches and Grand Ecore on the Red River. In 1881 the Texas and Pacific Railroad (T&P) came through the area building a depot at Pleasant Hill in Sabine Parish. One was also constructed at Robeline, just over the boundary line in Natchitoches Parish, and that town became the chief trading post for the area.

William Martin Webb and his bride were the first to ride the passenger train on the T&P from

Texarkana, Texas to Pleasant Hill. They rode from Pleasant Hill to Clyde by buggy and opened a trading post. Webb later acquired a post office for Clyde and was appointed the first postmaster. He established a pony express letter service to Hamilton's Ferry, located about 10 1/2 miles to the west. The rider would go to Hamilton's Ferry one day and back to Clyde the next. This east-west mail route greatly helped Webb's business.

The charter for the Town of Zwolle was granted June 12, 1898. It set the limits of the town at one-mile square. Charles R. Stockford was the first mayor and councilmen were Louis B. Gay, William Martin Webb, J.A. Franks, and J. W. Allen.

Timber has always played an important part in Zwolle. The H. J. Allen Lumber Company built the first sawmill in Zwolle in 1897, right after the arrival of the railroad. In 1901 a group of businessmen interested in the development of the timber industry in Louisiana purchased the Allen Lumber Company and formed a manufacturing unit called Sabine Lumber Company. The Hall, Gibson, and Driver Mill, the first hardwood mill in the state, was built in 1907 and remained in operation until 1914. Mansfield Hardwood Lumber Company opened a mill in 1928. In his book about the history of Sabine Parish, published in 1912, John G. Belisle wrote, "Zwolle has always been one of the best sawmill towns in the parish."

Just four years after its establishment, some two hundred forty-seven residents were registered in the census of 1900. As the forest resources continued to engender growth of the area, Zwolle's population had expanded, approaching one thousand by 1910. In 1930, the population was listed as one thousand two hundred fifty. According to the census of 1940, Zwolle was the largest town in Sabine Parish and carried the largest payroll.

As the timber industry remained stable, the early Zwolle area was a good growing area for cotton, corn, potatoes, truck gardening, hogs, cattle, poultry, and other farm products.

Oil was discovered in the Many-Zwolle chalk formation on Thanksgiving Day 1928. Wells were generally small and unsteady in production. During 1932, this area had a daily production of six thousand seven hundred sixty-six barrels of oil.

In 1932, operators had learned to treat the wells with chemicals, which would sometime restore and increase their production. In January, 1933, some seventy-five Zwolle area wells were treated by the acidizing process. On February 24, 1933, the Pugh-Hickman Company completed a well that produced three thousand barrels per day.

An article by Stan Durnin in *"Linn's Stamp News"* dated June 6, 1977, stated, "A large Spanish population is still residing in Zwolle and the surrounding areas. The populace is made up of about four thousand Spanish folks, one thousand Negroes and one thousand white Anglo-Saxon Protestants; three thousand in town and three thousand in the surrounding area."

So, from the early beginning Zwolle had a rich and varied history. Few other places in Northwest Louisiana can lay claim to the rich heritage that the town possesses. That heritage was only going to be enriched by a young lad who would be born in 1917 at the nearby Alliance community.

Chapter 3

The Brandons of Alliance

"I asked for riches that I might be happy,
I was given poverty that I might be wise."
—-from Prayer of Unknown Confederate Soldier

Quinton Brandon may have inherited his desire to protect and serve and to seek truth and justice from his ancestors.

Research on the Brandon ancestry has been furnished the authors by Kenneth Edwards of Alexandria, Louisiana and Keith Brandon of Hemphill, Texas.

Brandon was a descendant of the Branhams from England. His family changed their name to Brandon during the 1850's. Originally the Brandon family name meant "one who came from Brandon," "brandon" meaning "broom hill," the name of several villages in England, especially in Norfolkshire.

A famous Brandon in the 1500's was Sir Charles Brandon, First Duke of Suffolk. He was created Knight of the Garter in 1514, married Mary Tudor, daughter of King Henry VII and sister of Henry VIII and led the English troops in two invasions of France (1523 and 1544) and the Pilgrimage of Grace in 1536.

Another Brandon was England's public executioner in 1616. He gained historical note not because of his dexterity with the rope and ax, but because he was granted the arms of Aragon with a canton of Brabant.

It is believed the Brandons arrived in Virginia in the early 1600's and that the Brandons of the Alliance community are direct descendants.

Records indicate that Nathaniel Greene Brandon (grandfather of Quinton Brandon) went to Nacogdoches, Texas. He is shown to have joined the Tenth Texas Infantry during the War Between the

States and these Confederate military records state he was born January 31, 1847, in Shelby County, Texas. He died August 27, 1925, and is buried in Appleby, Texas. One of Nathaniel Greene's sons was Nathaniel Webster (Webb) Brandon, who was Quinton's father. Quinton's mother was Mattie Blackwell Brandon of the Alliance community. Her parents came from Alabama on a wagon train, settled in Louisiana, and later migrated to Sabine Parish.

Dr. George Douglas Brandon, a Leesville veterinarian and nephew of Quinton, said that his father Victor told him the boys used to kid their mother that her family was run out of Alabama for stealing hogs. He continued, "To my knowledge, this was not the case, however it used to infuriate her, and she once chased my dad out of the cotton field with a hoe for saying that."

Quinton grew up during the Great Depression and was born the fifth son of nine boys: Elmo, Harvey, Morris, George, Quinton, Victor, Howard, Nathan (Bob), and Alvin (Jack) and there were four sisters: Della Blankenship, Heloise Nabours, Eula Lee Nabours, and Lerah Holt. Quinton was born October 12, 1917.

His family was sharecroppers and worked for thirds and fourths. This meant the owner of the land they lived on got the third or fourth bushel, bale, animal, etc. that was produced on the owner's property. The Brandon family worked for the Knott family, the Alford family, and the Ott Williams family and lived in rent houses located along what is now known as Highway six. Quinton was born on the Alford place. The family moved to what is now known as "Hurricane Valley" in 1938-40. Three of the remaining brothers and several more of their relatives still live in this area. Ed Blackwell, Mattie's brother, was probably the first to live in Hurricane Valley. After his death, John Blackwell, Mattie's brother, farmed it. He sold Harvey and Elmo 80 acres each, and over the years, most of the Brandons lived there.

PHOTO FROM THE COLLECTION OF JEAN BRANDON

The Brandons of Alliance are shown in this 1940 photo. Seated in the rocking chair is Alvin, who was called Jack. The vacant rocker is for Alton, his twin brother. His nickname was "Itty Boy" and on May 9, 1933, he died from the complications of bronchitis at the age of twenty-one months. In pictures of the family afterwards an empty chair was always placed where "Itty Boy" should have been. In the second row are Howard and Nathan, who was called Bob. Victor, Morris, George, and Harvey are in the third row. Standing in back are Elmo and Quinton.

The "cash crop" was cotton, but they grew huge gardens filled with peas, beans, corn, onions, potatoes, and all of the other foods they ate.

One of the means of preserving food was canning. The women of the family spent many afternoons in the hot summer over simmering wood stoves using pressure cookers to prepare vegetables for the canning process.

Any meat that was consumed came from killing their own hogs and cattle. They had to wait until the weather was very cold because they had no refrigeration other than the "cold cellars" or putting meat in a spring or a well. They preserved meat by smoking and "salting" it. They also hunted deer, squirrel, rabbit, and turkey during the specific season.

Dr. Brandon said that there were few, if any, deer or turkey at the time. He continued, "Squirrel was an important source of meat for the dinner table. Coon hunting was a source of meat and the selling of their hides was an important source of cash money during the winter. This was done not only for economics but also for sport."

They made their own soap and candles and collected honey from beehives. They made ribbon cane syrup and ground corn meal. When they had more of these items than the family needed, they would sell or "barter" the rest of the supply to stores in town or other families in the area. In this way the family was able to obtain shoes, clothes, and any other items they could not make or grow. New items of clothing were purchased only before school started each year and, if crops were good, at Christmas.

A typical day would find Quinton and his siblings getting up before sunrise and heading to the fields where they worked until sunset. Even the very small children helped by carrying water to the field. One of the older girls would stay home to cook meals and do the housework. There was no running water, no indoor plumbing, and no electricity. Washing was done only one day a week and the task took the entire

30

Nathaniel Webster (Webb)
and Mattie Blackwell
Brandon.
Circa 1964.

The Brandon Brothers -
George, Quinton and Victor
October 1938.

day. Huge black pots filled with water were put on open fires and the water was boiled. Then the clothes were rubbed on a scrub board with home-made lye soap until they were clean. They were then hung on the clothesline to dry.

When the crops were harvested, the routine did not change too much. What kids were not in school would again work from sunup to sundown killing hogs and cows and processing the meat. They also cleared land so crops could be planted the next season. At that time trees were so plentiful they would cut them down, stack, and burn them.

Dr. Brandon said that his father told him the following story: "One winter, the boys needed shoes. Webb decided to butcher a hog and sell it in order to buy shoes for them. He was to sell it at Fisher, some ten or twelve miles away. Not having other means of transportation, he hefted it to his shoulder and began the long trek. Along the way, he passed some men working on the road. At the sight of him carrying the hog, they began to laugh and ridicule him. Webb picked a clean place to lay his hog and dared any and all to come across the fence. None did."

Sabine Lumber Company and Mansfield Hardwood were industries in Zwolle at that time. The Brandon children often wished they had jobs at the lumber company because they would hear the "whistle" blowing each day and knew the people working there were going home while they still had several hours of daylight to go before quitting time for them.

During much of Quinton's childhood his father worked as a detective for the KCS in New Orleans and would be gone for months at a time coming home only on week-ends. This left Quinton's mother and the older siblings to handle the day-to-day problems that developed. Quinton's mother was a hard working, no-nonsense kind of person. If one of them was causing trouble, all she had to say was, "Okay, I'll let Webb deal with you when he comes home." That was enough to make even the most mischievous child straighten up. They knew their dad had no misgivings about using a strap if Mattie told him one of them deserved it.

The older boys had already left home and Quinton found himself in the position of helping to keep his other siblings in line. Until the day he died, Quinton kept close tabs on all of his brothers and sisters. He never hesitated to let them know how he felt about any area of their lives, whether they liked it or not. He always felt responsible for taking care of them.

Their entertainment consisted of going to church on Sundays, house and barn buildings, chimney daubings, fence buildings, quiltings, and country-dances.

Once a tornado touched down at the Brandon home and did severe damage to their property. Most of the family members still get nervous to this day when storms develop. Until about ten years ago there

Nathaniel Webb Brandon, left, is shown with his son, Quinton. This picture was taken about 1946.

was a "storm house" built into the side of a hill in Hurricane Valley. Some of the children of the Brandon clan can remember going to that storm house at the first clap of thunder. After years of men, women, children and even a dog or two cramming into the confined space of the storm house, the discovery was made that a very large snake claimed this space as his "den." There is no telling how many stormy nights that snake was right next to some of them.

Alvin Brandon, second to the youngest son, had a twin named Alton. His nickname was "Itty Boy" and they all tell tales of the mischief those two toddlers got into.

Everyone had a fireplace back then and the Brandons were no exception. Quinton's mother was a firm believer that cleanliness was next to godliness and her home stayed immaculate at all times. She had just finished the "spring cleaning" which took several days back then with no modern conveniences to help out. Each bed had been freshly made with clean white sheets and the pine floors had been scrubbed white with lye soap. The whole house sparkled and shined. "Itty Boy" crawled into the chimney to play and by the time they found him, he had gotten black soot all over every freshly made bed and scrubbed floor. Needless to say the little man was in big trouble.

On Tuesday, May 9, 1933, when Alton was twenty-one months old, he developed bronchitis. Back then, doctors made house calls but by the time the doctor was able to get to the Brandon household "Itty Boy" was in very bad shape. His throat was closing up and he was choking and turning blue. The doctor had to do an emergency tracheotomy. There was no time to sedate the child as it was a matter of life and death. All of the siblings were there trying to comfort him in anyway they could.

His mother and some of the older children were forced to hold the little boy down as he screamed and struggled while the procedure was being performed.

None of them were ever able to wipe that

horrible episode from their memory and even worse was the knowledge that the tracheotomy was done in vain. "Itty Boy" could not be saved and died that day.

He died at 2:00 a.m. and his funeral was held the same day at 3:00 p.m. at Pilgrim's Rest Baptist Church with the Reverend J. M. Pate officiating.

In pictures made of the family after that day, there is an empty chair where he should be sitting.

Another sad incident that affected Quinton's life during his childhood was the death of his little sister Lorene. She died when she was about three years old. They remember her as looking like a miniature "Snow White" with raven hair and ivory skin. She died of dysentery. Quinton named his first child Lorene in her memory and his Lorene had raven hair and ivory skin also.

At a very early age Quinton learned that taking care of one's family should be a person's first priority no matter what the personal cost might be. When he became marshal, the size of his family just increased to include the whole town of Zwolle.

Chapter 4

The Early Years

*"Sometime in 1937, I realized
I was in love with Quinton."
—Nannie Maxey*

Quinton Brandon started attending Alliance School when he was in about the fourth grade. That was the time he met his future wife, Nannie Maxey, the daughter of Mr. and Mrs. Leo Maxey.

"He had moved from Many School," Mrs. Brandon recalled. "He quit school in the eighth grade and I graduated at sixteen years of age in 1937. At that time, the Brandon family lived across the bottom land from us."

On his U. S. Army records dated November 9, 1945, Brandon listed he had completed the tenth grade and on his Louisiana State Police application in 1948, he said that he had finished high school.

Mrs. Brandon realized sometime in 1937 that she was in love with Quinton. "We were married on November 29, 1939," she stated. "We went to Marthaville to a preacher's house to be married."

There is a funny story associated with the marriage. Mrs. Brandon said, "Quinton was raising hogs at the time we got married. The preacher wanted one of his hogs. Quinton told him, 'Yes, I'll let you have one, if you will marry me when I'm ready.' That's the way it happened."

After the marriage, the couple settled in their first home on land belonging to his brother, Elmo.

Their first year Brandon tried farming. Mrs. Brandon said that it rained so much that year they lost the crop. The story is jokingly told within the family that farming did not settle too well with him and he cursed enough that first year "...to send him to hell four times." After that first year and the crop being a

A Proud Daddy

Quinton Brandon with daughter, Lorene, and 1941 Plymouth. Photo taken 1948 in Hurricane Valley.

Quinton and Lorene fishing at Loring Lake; this photo taken in 1944.

Quinton and Lorene with Prize Brahma Bull at Hurricane Valley in 1953.

complete failure, he told his wife he was going to try something else because farming was "too risky."

But on his U. S. Army records, he said prior to entering the service, he had been self-employed as a farmer for seven years. He stated that he did general farming, raised cotton and corn, and tended livestock, in addition to driving a truck in connection with this work.

Dr. George D. Brandon tells the story of that first year, with a little different slant. "His patience wore thin, with the difficulties he faced," he said. "I can recall his brothers laughing and saying you could hear Quinton cursing his mules for a mile away. My father, Victor, said he and another brother were helping him break land one day and the wet ground became so difficult that Quinton ran out in the middle of the field and jumped up and down, cursing with every breath."

World War II had begun and Brandon went to work at the shell plant at Minden. They lived in Doyline and at first he commuted.

Mrs. Brandon said, "Our first child, Lorene, was born February 13, 1942, and as soon as I could travel, we moved to Doyline. I had been staying with my parents."

Sometimes thereafter, her husband got a surveying job and they moved to Karnack, Texas.

"It was there that we met Lady Bird Taylor, whose parents lived in Karnack and had a store there," Mrs. Brandon remembered. "She later became Lady Bird Johnson, wife of President Lyndon B. Johnson."

"Quinton would take Lorene to their store after work every day and visit with Lady Bird," she continued.

As World War II progressed, Brandon volunteered for the U. S. Army. Mrs. Brandon and young daughter moved back to Hurricane Valley with her parents to wait until he returned home safely.

Chapter 5

Off to the War

"All who shall hereafter live in freedom will be here reminded that to these men and their comrades we owe a debt to be paid with grateful remembrance of their sacrifice and with the high resolve that the cause for which they died shall live eternally."
—Gen. Dwight D. Eisenhower

If there was one thing that always stuck with Quinton Brandon, it was that he was proud of his country and proud to be an American. When duty called, he volunteered and headed off to see what World War II held in store for him.

Kenneth W. Edwards, who has studied Brandon's war years extensively, pointed out he rose from the rank of Private (E-1) to First Sergeant (E-8) in a little over two years.

Brandon officially enlisted in the army because several of his good friends and relatives were joining. On April 21, 1943, he was stationed at Camp Beauregard, north of Alexandria.

He went through extensive training from the time he enlisted. He took Basic Engineer Training at Fort Belvoir, Virginia. While there he studied for five weeks at the Engineer Demolition School on proper techniques of explosives. He also attended the Transportation Corp School on water navigation and piloting for three weeks.

Brandon's military records show he was in engineer basic training for three months, Ship Master with a rank of Technical Sergeant for twenty months and Administrative Non Commissioned Officer for four months, with a rank of First Sergeant.

Within a year, he went from Private to Tech Sergeant (E-6) and on April 18, 1944, along with thousands of others, was convoyed across the great Atlantic Ocean to England where troops were amassed for the final invasion into Europe and the German heartland. He served 14 months in England, Belgium, France, and Germany.

The ship which Brandon was on arrived April 26, 1944, a little more than a month from the D-Day invasions. He was a Ship Master with the 334th Harbor Craft Company and it was his job to blow up the iron girders the Germans had placed on the beach to tear the bottoms out of landing crafts.

These railroad track size rods were simple and very effective. Set down at an angle pointing out to sea, they simply disappeared beneath the waves at high tide. The Germans assumed that an attack force would have to invade at high tide to place the infantry as far on shore as possible. They were right. To attack at low tide exposed the invading force to hundreds of yards of murderous machine gun fire as they waded slowly to the beach.

The intention was that these rods spill the heavily laden soldiers into the sea to be drowned, pulled under by the incredible weight of weapons, ammunition and equipment they carried.

Part of Brandon's job was to eliminate these hazards. To say this was an awesome job would be a grave understatement. Each beach had thousands of these things and paths had to be cleared through them. Somehow, this was accomplished, by the likes of Brandon and his comrades.

Other duties included the moving about of boats harbored in English ports. He patrolled the English Channel for pilots, from both sides, who found themselves ditched in this watery space between England and France.

The Channel was one busy place. The Americans and the English had steadily increased their bomber and fighter traffic. The pilots of planes, that had been shot, tried to make it to the Channel to avoid becoming prisoners of war. Nursing a crippled plane to the

Channel at least meant the possibility of falling into friendly hands. Some made it, but many did not.

During this stint of inner-Channel runs, Brandon and his crew rescued two British pilots, one American pilot who was flying a Thunderbolt, a heavy fighter plane commonly referred to as a "Jug," and three survivors of a hopelessly crippled B-29 which had been riddled by gun fire during a bombing mission into the fringes of Germany.

In another story that Edwards told, Brandon went ashore on the beaches of Normandy on D-Day and was horrified at the bodies that lay all along the beach and water.

The mission of Brandon and his comrades was to blow up the pillboxes and bunkers after they had been captured. This was to insure if the Allies were pushed back into the sea, the Germans would have to rebuild the fortifications.

While Brandon's body was overseas, his heart was still in Zwolle. "We corresponded regularly through the mail," Mrs. Brandon said. "I went to the mailbox every day waiting on a letter. I remember one time he said he had not gotten a letter from me in a long time and then all at once he got some and sat down and read them all."

Brandon served as Administrative NCO with the Transportation Corp in the U.S. for five months. He was responsible to his superior officers for all administration in a company of four hundred ten enlisted personnel. He made clerical records including morning report, sick book, and duty roster. Brandon supervised the care and the equipping of all personnel and passed on orders received from immediate superiors.

Edwards' research showed Brandon was awarded two Bronze Stars, the American Theater Ribbon, the European-African-Middle Eastern Ribbon, Good Conduct Medal, and the Victory Medal II.

Paul Maxey of Zwolle, who was eighty-three on July 2, 1998, was Brandon's brother-in-law and served

Quinton Brandon - The World War II Years

proudly during the war.

"I was in Holland in November, 1944," Maxey recalled. "We were bivouacked off the highway in snow three inches deep and you could hear those bombs going over. Quinton came along and saw my 84th Division insignia. He went to the main office and asked about me and was told, 'We can't tell you where any man is.' Quinton replied, 'Yes, you can. He's my brother-in-law and I'm gonna find him.' One day, just after dinner, I was slipping my mess kit over my shoulder and there came Quinton with that big grin on his face. I told him that day and many times since that seeing him then was one of the happiest times of my life. He said that he had been on C rations for weeks, so I had them give him a good dinner. On November 19, 1944, I got wounded and it was about dusk dark. They put me in a barn and I was seemingly by myself. Then I said, 'No, the Lord is with me.' I didn't see Quinton again until we both got home the next year."

In the winter of 1944, Brandon and a couple of his comrades were separated from their unit in Holland. They found a warm barn, got in it, and went to sleep. Early the next morning they heard German words being spoken outside the barn. They trained their guns toward the door and as it opened, a startled farmer stared at them down the barrel of the guns pointed at him. German was widely spoken in that portion of Holland and once the man realized they were Americans, he happily invited them to share breakfast with him.

The meal was a warm milk gruel, hardly enough for two people, but they shared what they had with the soldiers. Their generosity with what little they had warmed Brandon's heart. The couple bowed their heads and thanked God for the meal. Brandon never forgot that moment—to see people with so little giving thanks for what they had. He said that he knew people who had almost everything and never gave a thought about God.

After the meal, he thanked them and upon

leaving noticed all the children were barefooted even though there was snow on the ground. The sight was enough to bring a tear to his eyes.

Days later, the American soldiers captured a town with a shoe factory and filled up a sack or two with shoes and took them to the family which had been so good to them.

Brandon told another story in his latter years of an incident during the final stages of the war in Europe. He and some of his buddies stole a jeep and went Absent Without Official Leave (AWOL) while in occupied Germany. They were absolutely sick of army chow and wanted some decent food for a change.

They drove into a German village and stopped at a restaurant that had a horseshoe single lane street going around it. Their first obstacle upon entering the cafe was that none of them could read the menu. Perplexed, but undeterred, Brandon thought, "What the hell," so he threw caution to the wind and ordered something from the menu for all of them. What the waiter brought out was described as saucer-size steaks that did not taste bad.

Just before they had finished the meal, they heard their jeep crank up. An ex-German soldier was stealing the jeep. The men grabbed their burp guns and ran to intercept the jeep on the lower side of the horseshoe. The would-be thief was machine gunned into eternity.

Brandon said that he never forgot the look on the dead man's face as he was flopped back on the seat, mouth and eyes wide open and piercing. As he pulled the dead man out of the seat, their eyes met and it was as if the dead man was pleading with Brandon for his life. The sight ran chills through him.

As if the incident was not bad enough on their digestion, a sight even more horrible for the GI's lay just before them. At the back door of the cafe lay a generous pile of dog hides. When they realized they had eaten dog steaks, they became very ill and stayed sick all the way back to the compound.

Brandon did not actually know for sure whether they had eaten dog meat, but they assumed the worse. This incident sickened him for the rest of his life. After that, army chow just did not seem so bad after all.

In a letter of recommendation, dated March 19, 1945, Captain Harold W. Smith, headquarters Eleventh Port, Normandy Base Section, European Theater of Operations, wrote of Brandon: "He has performed missions which required tact and on at least one occasion, a high degree of courage. His conduct has invariably been of the highest order and reflects credit upon him and the military service. I take pleasure in commending him as a superior person well deserving such advancement as is offered him."

After the Germans surrendered, Brandon was promoted to First Sergeant. He and many of the other soldiers were sent back to the U. S. to prepare to head toward the Pacific to fight the Japanese. The two atom bombs dropped on Japan put an end to the war and Brandon received an honorable discharge on November 3, 1945, at Camp Plauche, Louisiana.

After the war was over, Mrs. Brandon said that her husband did not get out immediately. "The army wanted him to take an officer's course and stay in, but he didn't want to," she said.

Chapter 6

Looking for Work

"It was always a challenge, as a young kid,
to be Marshal of Zwolle."
—*Quinton Brandon*

After his release from the army in late 1945, Quinton Brandon returned to Zwolle and started looking for work. He had had enough farming and did not want to go back to it to try to make a living.

At that time, Pete McCormick was a member of the Zwolle Town Council, where he served as treasurer and mayor pro-tem. He also operated Pete's Coffee Shop.

"In early 1946, Quinton came to Pete's Coffee Shop," McCormick recalled. "He and I sat down and we had a nice visit. He had just returned from World War II. As he left that day, he said, 'If you all need any help in law enforcement, let me know.' "

McCormick related, "In November, the council needed a marshal because Bill Adams resigned. We had a meeting, and I repeated to them what Quinton had told me. Two of our members and Mayor Joe B. Parrott went out to Quinton's home. There was another council meeting and Quinton was there. After some discussion, the mayor and the council hired him." Also serving on the council at that time were M. L. Corley, A. J. Rivers, Bob Smith, and Pat Click.

"Quinton believed in law and order and he had that God-given talent to enforce the law," McCormick said. "He was a good law enforcement officer; one of the best."

McCormick told this account of why Adams left, "He had a falling out with Mayor Parrott. Adams knocked him down in the street. I saw it. Mayor Parrott fired him on the spot. Adams wanted to stay

This faded photo was taken in 1946 after Brandon came out of service and was possibly in front of a movie theater in Zwolle.

A young Quinton Brandon is shown in this photo, possibly taken about 1948. He was still struggling to find a place in his life.

one more day, but the Mayor called Adams' twin brother, Bert, in Leesville to come get him."

James McComic, a retired sheriff's deputy from Zwolle, said he heard the story that Adams tried to put Parrott in jail and the mayor fired him. "I heard they hired Quinton, but Adams wouldn't leave," McComic said. "They had two marshals at one time."

Howard Brandon said that when his brother came back from the war, the council asked him to be night marshal. "It was rumored that Adams was a drunk when he was on duty and everytime Quinton heard this, it made him mad and he defended Adams," Howard explained. "One day Doc Parrott called

Quinton and told him to come to City Hall and arrest Adams because he was drunk."

Howard continued and said, "Quinton came, but told Parrott that he was mayor and would have to arrest Adams, that a night marshal didn't have that authority. Parrott did not have the guts to do so and just told Adams to resign and leave town. Adams did leave town and Quinton was hired. That's how it all began."

Roger Lopez, Zwolle's present mayor, said he has been told the story that at the time of the incident, one man ran into a store and told the owner, "There's a fight going on out there."

The storeowner replied, "That's nothing, there're fights out there all the time."

The first guy replied, "But this time it's the mayor and the marshal."

"Oh, in that case," the second man answered, "I'll go see it."

Brandon knew something about what it was going to be like to be marshal. His father, Webb Brandon, had served before him. Howard Brandon said that Quinton always admired the way people respected their Daddy. "Quinton also admired Daddy's bravery," he said. It is interesting to note Quinton's son, Jerry, dreamed of some day returning to Zwolle to work as marshal after his dad retired.

In an interview with *The Sabine Index*, a weekly newspaper published in Many, Louisiana, since 1879, on August 6, 1970, Brandon said that he had been interested in the marshal's job for a long time. He recalled, "While visiting Zwolle as a young boy, I saw the law violated a number of times and nothing done about it. I saw people mistreated and run over. It was always a challenge, as a young kid, to be marshal of Zwolle."

He continued, "Even during my tour of duty with the army, there was plenty of action, but I kept thinking when I got out, I would be old enough to get the marshal's job in Zwolle. After I got back from the army, I made application and got the job."

Mrs. Brandon said that she did not think her husband's relationship with his father caused him to want to go into law enforcement. "Quinton loved him," she remarked, "And took him back when he came from New Orleans and cared for him. He also did all he could for his mother."

Mrs. Brandon said that when her husband came back after the war, he was "...ready to get into it."

Chapter 7

The Zwolle He Tamed

"Some of the people were just plain mean."
—-An Old Timer talking about Zwolle

If Quinton Brandon was the tamer of Zwolle, then what made it a town that needed to be tamed? Today there are few people still living who accurately remember the Zwolle that was. The authors have made a diligent effort to get as much factual information about this matter as possible.

Zwolle had been a rough and tough town from its inception. There were some people who just liked to be mean. There were others who liked to drink. While, at times, the area was dry, there was always a supply of liquor in Zwolle, either legal or illegal. And when one mixed meanness and liquor, he ended up with arguments, fighting, cuttings, shootings, and killings. Folks urinated on the sidewalks. There was a time a woman or a black could not walk down the streets without being verbally abused.

The foremost opinion on why there was so much trouble is that Zwolle was an ethnic melting pot, composed of several different groups.

Talking to a reporter in 1981, Brandon pointed out Zwolle had the reputation as the toughest town in Louisiana because of a melting-pot population and some serious "moonshining."

The Indians, of course, were the first group in the Zwolle area. Then came the French and Spanish, who inter-married with the Indians. The Anglo-Saxons came in the early 1800's and blacks brought in as slaves followed this. Other ethnic groups include the Czechoslovaks and some in Zwolle today say Italian blood flows through their veins.

Glenwood Bullard, the son of the late Mr. and

Mrs. Clarence G. Bullard, grew up in Zwolle, and he has a very keen insight of the lawlessness of the area as learned from his parents.

"The Czechoslovakians were barrel stave makers, who lived in camps down on the Sabine River," Bullard said. "They cut white oak trees and made barrel staves. They worked hard and when they came to Zwolle on Saturdays, they believed in playing hard."

Bullard continued, "My dad said he remembered the Czechs coming to town on Saturdays and they would bring with them the big knives they used to cut staves. My daddy said they were the sharpest knives he ever saw and they would use them, if they had to. You didn't cross those people. They thought you should mind your business and they would mind theirs. If you meddled in their business, they didn't back down."

"People around Zwolle liked to drink, raise hell and be mean," Pete Abington, Many business leader observed. "There was little education back then. If you went up there, you better know what you were doing."

John Henry Procell, lifelong resident of the area and former Zwolle Council member, said there were saloons in town after World War II ended. He stated, "There weren't supposed to be any, but there were. Emmett Stoma, Tom Stoma, and Lem Dyess all had saloons. The population of Zwolle at the time was about 1,200. Drinking and fighting were the big problems. When I was young, the police didn't mind if you were drinking in town, but they didn't want you to fight or anything else bad. Quinton broke that up. He was a good officer."

Howard Brandon recalled that in the early days the law allowed people to get drunk as long as they stayed in a business. "They were not supposed to be out in the street," he stated. "They would stay outside until they saw the law coming, then they would run inside a business."

Paul Maxey said toward the beginning of the

war, he saw a man ride up on a horse and sell some whiskey to another man who was waiting in a parked bus. Maxey stated, "Drinking and bootlegging were the main problems. The place was in ramshackles. It was a terrible place to live."

Maxey remembered during the 1930's there were seven saloons in Zwolle. He continued, "Later it went dry, but the bootleggers took over. There were fights and cuttings. Emmett Malmay got his belly cut wide open on the streets of Zwolle."

He said that he was raised in the country and as a boy of seven or eight, he would come to town with his daddy. "I would be scared," he recalled.

Maxey told a very interesting story: "When I was about seventeen or eighteen years of age, I was in Lem Dyess' Saloon one night. This fellow was drunk and was talking louder and louder. One of my uncles told me to leave: that this drunk had mistaken me for someone else and was going to kill me. He said, 'You better leave' and I did."

W. F. Jeter, Jr., who was a deputy marshal in Zwolle and also served as a sheriff's deputy, said the town was dry when Brandon took over as marshal. "The folks then started bootlegging and made more money than if the bars and saloons had remained," he said. "Acey Drew had a liquor store where J. O. Kimbrell's is now; Stoma's was where the dry cleaners is, and there was one more but I can't remember the name."

A person who asked not to be identified, said he drank a little wine back in the early 1940's, before Brandon became marshal and told this story: "I went to the marshal at the time and told him I wanted some wine. All he said was, 'Follow me.' We went to his house and he had a big refrigerator and it was full of liquor."

Milton McFerrin of Zwolle, a former deputy marshal, pointed out at a time when Zwolle was dry there were a lot of bootleggers in the area. He stated, "Sheriff T.M. (Pappy) Phillips got Zwolle Marshal

Cicero Merritt to get evidence on a bootlegger out in the country, not in the town. He had to shoot the man and was found innocent, but was sued over it and had to pay."

Another reason for the early lawlessness cited by Mayor Lopez is that Zwolle "...had never had strong law enforcement like Quinton provided." Another reason pointed out by McFerrin was, "Many people hated law enforcement. A lot of people were mean. Back then, you didn't have to have a reason to be mean. I had a friend in Ward five tell me, 'They weren't tough, they were ignorant.' "

A fifth reason cited by Bullard for making Zwolle so rough and tough is that it was a trade center. It was a Saturday town. The people from the outlying areas would come to town to make purchases, trade, and take care of business, in addition to visiting and drinking and fighting and cutting and shooting.

Stated Bullard, "People would not see each other during the week because they were working. When they came to town on Saturdays, if they had differences, they would settle them. The horse pens, where they bought and traded horses, was one of the places people fought and settled their differences."

Another reason for the character of Zwolle was the large number of family feuds and family grudges in the area. James McComic commented, "They've been known to kill members of the opposite family in these feuds."

Commented Jeter, "People would come to town on Saturdays. They would get drunk and start raising hell. The people who lived out in the country would have grudges. They would come to town and try to settle them."

A seventh reason cited was that World War II was over and the Great Depression had ended just before that. McComic said, "A lot of boys who had gotten out of the service were always in town causing trouble."

George Autrey of Sugar Land, Texas, lived at Negreet in the years before World War II, and served

Sabine Parish in the late 40's and early 50's as a Deputy Sheriff. He said the returning soldiers were called "wolves" and had just about taken control of Zwolle.

McFerrin stated, "When the veterans were returning from the war, their attitude was, 'I'm a veteran and I can do anything I want to.' They would tell you that."

Pete McCormick recalled, "After the war, the young boys were coming home and were ready to celebrate. Sometimes it got rough. Most of the problem people were not from Zwolle, but from the outlying areas. There were some from Zwolle though. It was mostly on weekends, but also some during the week. There was fighting. People would hang around on the streets."

Murray Sepulvado, seventy-four, was born in the Zwolle area and spent four years in the U.S. Navy during the war. He recalled after the Great Depression and war "...people were trying to improve their lot in life." He continued, "They didn't have any cars. People rode horses. People were uncivilized back then. We had been overseas and we saw so many uncivilized people and when we came home, we were uncivilized, to a certain extent. The town was not civilized. People made their own laws."

Sepulvado concluded, "They made white lightning and homebrew and they bootlegged. In every stump hole, you could find beer that somebody had hid."

Howard Brandon cited another reason for it being such a rough place. He explained, "Zwolle and Leesville were the only two towns in the area where you could buy liquor and the soldiers stationed at Camp Polk loved to come to Zwolle. They said they could find the strongest liquor and the wildest women in Zwolle. It was said at the time that no decent woman could come to Zwolle after sundown on any night of the week. The men who did venture out said you had to literally walk over a lot of people who were drunk or had been in fights and were laying out on the sidewalks and in the streets."

A reason James Cotton, a native of Spanish Lake and a Many resident for years, pointed out was the "hard times." He said when oil was discovered in Zwolle in 1928, "...it helped bring Zwolle out."

Concerning hard times, Bullard said the old sharecropper system, of which the Brandon family was a part, was operating in the Zwolle area. "That was not good," Bullard said. "There was an unscrupulous side to that story." So many landowners took advantage of sharecroppers either through dishonesty or because the sharecroppers did not have a knowledge of financing and business matters, or both.

Another reason for so much trouble, which Bullard pointed out, is Zwolle was a stop on the KCS and this was always bringing new people in and out of town.

Bullard concluded, "I remember hearing a story about a row of ties stacked in Zwolle, or maybe it was a loading dock, I can't remember which. Anyway, it had something to do with the railroad. Certain ethnic groups didn't go on one side of the deadline and another ethnic group didn't go on the other side. Depending on which ethnic group you were in, you stayed on your side. If you did venture on the wrong side, then there was trouble."

Maxey said that there were two horse lots in Zwolle, located side-by-side. The owners fell out with one another. "One of them hit the other with a walking cane," he said. "The other then shot and killed him right there. Dr. R. L. Parrott was called in, but there was nothing he could do."

Another story Maxey told, "I was on the streets one day and there was some sort of commotion on the corner where the red light now is. There was a man and his brother-in-law and everytime they met, they would fight. On this day, they started fighting on the sidewalk and I saw them roll out into the street and stop traffic."

Tom Phillips of Sunshine, Louisiana, son of

Sheriff Phillips, remembered there were pool halls in Zwolle where the men would congregate. "The windows would be painted head high so nobody could see who was inside," he said. "They all had back doors, so a person could run out, if he needed to."

Dr. Richard J. Oosta of Many moved to Zwolle in 1963 and said even then there were a lot of people who would get boozed up and fight. "I never felt uncomfortable living there," he stated. Bullard said that he enjoyed growing up in Zwolle and never felt threatened.

Mrs. Maxine Holmes and her husband, Woody, now live in Jonesboro, Louisiana, but in 1942 moved to Zwolle. Said Mrs. Holmes, "I wasn't comfortable walking down the street when we first moved there. When we left in 1964, I was very proud of Zwolle. Quinton was an outstanding person and had a good family. I am very proud of the way Zwolle has progressed."

Autrey recalled that most boys from Sabine either went to the war from 1941 until 1946 or were away at school. He recalled that sometime in 1946 he was on a bus traveling from Shreveport to Many.

"The driver had made a right turn in Zwolle and suddenly stopped in front of Keelen's Drug Store," Autrey said. "Then we saw a man running across the street and turning to fire a pistol back across the highway toward the railroad. In the vicinity of the railroad, we could see flashes from other weapons returning fire. The bus driver announced, 'Don't be alarmed ladies and gentlemen, this is just Zwolle.' I later learned that Quinton, who was marshal, and his deputy, Ben Isgitt, responded to a complaint and were going to check on a stranger in the area when the man ran and started shooting."

Autrey said based on his observations in the late 1930's when, even toward the end of the Great Depression, there was a considerable amount of oilfield and sawmill activity and somewhat lax law enforcement, leaving an opening for criminal activity.

He continued, "In later discussions with such people as special deputy sheriffs, Lee Meshell, Frank Martinez, and Steve Paddie of Ward five and Mayor Joe Parrott, whiskey and beer, including homebrew and homemade corn whiskey contributed to small time criminal activity. This coupled with the return of young war veterans, many of whom were of Spanish descent and customs with their machismo and hot blood, and with government money in their pockets, led to a seemingly insurmountable problem. The "wolves," as they were sometimes called, had just about taken control of Zwolle."

McComic said in the late 1940's, when he was a child, Zwolle was still a pretty rough place to live. "I delivered papers and my last drop was to the priest at St. Joseph's," he said. "I had parked my bicycle and was walking on the bridge over the railroad track one Sunday morning. I looked down and saw a man's arm on the railroad track. I can still remember seeing the ring on his finger. The arm belonged to a soldier from Ft. Polk who had been killed in Zwolle that Saturday night. Zwolle has always had a bad name. There was always a lot of fighting, cutting, and trouble."

Guy Wayne Maxey of Zwolle, Brandon's nephew, said, "Back in the 1940's it was wild here. I've seen several good fights. I've heard of Acey Drew's Saloon, but that was before my time."

McFerrin said that Zwolle had been a very unlawful place. "Many people were killed over nothing more than a dog or a hog. A person who had stolen a hog would sometime get a tougher sentence than someone who killed a man."

From early on, Zwolle was a rough, tough, mean, rowdy town, for many different reasons. The man who would take on the task of trying to tame it certainly had his work cut out.

Chapter 8

His First Call to Duty

*"Quinton Brandon served as Marshal of Zwolle when
probably no other man could have done the job."*
—*Sheriff T. M. "Pappy" Phillips*

Zwolle was known far and wide as one of the
roughest spots in this area back in late 1946 when
Quinton Brandon took over as marshal. Old-timers in
the area today still recall the days when outsiders
were unwelcome, when there was public drunkenness,
fights, shootings, cuttings, and when residents were
wary of walking the streets at night.

"When I first came to work here," Brandon
recalled, "this town was tougher than a nickel steak."
He continued, "I had to fight every day to stay here.
I've been shot at, cut up, kicked around, and hit. Used
to be a day didn't go by I didn't have to fight somebody.
I can't count the black eyes that I've had, but I always
got my man."

Did he ever lose? "I didn't get into a fight so I
could lose," he said, eyes twinkling, "But I admit there
was some doubt midway through as to the outcome of
some of 'em."

Sheriff Phillips remembered that in 1946 the
mayor and members of the town council would have to
go with the marshal on the streets of Zwolle on
Saturdays to keep order. He and Brandon both
recalled that during the time when Bob Adams was
hired as marshal, things got so bad he had to leave.

In a 1981 interview, Brandon said it "...wasn't
that long ago when all of Zwolle was the bad part of
town."

In an interview in his later life, Brandon stated,
"There used to be a saying that more men died with
their shoes on in Zwolle than in any other town on the

61

Brandon, young and proud, is shown with badge, pistol and hat in this early photo. Circa 1946.

Kansas City line. And I guess for its size, that was true."

Brandon continued, "This was a weekend town, and people would come in wagons or on horseback. Most of the trouble would start in bars with drinking leading to fighting and cuttings and shootings."

On some nights he would have to take on half a dozen roughnecks and lumberjacks, sometimes two or three at a time. He said, "I got my scratches and bruises, but I always got my man."

In a 1973 interview, Brandon and Phillips talked about the gambling and bootlegging that flourished in the Hale Quarters. Jim Hale had about two hundred rent houses in the late 1930's and 1940's. "He did many things for the people," Phillips recalled. "During the depression he collected little rent because the people were only working a day or two a week. He planted truck crops and would give vegetables away."

Pete McCormick recalled that Hale also had another cash crop.

McCormick stated, "Back when Quinton took over, they were still using untaxed whiskey. Some of it was bootleg whiskey and other was homemade white lightning. Jim Hale was big time in the whiskey business. Pap tried to catch him, but couldn't. Pap called me one time and said the FBI was coming. They went to an old barn Hale had and got seventy-five gallons of whiskey."

The sale, legal or illegal, of alcoholic beverages has long been a point of contention in Sabine Parish. Back in 1885, the sale of intoxicants was forbidden. In January, 1898, the Police Jury adopted an ordinance fixing a fee of $2,000 for a license to sell liquor. It was the record high fee for a license. The intention of the Jury was to completely discourage any attempts to open saloons in any of the towns of the parish where voters might wish to have them. On October 16, 1934, Sabine voters cast their ballots to prohibit the sale of beer and wine.

George Autrey recalled Sheriff Phillips hired

him as a deputy in August, 1947. "I was twenty-four at the time and the other field deputy was Bill Davis, about sixty," Autrey recalled. "Mr. Davis was my mentor. He and I and, later, Oliver Elliott, who had been a state trooper, worked a lot with Quinton. Most, if not all of the town marshals, carried special deputy commissions from the sheriff. We soon came to respect Quinton for his law enforcement ability, integrity, affable nature, and devotion to his family. We also became close friends. While we enjoyed a good relationship with Quinton, we also worked well with officers in the other communities and the special deputies in the rural areas. However, our most active area was Zwolle and the surrounding area. While Quinton was ready to fight when it was absolutely necessary, he had a standing rule, to never use more force than necessary to make an arrest."

Autrey recalled an event that happened on December 23, 1947, at about 9:00 a.m. He told his story, "Bill Davis and I were in Zwolle in a new 1948 Ford that was assigned to me. We were at the curb in the main business block and Quinton had joined us and was sitting on the right side of the front seat with the door open. I noticed a noted bootlegger from Many, driving by in a 1942 Chevrolet Fleetline from the direction of Shreveport."

"Quinton said, 'Look at that rear end, he's got a load of whiskey.' " Autrey told. "I backed out and turned and drove one hundred miles an hour to Many where the bootlegger was sitting at a traffic light. When we pulled beside him, he turned right across the curb and headed out the Texas Road. When we crossed the rough railroad track on the edge of town, the bootlegger's hood flew up and he drove by peering under the hood, but not well. We followed him out a gravel road with him weaving and throwing gravel. Quinton and Bill were advising me on how to pursue. Five miles out, the driver hit the back wheel of a tie truck and wrecked. He had seven cases of bonded whiskey and some special bottles for special

64

customers. We pleased the sheriff, who was running for re-election and needed an interesting event such as this."

Another time, Autrey said that Brandon called and said a troublemaker had threatened some Zwolle citizens and when the marshal got involved had gone into his shack and locked the door, saying he would shoot anyone trying to take him.

"I got there and noted that a crowd had gathered," Autrey continued. "Quinton said he needed a witness and a backup. The suspect would not respond when called, so Quinton kicked the door down and went in with me on his heels, expecting a shotgun blast at any time. To my relief, he was in bed with covers over his head and the gun leaning against the side. Quinton said, 'I didn't think he was mean enough to shoot us.'"

Bill Leslie, a former sheriff's deputy, recalled when he came to Sabine in the early 1940's there were three town marshals. He explained, "There was Otha Gregory at Pleasant Hill, George Cook at Many, and Quinton Brandon at Zwolle. All three were close friends and were of the same cut; they believed in enforcing the law by force. Mr. Gregory was the eldest and possibly the most forceful. He had Pleasant Hill so subdued that all he had to do to make an arrest was to

QUINTON BRANDON

INVESTIGATION SECTION
LOUISIANA FORESTRY COMMISSION

WOODWORTH, LA.
TEL. LECOMPTE 7200

Business Card - 1948

get word to the culprit that he was wanted and that person usually turned himself in. No one wanted Mr. Gregory to come after him because the consequences would be too severe."

Leslie continued, "This was the procedure of all three marshals. When Mr. Gregory grew too old to serve and Sheriff Cook died of cancer, Mr. Brandon became the last of the old time marshals. Although he lived to serve many years after the others, he became the last of his breed."

In an article in the April 4, 1974, *Shreveport Times*, Brandon told reporter Danny Anderson in "two short" years, he had changed Zwolle of all its bad ways. The article stated, "Practically alone, Brandon started Zwolle on the path to what it is today, respectable, clean, and virtually crime free."

In later years Brandon would tell that he served as marshal for two years the first stint, but the fact is he served only about a year until December, 1947, when he accepted a job as an investigator with the Louisiana Forestry Commission.

In an article in the April 2, 1948, issue of *The Index*, it was reported Brandon had visited the newspaper office to "...report the arrest of several offenders of simple arson, setting fire to forest lands."

In conclusion, the article said, "Mr. Brandon is a capable officer, having worked with Chief Investigator James V. Smith last fall when fires burned many acres of forest land in Sabine and adjoining parishes."

The writers of this book were unable to verify why Brandon left Zwolle as marshal and why, in later years, he seldom listed among his accomplishments that of working with the Forestry Commission.

Chapter 9

The First Year

"He said I got the whiskey and Pap ate the ribs."
—-Quinton Brandon

When he took that job as Zwolle Marshal in November, 1946, Quinton Brandon probably did not know what he was getting into. But, he had all the characteristics necessary to serve in the hostile climate of that rowdy town.

First of all, if he stayed, he would have to be brave. There would be nothing in the world of which he would be afraid. And if he ever did get afraid, he would never be able to show it. He must be a dedicated man; dedicated to the finest principals of law enforcement and dedicated to justice and what is right. And he must be determined.

But even more important, he must be dedicated to persevere. He must stand up to the obstacles that would be thrown in front of lady justice, whatever they may be. He must be loyal; he must be solid; and he must be able to be among those who could be counted upon. When the going got tough, he must be able to keep going. He must be prepared to put in a lot of long, hard hours with little pay. He would have to look death in the face, again and again. He must be prepared to face the grim reaper, because he never knew when the hand of death might knock on his door. Could he make the grade? Only time would tell.

In a story in the June 7, 1973 *Sabine Index*, Brandon recounted, "Back in those days, we had no cars. We had to police on foot."

One Saturday night Sheriff Phillips and Deputy Glen Phares came to see how things were going in Zwolle.

Brandon related, "I told them I had a warrant to search a fellow's place for bootlegging and asked them to go with me. When we got there, we found a big pan of barbecue ribs. They looked so good that Pap started eating them. We found the whiskey and later the man said he lost two ways that night. He said I got the whiskey and Pap ate the ribs."

Back then, the town jail was called the "calaboose," Brandon told *The Shreveport Times* on March 27, 1978. "It wasn't fit to lock a man up in. But I locked them up there anyway, with them fighting and scratching all the way."

Brandon told *The Shreveport Journal* on August 19, 1978, during the early years that he was instrumental in changing the town from wild to what he describes as one of the most peaceful towns in the region.

He said in the 1940's and 50's a stranger just did not stop in Zwolle. "In the early days, it was rough," he said. "In the late 40's I had to fight every day to stay here. In the early 50's, it was still rough."

The roughness, Brandon said, stemmed mostly from "moonshine" and its resultant drunkenness and when he tried to curb it, he ruffled quite a few feathers, including some public officials. He arrested the Mayor and one Councilman in the late 1940's on charges of drunk and disorderly. The Councilman reportedly tried to shoot Brandon.

He continued, "I've been shot at, cut at, I've been kicked around, and hit. I would break it up and then have to fight when I tried to corral them."

Brandon came on strong. He was a throwback to the days of the old, Wild West. He was of Wyatt Earp, Matt Dillon, and the characters played by John Wayne, all rolled into one. He loomed as big as life and larger. At that time, Zwolle was known far and wide as one of the rough spots in the area. Old-timers recalled the days when outsiders were unwelcome and residents were wary of walking the streets at night.

In the March 26, 1978, *Baton Rouge Morning Advocate*, Brandon said, "It was rough when I started out and I had to fight every day to stay here. Most of the trouble would start in bars with drinking leading to fighting and cuttings and shootings. The first term I walked the streets to police this town, and they tried me out thoroughly for awhile. I came out with a few scratches and bruises myself because it was mostly fist fights back then."

"Some families were tougher than others and there were a few clans of rough-runners who gave me more trouble than others," said Brandon, but he declined to name anyone in particular at the time because they, like the town, were peaceful.

"One thing I'm proud of accomplishing is that when I first started out, a black man couldn't walk down that sidewalk out there without getting knocked down. I always believe in equal law enforcement for black and white and I've got a wonderful relationship with the black community here," he said.

Equal treatment was an alien idea almost everywhere back in those days and Brandon said, "It drew much opposition at first, but when they saw I meant business, it quieted down in just a little while. When they were having racial problems in other areas around here, there were none in Zwolle and integration of the schools went off perfectly."

Timber was the main occupation and bar room brawling the main recreation when Brandon strapped his gun on his hip and began enforcing the law. He was willing to take on all comers and soon his reputation as a tough lawman traveled far and wide. It was rough back in the early days, but Brandon managed to walk tall and soon enough he earned the respect of many.

Sherman Tatum, a retired Sabine educator, said that he remembered a story shortly after Brandon took over the job. He related, "By Oakerson's station, there was a big stack of railroad ties. It was a good place for people to congregate, talk, and drink. Sam Bison came to town from where he lived west of Noble. Quinton thought he and some of the others had been drinking and confronted them. The truth was that Sam had not been drinking, so he defended himself. He and

Quinton got into a fistfight and he gave Quinton more than he wanted and then some. A few days later, Quinton went up to Noble and stopped at a store and inquired of the owner about Sam, "Is that guy a prize fighter?"

"The answer came back, 'No,'" Tatum said. "Then Quinton said, 'Well, that man, to be as small as he is, hit me harder than anyone else ever hit me.'" Archie Anderson of Converse also remembered the story.

Don English, chief of police in Mansfield, stated, "Before he took over, I heard a lot of tales about Zwolle. They say people were afraid to stop at the red light. When he became marshal, he put a stop to that kind of stuff. I don't think he had a scared bone in his body."

Ralph Shelton, a deputy in DeSoto Parish from 1950-1956, said that bootlegging was bad in Zwolle. "Brandon really took care of it," said he. "Those he beat up respected him. As a law officer, he was tops. He was trying as best he could. He believed in living right and doing right."

In the September 6, 1979, interview, Brandon said that he recalled a time when, "I used to paint my face black and go into the quarters to buy illegal liquor." He added, "It worked, too. They would actually sell me liquor."

"When he went to work in the 40's, he had a tough job," Vernon Parish Sheriff Frankie Howard said. Mayor Roger Lopez stated, "Quinton was fair. I know many times he was told, 'If you didn't have that gun on, I'd whip you.' Why, Quinton would pull his gun off and fight them."

Pete McCormick stated, "I saw Quinton arrest nine boys at one time for being drunk and fighting."

He continued, "I really don't agree that Quinton tamed Zwolle. He tamed those drunks. They were fighting. People would hang around on the streets. Quinton would arrest them."

"Quinton was one good officer," McCormick said. "He didn't take any foolishness. He was impartial. A boy one time told Quinton he wanted to talk to him.

He got in the car with Quinton and then started trying to beat him up. Quinton got two black eyes out of the deal."

Murray Sepulvado stated, "Quinton made his own laws and made it work. Nobody knew what the law was back then."

B. C. Isgitt, Jr. of Belmont said that his daddy worked for Quinton for two years. He related, "In the mid-1940's, there was a bank which was across from the Sabine Clinic. Someone was shooting at Quinton and my daddy. They were shooting from somewhere around the railroad tracks. They never knew who it was." The Junior Isgitt ended up working for Brandon on weekends for 12 years.

Kenneth Edwards stated, "Many people got a taste of Zwolle hospitality from Quinton, if they got out of line. Dick White, in his early days, made the mistake of acting up in town one weekend with several friends. He told of being thrown in a tiny jail cell with a host of others. They were packed so tight in that tiny cubicle that they could hardly sit down. That miserable night spent in a packed jail in Zwolle left an everlasting impression on Dick, as he told of it to three generations."

In closing, Edwards said, "Some of those he arrested would give Quinton a hard time. When he got enough, he would lock up his gun and simply have it out with the offender. Sometimes a physical thrashing would calm down those who were not quite as mean as they had once thought."

Chapter 10

Off to the State Police

"What is known is that Quinton slapped him in public."
—-*Source Who Asked To Remain Anonymous*

A search of Quinton Brandon's records with the Louisiana State Police turned up several interesting items. First of all, the records show he was unemployed at the time he filed an application for the job and second, he resigned a jump ahead of being fired.

First, one must go back to the beginning of the story. In early July, 1948, the move started for Brandon to obtain the trooper's job. The first correspondence in the State Police file is a letter from the late Paul Ebarb, who ran a general store in Zwolle. He wrote to State Senator Albert Asa Fredericks in Natchitoches. The correspondence, dated July 10, 1948, asked him to intercede on behalf of Brandon for the job. Ebarb wrote that Brandon is well qualified for any position in law enforcement.

J. G. Grant, Director of the Louisiana Department of Public Safety, acknowledged Frederick's letter and sent a job application to Brandon.

The application, dated July 23, 1948, showed Brandon was thirty years of age at the time, was six feet one inch tall and weighed one hundred seventy-two pounds, and did not own a home. The only property he did own was a car, valued at fifteen hundred dollars. The application said that he had seventeen months experience as marshal and ten months with the military police. Brandon's war records show he never served in the military police.

An unusual part of the application showed he was unemployed. It showed his previous experience was as marshal but no reason was given for his not being marshal at the time of the application. It also showed he had acquired a high school education, which his U. S. Army records did not show. The references listed on the application were Sheriff Phillips, W. M. Knott, Paul Ebarb, and F. A. Keelen.

A second letter in the file is to Lieutenant Governor William J. (Bill) Dodd from Pete McCormick. He wrote Dodd, "I know you are a busy man, but I am sure you won't mind me asking you a personal favor. A friend of mine, Quinton Brandon, has his application in for a state trooper job. If you can, please say a good word for him. Mr. F. E. Cole, our Representative, has already recommended him. I am sure Senator Fayette Gay has or will recommend him and also, the council, and the mayor of Zwolle and I. He is already a peace officer, a war veteran, and an outstanding man with lots of friends. He is one hundred percent Long Administration. Dodd, if you can help in this matter it will be appreciated."

Dodd replied August 9, 1948, saying he was referring the letter to Grant. Dodd said personally that he would like to see Brandon have the job. He closed his letter saying he expected to be in Zwolle before long when he had enough time to visit around with "...all you old ex-rabbit hunting partners."

A letter from Major M. R. Roden, Assistant Superintendent of State Police, dated November 18, 1948, said that Brandon was to report to State Police Headquarters in Baton Rouge November 28, 1948, for employment. It stated, "You will come prepared to stay at these headquarters for at least two weeks, during which time you will attend the division's training school and will then be assigned to Troop H, Leesville for duty." Troop H included Sabine, Vernon, DeSoto, and Beauregard Parishes.

An employment record for Brandon, dated November 29, 1948, showed his date of appointment as December 1, 1948, at which time he took the oath of office, and his beginning salary was one hundred sixty dollars per month.

The records showed that Brandon earned a total of 95.8 points on his student's final rating sheet. The passing standard was 70.0 and Brandon scored 25.8 over. The record also stated his conduct and attitude were both excellent during the school.

During his tenure with the state police, the Brandon family continued to live in Sabine Parish, until September, 1949, when they moved to Leesville.

There is nothing else in Brandon's file until October 18, 1949, when a special order was issued saying Brandon was assigned to two-weeks' tour of duty at the Louisiana State Penitentiary at Angola, November 1-15, and afterward reported back to Troop H. It stated the regulation state uniform was to be worn.

In Brandon's employment record, it showed effective November 1, 1951, his salary was increased from two hundred fifty dollars to two hundred sixty dollars per month.

A letter from Brandon to Captain Wingate M. White, Commander of Troop H, Leesville, dated March 7, 1952, asked that his resignation be accepted at the close of business that day. Brandon wrote he was resigning in order to accept a job as marshal in Zwolle. Prior to that, Brandon's brother, Elmo, had been serving as marshal for about a year and a half. He resigned that position effective March 7, 1952.

Captain White wrote of the resignation to Colonel E. P. Roy, Director of the Department of Public Safety in Baton Rouge on March 8, 1952. He stated, "I regret losing Trooper Brandon as he has been a good officer, but he felt his interest is best served by this change."

A former state trooper, who asked not to be identified, told Dr. George D. Brandon, an incident happened which caused Brandon to resign because he felt he was going to be fired.

The trooper said that it was known at the time that the Earl K. Long administration required

Quinton Brandon was Officer No. 469 for the Louisiana State Police. This picture was taken about 1949.

financial support from state policemen. A contribution of fifty dollars was required of each, he said. This was in the time period when the Long vs. Robert Kennon battle was raging. There were seven troopers who did not give to Long and were discharged but were reinstated when Kennon took office.

Shorty Owen of Leesville, the trooper said, was the point man for Kennon in Vernon Parish. Subsequently, when Kennon was elected governor, he appointed Owen as Director of the Department of Public Safety, which controlled the state police.

The trooper continued, "Prior to Owen's appointment, Brandon had humiliated him in public during a parade on Third Street in Leesville. The specific cause for the affair has not been learned, but what is known is that Quinton slapped him in public. I am told that after the appointment, Brandon felt he had no future with the Department."

Concluding the story, the trooper said, "As a sideline, Governor Long in a public address denied his requirement for troopers to support him and used the 'Good Lord' as his witness. Some folks looked up, expecting a bolt of lightning."

R. V. Bolton, a retired State Policeman, concurred with the above story, adding, "Brandon said that he wasn't going to give Owen the satisfaction of firing him."

Bolton said Brandon "...was the most dedicated law officer I ever knew." He added, "He was strictly business to a fault; he wouldn't bend."

"I once assisted Brandon in trying to apprehend an AWOL soldier," Bolton tells. "It is funny now, but it wasn't at the time. The man was supposed to be holed up in a house somewhere northwest of Zwolle. Brandon planned for us to all sneak up on the house one morning before daylight. It was a cold, frosty morning and we crawled on our bellies for thirty minutes to sneak up on him. I almost froze to death and when we got to the house, the soldier wasn't even there."

Bolton concludes, "I assisted him from time to time on raids on bootleggers in Sabine Parish. " We would arrest them and they would make more money in jail than when they were out," he said.

"I loved Quinton," said Roscoe Rains, a retired state trooper from Leesville, "I could always depend on him day or night." He continued, "You could depend on his word. I could sum him up as a lawman with just a few words; you couldn't buy him, nor could you scare him. He put his heart in his work. At times, he infuriated me for the zeal he had for police work."

Rains continued, "He would usually go home to Zwolle on his days off. Once, on his way home, he stopped at Sandel, just south of Florien, and learned that the Rawls brothers were in a drunken brawl. Since he was off duty, he should have just gone on, but instead, he went and got involved, finally broke the fight up, arrested them, called me and I had to stop what I was doing and go up there to bring them in."

In another story, Rains said, "There used to be a bar on Third Street in Leesville, that was owned and operated by a fellow who was just plain mean and untrustworthy. That was back in the days when they had slot machines and we would raid his bar every weekend and confiscate the slots, but then he would just have the slots back the following Monday."

Rains continued and stated, "The proprietor was mad at Brandon for the last raid and one night he called the state police office, disguised his voice, and pretended he was an informant and to let Brandon know there were some machines he had missed in the last raid. I recognized the voice and knew it was a setup. He was going to lure Brandon to his bar and kill him. The fellow always carried a concealed pistol and I knew it would be Brandon or him if Brandon went back down there. I got Brandon up to the office, got his gun, and kept him at the office all night. I knew if I didn't and he went to that bar, there would have been a killing."

And in a surprise in the state police file is a letter

from Brandon to Colonel Francis G. Grevenberg, Superintendent of the State Police, dated September 1, 1952.

Brandon wrote, "I wish to request reinstatement to the position of trooper, which I resigned March 7, 1952. I resigned because I had been informed I would be discharged for political reasons. I am applying for reinstatement because I believe my record with the state police fully justifies the request. I will appreciate hearing from you in connection with this request and will state that if you do see fit to grant my request you shall not have cause to regret doing so."

The filed letter showed no reply. The line had been drawn in the sand. Brandon would not cross back over.

Chapter 11

Another Man Bites the Dust

*"Mr. Brandon thought he might be killed
and had no other choice."*
—-Milton McFerrin

The "dog days" of summer were approaching. The month was August of 1951. The summer had been good, not too hot, and there had been rain along the way.

On this Saturday, August 17, Nathaniel Webster (Webb) Brandon was working as a deputy marshal for Zwolle. He had served the town as it's marshal for either two or four years, depending on whom you ask. That was back in the mid-1930's. Joe Parrott followed him in that position.

On this day he was filling in for his son, Elmo, who was marshal. Howard Brandon, Elmo's brother, recalled that Elmo had a doctor's appointment out of town and had asked their daddy to fill in.

There was a big crowd in town that Saturday. It was usually that way on Saturdays in Zwolle, if the weather was good. Because of the heat, a lot of people left about noon, but there was still a lot of people around.

It had been a relatively quiet day and Webb Brandon was glad. He was sixty-eight years old at the time. He felt he had already given law enforcement a good part of his life, but when his son asked him to fill in, he could not refuse.

W. F. Jeter, Jr. remembered the marshal then did not have a car, so he had to make his rounds on foot.

Webb Brandon got a report that there were a couple of drunks at the pool hall, down on the corner where E. B.'s Hot Tamales is now located. He went inside about 1:20 p.m. and approached Calvin Leonard, thirty-one, and Tommy Johnson, both of Zwolle. He

81

arrested Johnson for being intoxicated, but Leonard escaped.

Brandon brought Johnson out on the sidewalk and started to jail with him. At this point, Leonard came up behind Brandon and threw him to the sidewalk. Both men struggled for Brandon's pistol and in the scuffle four shots were fired. One hit Leonard in the chest and he died.

Milton McFerrin of Zwolle was almost a witness to the shooting. "I was standing in the door at Western Auto about seventy-five feet away," McFerrin explained. "When I saw them, they were on the concrete sidewalk. A man was on top of Webb. He had jumped on him from the back. When he jumped on Webb, some of those nearer stated he said, 'Let's kill the old son-of-a-b——.' I did not hear him say that, but it came out in testimony. The first shot blew out a tire on a car that was parked nearby. The second shot hit the roof over the sidewalk. The third shot killed Leonard. I saw Mr. Brandon push him off. When I got to Calvin, he was lying on his stomach on the sidewalk. He used his arms to push his face up just a bit from the concrete and fell back. He was dead."

Dr. George D. Brandon said he learned that after the shooting of Leonard, his grandfather had given Johnson the ultimatum, "hell or jail," and he readily chose the latter.

That afternoon at 3:30, Dr. Swepson F. Fraser, acting Sabine coroner, called an inquest. After hearing the testimony, the coroner's jury rendered a verdict of death by gunshot, fired by Brandon, and referred the case to the grand jury.

The next day, Leonard's brother, J. W. Leonard of Shreveport, swore out a warrant charging Brandon with murder. On Monday, Sheriff's Deputy George B. Autrey, served Brandon with the warrant at 11:00 a.m. Webb Brandon was taken to jail in Many where several Zwolle citizens provided the two thousand dollar bond to free him.

Leonard, who suffered fifty percent physical

82

*Webb Brandon wearing
holster and pistol.
Circa 1924*

*Webb Brandon while
working for KCS in New
Orleans. Circa 1952.*

disability from a wreck overseas during World War II, had attended Zwolle High School. He was buried the next Monday at 5:00 p.m. at Fender's Cemetery.

The fall term of the grand jury met in mid-September. No true bill was returned against Brandon; thus, the case was dropped.

"The grand jury did not bill him," McFerrin remembered. "There were some witnesses who were no more than ten feet away and their testimony was that Leonard jumped on Mr. Brandon's back. Leonard said, 'Let's kill the old son-of-a-b——' and Mr. Brandon thought he might be killed and he had no other choice."

Jeter related, "Leonard had started back to attack Webb when he got shot. It was in self defense."

Autrey recalled, "Calvin Leonard was one of the 'wolves' and did a lot of drinking and some strange things. He had no permanent address that I was aware of, but stayed with his brother on the Sabine mill side

83

of Zwolle some of the time. The reason for his attack of Mr. Brandon was not fully determined, but the indication was that he thought Webb was too strict and needed a beating, even though he was getting along in years. Calvin was the one with the nerve to do it."

Autrey continued, "According to five witnesses who were in the cafe, Calvin jumped on Mr. Brandon's back and pulled him to the sidewalk. No two saw it the same way, but all of those sage men agreed that after Webb was pulled to the sidewalk and during the melee, a pistol was fired and Calvin died as a result. I think the pistol was a .32 carried in Webb's pocket. The witnesses all thought the shooting was justified."

Howard Brandon told an interesting story about the time that his dad was marshal. "There was a rule a person could drink as long as he was inside a place of business and the owner did not object," Howard explained. "Many times it was like a game and a person would come out of a business very drunk and then when he saw the marshal approaching, he would run back inside the business to avoid getting arrested. Acey Drew was famous for this and he and Webb played the game often."

One night, Drew was not fast enough and Brandon arrested him. Howard, Webb's seventh son, was about eight or nine at the time and had gone with his dad as he was making the rounds. He recalled Drew was furious when Brandon arrested him and put him in jail and shouted every foul name he could think of. Howard said that after about thirty minutes of this, his dad took off his gun belt and walked into the jail cell, locking it after him. Howard heard all kinds of noises and was getting worried about his dad, but after a few minutes Brandon unlocked the cell and walked out. Drew was sprawled out on the floor and it was very peaceful the rest of the night.

Webb Brandon was a sharecropper and first took a job as deputy sheriff at seventy five dollars per month to supplement his income. Later he took the job as Zwolle Marshal and then as a deputy marshal.

Prior to the shooting he worked in New Orleans as a detective for the Kansas City Southern Railway Company. Mrs. Brandon and the children continued to live in the Zwolle area and Brandon would visit as he could.

Dr. Brandon said while Webb was working in New Orleans that he killed another man. "It has been my understanding that he worked in a rough area of the city along the river," he stated. "The exact circumstances of this shooting remain unclear; not many of the family talk about it, but some controversy apparently did exist about the justness of the killing."

Webb Brandon's earthly life came to an end December 1, 1959, when he suffered a heart attack while deer hunting near Zwolle. He was laid to rest in the Zwolle Cemetery. He was seventy-six. His widow continued living in the Zwolle area until her death on April 30, 1967, at seventy-nine years of age.

Webb Brandon had lived a long life and had dedicated a good part of it to law enforcement. He was now gone and it was up to his son to continue to carry the torch. Quinton was marshal in Zwolle. Before he passed on, Webb Brandon had to have felt proud to leave law enforcement in such good hands.

Chapter 12

Back to Zwolle to Stay

"Wherever 'ore this world I wander,
There's no place like home."
—A Song, "Home Sweet Home"

"I returned to Zwolle in 1952 because the town needed me," Quinton Brandon said in a 1972 interview with *The Shreveport Times*. "I thought I had done a pretty good job during my first stint but when I left to go with the state boys, something happened to the town. Seems like it began to go backward instead of forward."

Brandon returned to find Zwolle just as rough as ever. Starting from scratch, Brandon tried to restore some law and order and for fourteen years, thereafter, he was the only law in Zwolle.

"I even used my own car until 1966 when the town bought me a patrol car," said Brandon.

Brandon resigned from the state police effective March 7 and the same day, his brother, Elmo, resigned as Zwolle Marshal after serving about a year and a half. The next day, March 8, Brandon took over as marshal.

"The people of Zwolle encouraged me to come back and take the job," Brandon said in a 1978 interview with The Shreveport Journal. "Over a period of years the town cooled down. They learned to respect law and order. I'll give education a lot of credit."

Kenneth Edwards, came up with this story: "In 1951 Brandon was approached by the 'founding fathers' of Zwolle. It appeared since his departure as marshal, crime had risen dramatically. They were desperate to have him back to tame the wild town as he had done before. He initially turned them down, but they came back with a 'deal he couldn't refuse.' He was offered the grand sum of $250 a month to tame one of the wildest areas of the state. At first, he had to patrol the entire town by foot since he did not have a car."

Part of this story does not jibe, since state police records show he had been given a raise from two hundred fifty dollars per month to two hundred sixty dollars per month effective November 1, 1951. The reasoning could have been that Brandon figured he could live cheaper in Zwolle than in Leesville and could also pick up a few dollars doing other things.

Pete McCormick, recalled, "Quinton came back. He said the state trooper job was not what it was cracked up to be and he could live cheaper in Zwolle. He knew everybody here, anyway. He wanted the job back and we were glad to give it to him."

Mrs. Brandon recalled, "The Zwolle officials came and wanted him back. They made him a good offer and he came back."

So Brandon had made the decision to come back home and once again make an attempt to tame the town he loved.

Chapter 13

It Ain't No Easy Run

*"The troopers he worked with were afraid
he would get killed working up there."*
—Trooper R. V. Bolton

"I was working for the town and Quinton was the only police officer, " Milton McFerrin, a long time friend said. "I didn't like that. There was an event that happened at a downtown cafe that really brought the seriousness of the matter home to me.

"A man knocked Quinton through the plate glass window to the sidewalk. Quinton went back in and arrested him. He started walking to jail with him. As this was going on, I started up that way in my pickup truck, but I didn't know what had happened at the time.

"When I got up that way, I saw Quinton and the boy and there were three or four others trying to take the prisoner away from him. It looked like a battle was fixing to start. Something had to be done.

"Quinton was outnumbered. I stopped, took a piece of pipe out of my truck and followed them to city hall. We got them dispersed and I told Quinton how concerned I was about him doing this alone.

"I only weighed one hundred forty-seven pounds at the time, but I started riding with him at night, not as a deputy, but as a friend. I think an extra person with him helped keep down some of the trouble. Quinton went before the city council, without me knowing it, and asked that they hire me on weekends and holidays. He got it okayed and brought my badge and commission to me. I worked for Quinton for about six years. I wouldn't have done half as much for any other man. He was a real friend. W. F. Jeter, Jr. took the job as deputy when I left."

R. V. Bolton of Leesville, a retired state trooper, said, "I was a radio operator at Troop H in Leesville in 1953. Brandon had already taken the job at Zwolle. He had it rough and the troopers he worked with were afraid he would get killed up there."

Several persons said the sheriff's department used Brandon to assist them in answering calls in that area, even though for years he was not deputized to act outside Zwolle. It didn't matter to him; if he was needed, he answered the call.

One person said that the sheriff's department used Brandon because they had some deputies who were afraid to make the calls. "Quinton knew he was being used," the person said. "He always said, 'If we needed them, they would help us.' "

McFerrin said he remembered the sheriff's department coming and getting Brandon. "At the time there were three field deputies, George Autrey, Oliver Elliott, and Wallace Firesheets," he said.

When Brandon ran for Sabine Sheriff in 1967 and carried Wards five, eight and ten, winning Sheriff Harold Sandel decided it would be to his best political interest to make Brandon a deputy, commission him, give him a badge, and pay him a little something. Every other sheriff followed suit. Sheriff George Cook, who beat Sandel four years later, had gotten upset with Brandon for supporting Sandel. He wondered whether he should commission Brandon, but W. F. Jeter, Jr., who worked for both Brandon and Cook, said he finally decided to deputize him.

Jeter said that one of the reasons Brandon was successful was he had a mayor, M.H. Burkhalter, who backed him up. "If Quinton brought them to mayor's court, Burkhalter found them guilty," Jeter related. "Burkhalter's attitude was, 'If you weren't guilty, you wouldn't be here.' "

At this point, Brandon started gaining a statewide reputation as an outstanding law enforcement officer. His fellow law officers may not have known him personally, but they soon heard about him. So had the general public. His reputation as a tough, hard-nose officer began to spread.

Vernon Parish Sheriff Frankie Howard remembered his late father, Robert Howard, Marshal of Hornbeck, use to assist Brandon in making liquor cases.

"There was a lot of bootlegging going on at the time," Howard related. "I would go to Zwolle and make buys. They would rent an unmarked car for me. I'd tell the officers where the liquor was stashed and they'd go in and confiscate it. The cases were based on my testimony. They were selling quart size Falstaff back then. It was the popular beer. They would buy it for fifty cents and sell it for one dollar."

"Quinton stayed after the bootleggers," Guy Wayne Maxey, said. "I heard the story he was under a house in the quarters one time trying to make a case and a woman poured a kettle of hot water through the cracks in the floor on him."

The jail at the time was an old brick building they called the calaboose. It was twenty feet long by ten feet wide and the walls were of one-foot solid red brick. The top was made of concrete about four inches thick. The building was divided evenly into two cells. Each cell had a door in front, a window on the end and a window in the back. The doors and windows all had bars. The building is still in the alley behind the Paul Ebarb Company.

"It would only hold eight prisoners," McFerrin remembered. "That's what we had beds for. Sometimes we'd stack them. If we had more prisoners than room, we'd see who had sobered up and release them so we could put somebody else in. Sometime we would take the prisoners to the jail in Many."

Brandon was back to stay and making headway. He had gone through a lot of testing and more was to come.

Chapter 14

Little Rennie Travis

"He worked for my daddy operating a dozer. He worked hard, stayed drunk, and wanted to fight. He was just as good as could be when he was sober and would help you in any way. When he was drinking, he was mean. And he drank all the time."
—Gailor Phares

Everyone who can remember little Rennie Travis today, recalled that he was a good guy except when he was drinking. The problem was, they said, he drank all the time. Another problem he had was the Brandons of Zwolle.

Sometime, no one can put a date on it, he was in Zwolle and had a run-in with Webb Brandon. It could have been when the elder Brandon was marshal early on, or it could been when he was a deputy.

W. F. Jeter, Jr., remembered hearing about the matter. "Travis thought he was rough," he said. "Uncle Webb arrested him, is the way I understand it. Rennie took the pistol away from him . Uncle Webb went to his office or somewhere and got another pistol. Rennie had shot at Webb, who returned fire and hit him." That was the beginning of it.

James Cotton recalled that after Little Rennie recovered, his daddy, Rennie L. Travis of Many, "...hauled him around in the back seat of an old model Chevrolet." Cotton continued, "I can remember it like it was yesterday. Little Rennie looked like a dead man back there."

Cotton concluded, "He was a drinking man. He believed in riding bulls and fighting."

Ernest Rodriguez of Many was about thirteen or fourteen years old in the early 1950's and used to drive a hay truck for Little Rennie. "One day I was driving and hauling hay from south of Zwolle to put it in storage on the old Zwolle-Pleasant Hill Road. Little Rennie was on the passenger side. He always carried a little bottle around with him. When he had a drink or two, he liked to sing. He was singing, 'Give me back my boots and saddle,' which was his favorite.

"As we crossed the railroad tracks in Zwolle, he said, 'There's my friend Quinton Brandon. Let me go see him.' I stopped and he got out. I stayed in the truck. The next thing I knew they were talking loud, and shaking fingers at each other. Then Quinton put a choke lock on him and started dragging him across the railroad tracks, headed for the jail.

"I sat in the truck for what seemed like an eternity. I didn't know what to do. Finally I saw Quinton coming and I told him I was driving for Little Rennie and didn't know what to do. He told me to go ahead and deliver the hay and come back in a couple of hours and pick Little Rennie up."

"I didn't know there was a feud between the two. I understand everytime they met something like that happened."

The chapter ended Friday, February 10, 1956, when little Rennie Howard Travis died in a Shreveport hospital. He was only thirty-nine. The booze and hard living had taken their toll.

Chapter 15

Building City Hall

"I'd have to fight 'em to get 'em to the jail,
and then I'd have to fight 'em again
when they saw where I was gonna put 'em."
—Quinton Brandon

In Zwolle some forty-five years ago, the "calaboose," a dismal, two-compartment, brick, concrete, metal and wood jail located behind the present City Hall, overflowed with prisoners every weekend. It was the only jail Zwolle had and even the marshal was ashamed of it and hated having to put a human being in it.

"I'd have to fight 'em to get 'em to the jail, and then I'd have to fight 'em again when they saw where I was gonna put 'em," stated Brandon.

In 1953 Brandon threatened to quit unless the city fathers built him a decent jail. They did, and when Brandon was marshal all the cells were often filled on weekends.

It cost approximately eighteen thousand dollars to build and the city only had nine thousand. The city borrowed seven thousand dollars from Brandon's brother, Harvey, and built the City Hall. The city paid Harvey back as soon as it could.

The City Hall housed the Mayor's Office, Marshal's Office, Fire Department, Waterworks Department, a four-cell jail of steel construction and an auditorium thirty-two by forty feet.

Dedication ceremonies for Zwolle's new City Hall and Fire Station Building and the opening of the Peoples State Bank Zwolle Branch were held Saturday, November 14, 1953.

The all-day program began at 9:00 a.m. and included a barbecue lunch furnished through the courtesy of the merchants and businessmen of Zwolle.

The town officials at the time were M.H. Burkhalter, mayor; Max Brown, secretary; C.G. Bullard, treasurer; Hoyt Maxey, street commissioner; Louis Lefkovits, mayor pro tem; W.L. Gaul, alderman; Milton J. McFerrin, waterworks superintendent; R. A. Fraser, Jr., city attorney; Quinton Brandon, marshal; and Cicero C. Merritt, deputy marshal.

In 1953 Zwolle had an annual payroll of one million dollars; yet for sixteen years the town did not have a bank. The businessmen of Zwolle and the Zwolle Lions Club negotiated with Peoples State Bank of Many to establish a branch in Zwolle. The new bank was located on Port Arthur Avenue across from the Sabine Clinic.

Bank Officials then were J.J. Blake, Sr., president; J.S. Pickett, Sr., vice president; J.M. Jordan, cashier; John J. Blake, Jr., assistant cashier; Beatrice Davis, assistant cashier; Jack R. Jordan, assistant cashier; and Charlsie Ross, Ann Thomas, and Lorraine Rhodes, bookkeepers.

At that time deposits were insured for up to $10,000. Very few people in 1953 went over that amount, as $10,000 was an extremely large amount for one person to have.

The Reverend Howard Bryant, pastor of the First Baptist Church of Zwolle, offered the invocation at the ceremonies. Mayor Burkhalter opened by stating the dedication of City Hall and opening of Peoples State Bank Branch was Zwolle's finest hour. He praised Brandon for the great progress he had made in developing the police department into a well-trained, well-dressed, and efficient law enforcement organization.

Principal speakers were Mayor Clyde E. Fant of Shreveport and Claude Morgan of Alexandria with the Louisiana Municipal Association. Additional speakers included Judge Edwin M. Fraser, Judge William H. Ponder, State Representative J.M. Belisle, Mrs. Cora Schley, representative of the Louisiana Review and the

One of Brandon's finest accomplishments was the construction of a new City Hall, including a four cell jail, in 1953.

Louisiana Municipal Association; Paul Ebarb, school board member; and the Reverend Hatten, pastor of the United Pentecostal Church.

Many of these speakers praised Brandon for his role in providing the marshal's force with adequate equipment to handle law enforcement problems in a manner equal to that of police departments of larger towns.

In 1953 the marshal's patrol car was equipped with a two-way radio which permitted him to work more closely with the Sabine Parish Sheriff's Office and the Troop H State Police Headquarters in Leesville. He also made sure the marshal's office had modern and up-to-date equipment for fingerprinting. At the time such was considered "state of the art" equipment and Brandon had done a lot of finagling in order to obtain them.

The Reverend F.C. Collins, pastor of First Methodist Church, offered the benediction and blessing of the food.

The barbecue lunch served during the

97

dedication was listed as beef barbecue, but knowing how much Brandon loved barbecued goat one can bet there was some goat barbecue slipped in there somewhere.

During his entire lifetime Brandon was extremely proud of the City Hall Building. During his tenure he placed a large picture of himself (he had it made especially for that purpose) on the wall at City Hall. That huge picture was the first thing one saw when walking in. It was his way of "claiming territory." Without saying a word, he let people know they were on his turf and were expected to show respect for the law and order he represented.

Chapter 16

It's Rodeo Time

"I'll never forget how the announcer used to introduce him, 'And now ladies and gentlemen make welcome the Cowboy Marshal, Quinton Brandon!'"
—James McComic

Being a country boy, Quinton Brandon always loved animals and the rodeo. George Autrey, was raised at Negreet prior to World War II and remembers the Brandons from Alliance. "Quinton and his brothers were friendly and very athletic," Autrey remembered. "Some weekends, cow pasture rodeos were held at various farms in the area. The Brandons were noted for their riding ability."

In 1954, Brandon and W. F. Jeter, Jr., who were good friends, decided to go into the rodeo business. Brandon's mother was Jeter's grandfather's sister.

Jeter said that he and Brandon had been going around to different rodeos and had started talking about organizing their own. Said he, "We decided to use Sabine boys in the rodeo. We bought some good stock. We did it more or less for pleasure."

They constructed a rodeo arena on the road leading to Dr. Lloyd H. Murdock's farm, about a mile south of Zwolle. The land was leased from Jim Hale.

The first performances of the Brandon and Jeter Rodeo was October 1 and 2, 1954. To close the season, they held other rodeos October 28, 29, and 30.

In a news story in the May 6, 1955 *Sabine Index*, Brandon announced that he had purchased Jeter's interest in the rodeo and was the sole owner. In the same issue Brandon announced his first rodeos of the season on May 6 and 7.

Jeter said that he had gotten "tired of fooling with it." He continued, "I had bought a truck and

Governor Earl Kemp Long paid a visit to Brandon's Rodeo in Zwolle on July 1, 1955. The marshal listens to Long's talk.

tractor and was hauling dirt. So I had to work to make a living."

The year 1955 had to be Brandon's best season. He had performances in Zwolle on May 20 and 21, June 3 and 4, June 17 and 18, and July 1 and 2.

The July 1 and 2 performances were sponsored by the Zwolle Lions Club and the July 1 issue of *The Sabine Index* announced that former Governor Earl K. Long would be attending the Friday night performance.

Jeter said that he can not remember Long attending the rodeo, but does remember former Lieutenant Governor Bill Dodd, a native of Zwolle, and former Governor John J. McKeithen attending some performances.

In the July 8, 1955 issue of *The Index*, Brandon announced his rodeo would be held every Friday night. He held rodeos on July 22, July 29 and 30, September 2 and 3 and then on September 15, 16, and 17 he took the rodeo on the road with performances at Leesville. He closed out the 1955 season with performances at Zwolle on October 21 and 22.

The 1956 season started with rodeos May 11 and 12. On July 6 and 7, the Lions Club again sponsored the rodeo. On August 3 and 4, St. Joseph Catholic Church sponsored it. Brandon closed out the season with rodeos on November 9 and 10.

The last mention of the Brandon rodeo, was on October 10 and 11, 1958, when it was announced that Henry Sublet would produce a rodeo in the Brandon Arena.

In addition to Leesville, Mrs. Brandon said that her husband took the rodeo to Marshall and Center, Texas and Mansfield. "He loved the rodeo and fooling with animals," she recalled. "He did it more or less as a hobby. He thought he could make some money, but he did not. He wanted people to have a good time. A lot of people he didn't even charge an admission."

Dr. George D. Brandon recalled that his uncle loved rodeos. Stated Brandon, "He once took his son Jerry, myself, and his nephew, Stanley, to a rodeo in Gladewater, Texas. As I recall, we got there early and were hungry. Quinton bought us a watermelon and we went to the outskirts of town to a scenic hillside and filled up with watermelon."

Rocky Brandon said that his father's quarter horse was named "Boss." Said he, "The horse was very big and no one other than Daddy could do anything with him."

Former Sabine Sheriff Alfice Brumley remembered that he used to clown at the Brandon rodeos.

The late Luke Litton became a good friend with

Brandon in the early 1940's. They worked at the rodeo together. Litton purchased a bull from Brandon and named him "Quint."

Howard Brandon, Quinton's brother, said one night that he, Emmitt Parrie, C. C. (Tobe) Nabours, Charlie Pearson, Earl Brandon, Bob Brandon, W. F. Jeter, Jr., and Dink Basco were in Leesville helping Quinton put on a rodeo. He told the story, "Someone brought in a bottle of whiskey and they started passing it around. One bottle led to another and another until they were all just a little bit tipsy. Quinton kept coming around and he finally told them, 'Boys, I know what you're doing and I don't like it one little bit. If you were in Zwolle, I'd take you all to jail.' They all knew he meant it.

"Late that night they were driving home, all worn out, sleepy and 'hung over,' but not too 'out of it' to know they had better get everybody home without going through Zwolle, because they were afraid Quinton would be waiting for them. It took a long time and a lot of extra gas to bypass Zwolle, but it was a good thing they did because Quinton sat up all night waiting at the city limits to catch them."

Rocky said that after his father quit the rodeo business and sold his stock, some of his steers were so good they ended up in the National Rodeo Finals. He also remembered the last rodeo he and his father saw. It was October 1, 1976, in Pineland, Texas. "I was riding a bull in the rodeo," he remembered. "I was the last rider. Daddy came up to me and said, 'Son, the money is still out there.' I won the bull riding and he was proud." Terry Brandon, Rocky's cousin, won second in the bull riding that night.

"When I started riding bulls Daddy gave me his chaps and picked at us for using a glove and rosin, but he loved going to the rodeo with me and I think he was proud of me," Rocky continued. "Daddy was not one to praise, but I could tell."

George Autrey, remembered a Thanksgiving Day when he had dinner with the Brandons, including

Quinton Brandon is shown on his horse in this photo. Since he is wearing a U.S. Army uniform, it is assumed this photo was taken when he came home on leave.

father Webb. He related, "Webb steered us into a conversation about who could ride the best. After dinner and a lot of daring, we went to the rodeo arena and drove some horses up."

"One was a big horse named 'Charlie' and the other was a small horse that I referred to as 'Spinning Wheel,' " Autrey continued. "I rode first on 'Spinning Wheel' who came out spinning. I had gained some balance when he reversed direction and I landed on the back of my head and shoulders. Quinton rode 'Charlie' to the far end of the arena and triumphantly got off on the fence. However, 'Charlie' turned his rear end to him and kicked his leg. I left there with a sore neck and feeling that every muscle in my body was injured and Quinton with a very sore leg, but claiming victory because he rode the farthest. Webb thoroughly enjoyed it."

So early on in life, Brandon's love for the rodeo was nurtured. And while his rodeo in Zwolle did not prove successful for an extended period of time; nevertheless, he was doing something he enjoyed and something he hoped his friends would enjoy. He carried his love for the rodeo with him all his life.

Chapter 17

Billy Goats, Barbecue and
The Village Vet

"If the barbecue got to running short,
Quinton would just add more red pepper."
—-Lee Raymond Isgitt

In these parts Quinton Brandon was generally recognized as one of the best at barbecuing goat meat. In his heydays, he had regular goat barbecues that were the talk of the area at his Brandon Arena and then later at his Billy Goat Ranch.

Retired State Trooper Lee Raymond Isgitt of Many remembered it all very well. He explained, "Once or twice a year we would go out there. We would get some of his goats and butcher them at the canning center in Zwolle. We'd take them out to his place for the barbecue."

Isgitt continued, "Sheriff Phillips and Judge William Ponder would usually invite some people. If they invited too many people and the goat meat started running short, Quinton would have to 'make do.' That to Quinton meant adding some more red pepper to the barbecue. That would make the folks eat less meat and drink more kool-aid."

He remembered that he, Smiley McDonald, and Oliver Elliott would help out with the barbecues.

W. F. Jeter, Jr., said that they would sometime have fish fries. "We would invite all the parish officials," he recalled. "Sometime some of the state officials would come."

Paul Maxey recalled that each July fourth Brandon would barbecue a goat. "If he didn't have one, he would buy one," Maxey said. "He would invite mostly kin folks. He did that for several years."

Bertha Sepulvado of the Zwolle area said that one day Brandon called in on the radio and said he had some billy goats for sale. "I heard my daddy, Walter Sepulvado, talk about Mr. Brandon for years, but had never met him," she said. "I called him and when he said, 'Hello,' I thought that was the sexiest voice I ever heard. We went to get the billy goat and I told him, 'Mr. Quinton, with my husband here, I've got to tell you that you have the sexiest voice I have ever heard.' He just died laughing. I loved his voice. It was very beautiful; very deep. He loved animals. I still have some of his brand of billy goats."

Dr. George D. Brandon remembered when his uncle bought a small farm out toward Hurricane Valley. "Even though farming was not his occupation and he hated it early on, he still enjoyed the husbandry of animals and the bounty of the soil," he stated. "The place had a stand of young pine timber and he made plans to have it pushed down so he could have a pasture for his livestock, primarily the goats. One of his brothers told him he should let the trees stay and grow, as they would be valuable one day. Quinton replied that he didn't want trees; he wanted goats. Up until his death, he kept goats, a freezer calf, and hogs on his place and enjoyed caring for them. As much as anything, however, he enjoyed sharing the bountiful harvest when the animals were butchered. Up until his death, he and Aunt Nannie had a small garden behind their home."

James Cotton said that he remembered Brandon and maybe, Earl Brandon, dressing goats and selling them for Fourth of July barbecues.

In addition, Brandon was known far and wide around Zwolle as a non-professional veterinarian. Recalled Jeter, "We used to castrate horses, tend sick cows and just about anything that needed to be done. We would catch cows for people."

He continued, "I remember one morning just before daylight was breaking, someone called about some cows being loose in Zwolle. We were on our horses chasing the cows. Quinton's horse 'Boss' stumbled in a hole and fell over on him. I thought it had killed him. He hurt his back and it took him quite a while to get over it."

Cotton said that he also remembered one time Quinton and the late Oliver Elliott caught a pair of mules for Warren Cutrer, Elliott's father-in-law. "Mr. Cutrer couldn't catch them," Cotton remembered. "So he called Quinton and Oliver in. They set some kind of snares and caught those mules."

Brandon is shown with twin calves delivered by his nephew, Dr. George D. Brandon, Leesville veterinarian, in 1977. "He talked me through this delivery," Dr. Brandon said of his uncle.

"He was a good vet," longtime friend John Patton of Zwolle remembered. "At one time I had some horses. He treated them for diseases and was also a surgeon. He and his father drove to Oxford, where I had my horses, and he neutered one. My dad was there and after the operation, I enjoyed seeing the two older men sitting under a tree talking. That was very enjoyable."

"He never charged anything for the work he did," son Rocky said. "He only charged for the medicine."

He concluded, "Daddy would cut a colt and say he was performing brain surgery '..taking his mind off ass and putting it on grass.' "

Chapter 18

Taking Care of the Cemetery

*"Let's always remember and honor
those who have gone before us."*
—*A Thought*

"One of my proudest accomplishments is taking care of the Zwolle Cemetery," Quinton Brandon told reporter Richard Munson for a story in *Baton Rouge's Morning Advocate* March 12, 1981.

"That place was like a jungle not too long ago," Brandon said. "Now it's pretty damn clean. Know how I keep it up? I use drunks! It keeps them out of trouble."

W. F. Jeter, Jr., remembered, "If a man was in jail and couldn't pay his fine, Quinton would put him to work in the cemetery. People would make donations and he would buy mowers and the tools to work the cemetery."

"I think he knew where every grave was, and he knew something about the person buried there," retired District Judge John S. Pickett, Jr., of Many recalled.

"He took care of the cemetery until he had his stroke," Mrs. Brandon said. "The cemetery was a wilderness when he started in about 1957. After his stroke, they formed a committee and he worked with them until he passed away. He would use his children and friends to take care of the cemetery."

Dr. George D. Brandon remembered, "On occasion, my uncle would hire his son, Jerry, and myself to mow the cemetery. That was before the days of weed-eaters and he would give us each a hoe to trim around the edge of each tombstone, in order for the cemetery to look as nice as possible. He always had respect and reverence for the graves. If someone died,

109

and there weren't sufficient mourners, he would round up people off the street or out of the jail. If someone died a pauper and sufficient funds were not available for burial, he would take it on himself, to collect money for them to be buried properly."

In a letter to the editor in the September 10, 1981, issue of *The Index*, Brandon announced to the "people concerned with the Zwolle Cemetery" that he was resigning as caretaker.

He wrote, "For the last 25 years I have been responsible for the maintenance of the Zwolle Cemetery. Many think the town was responsible, but that is not true. I was responsible at my own expense and through yearly donations from the elderly on fixed incomes."

He ended, "Due to recent sickness and lack of donations, I am giving up any responsibility concerning the cemetery as of October 1, 1981. As far as my interest goes after this date, I will only claim responsibility for my family plot."

It seemed such a bittersweet ending to something that had been so near and dear to his heart.

Chapter 19

The FBI Comes to Visit

*"The Marshal was not perturbed
by the intrusion of the FBI."*
—-Unnamed Source

In the dog days of summer 1998, Delane Christianson sat in the kitchen at Mrs. Quinton Brandon's Zwolle home and recalled from his storehouse of fond memories those of his departed friend. He and wife, Phyllis, had started to Alabama, but were stopped short in Zwolle by Hurricane Georges.

Born in Harlan, Iowa, Christianson spent from 1948-1980 with the Federal Bureau of Investigation (FBI) and it was during this period that he met Brandon. After leaving the FBI, he continued living in Omaha, Nebraska, where he opened a private investigation agency, from which he was now retired.

In 1958, Christianson was assigned to Shreveport as the resident FBI agent. He covered Sabine, in addition to DeSoto, and Red River Parishes.

"I first met Quinton in March, 1958," Christianson recalled as if it were only yesterday. "Actually, I met Nannie before I met him. I was looking for him and came to his house. I found out again that behind every good man there was a good woman. She invited me in and made a cup of coffee, and I visited with her until Quinton came."

Although Christianson would not admit it, information had surfaced that he came to visit because it had been alleged Brandon was in possible violation of Federal Civil Rights statutes. The story had it that when he advised Brandon why he was there, the marshal was not perturbed by the intrusion of the FBI and simply supplied him with the facts. After the

Delane and Phyllis Christianson of Omaha, Nebraska, shown at right, were special friends of Quinton and Nannie Brandon. They first met in 1958 when Christianson worked for the FBI. The picture was taken in October 1984 at the Tamale Fiesta.

investigation was completed, the matter was never pursued. From their initial contact and subsequent visits, Christianson learned that Brandon's word could be relied upon.

"We immediately became good friends," he continued, "And we remained that way until his passing. My friendship continues with his family until this day. As the years went by, our friendship continued to develop. In life, you have a lot of friends, but you don't have many real friends and Quinton was a real friend."

Christianson was transferred from Shreveport to Omaha in March, 1965, but the friendship with Brandon continued to be strong. "I would come down and visit at least once a year," he remembered. "I would bring some judges, attorneys, and my kids from Omaha to fish Toledo Bend. We'd stay a week sometimes. He would always come out and spend at least one night with us. He and Nannie would bring some barbecue and pecan pie. He was a very accommodating person."

"He was a person I could always rely on," Christianson continued. "Of all the police officers I ever met, he was the most dedicated. He used to say he had three priorities in his life, God, country, and family, in that order."

"Back in those days, the FBI was more of a reactive organization," he recalled. "It is now a proactive organization. We had a reactive responsibility back then—bank robberies and any violation of federal law. I could always rely on Quinton when I had a problem in the Zwolle area. He would either go with me and help me, or he would give me the names and directions."

Christianson continued, "I remember one time, we had a drug case where a person who lived in Zwolle was supplying drugs to Shreveport. We arrested the person responsible and if it had not been for Quinton, we would not have made the arrest."

In sizing Brandon up, Christianson stated, "He always told you what he thought, even if he knew you wouldn't like it. He was dedicated to his job. When he enforced the law, he never let politics or personal preference get in his way. If you were his friend and violated the law, you were arrested. Quinton was like a lot of people in law enforcement: he did a dedicated and honorable job, often to the detriment of his family. And I mean the long hours he put in, the nights he got called out, and the years he went without a vacation."

"Quinton and the late Oliver Elliott, a deputy with the sheriff's department for many years, were close," Christianson remembererd. "They used to barbecue goat. Quinton liked things hot. He'd put a lot of pepper on the goat. Then he and Oliver would get a big kick out of watching the look on people's faces as they bit into that goat with all the pepper on it."

"His friends meant a lot to him," he continued.

"He found out one of the guys he was in service with had cancer. He immediately took a flight to Virginia to see him. That's the kind of guy he was."

In conclusion, Christianson stated, "I never met another law enforcement officer with whom I enjoyed such a wonderful relationship. After I retired, our families got even closer. I'll always remember Quinton and the wonderful times we shared, and I still love to visit his family today. Good, true friends are few and far between and that's why I valued his friendship and still value his family's friendship so much."

Chapter 20

A Man to Help

*"Mr. Brandon was one of those searching
the river and he found the body."*
—-Mayor Roger Lopez

Zwolle Mayor Roger Lopez recalled Quinton Brandon as a man always willing to help his neighbor.

It was May 19, 1960, and Glen Patrick Martinez, seventeen years old, and a classmate, Steven Garcie, were swimming in the Sabine River. They and several classmates had been on an overnight camping trip.

Martinez drowned in a deep hole in the river, as Garcie attempted to rescue him. Martinez was holding onto a stick as Garcie, who was not a good swimmer, attempted the rescue. Martinez suddenly let go of the stick and disappeared.

He was the son of Mr. and Mrs. Gilbert Martinez.

"That was back before the days of diving teams and search and rescue teams," Lopez recalled. "Mr. Brandon was one of those searching the river and found the body. I remember seeing him come up with the body."

Lopez continued, "He was helping and found the body, even though the search was not his duty. He took time out from his job and went and found the boy's body." Brandon had no jurisdiction at the time outside Zwolle, but always went where he was needed.

According to a report in the May 27, 1960, edition of *The Index*, Brandon recovered the body about two hours after the drowning.

George Autrey, who was a Sabine deputy starting in August, 1947, recalled another sad note. He said that two young girls drowned in the Sabine River near Ebarb while on a family outing. Autrey told the story, "The area was hardly accessible by car or truck.

However, during the night, after one body had been recovered, Quinton and I bounced a Ford in and placed the body in the back seat and hauled the remains to the Many Funeral Home and the coroner. Later, about daybreak, the other body was recovered and we repeated the chore. A family member accompanied us."

Early on, Brandon as well as Autrey, had been taught to help his neighbor. And as a law enforcement officer, there would always be plenty of helpful acts to perform.

Chapter 21

A Good Piece of Work

*"Mr. Brandon began to methodically investigate
and build his case piece by small piece."*
—-The Sabine Index

Paul Ebarb Company was robbed on February
24, 1964, and Marshal Quinton Brandon did one of his
best pieces of work in solving the crime. Netted by the
thieves was $1,665 in cash and notes and account
records of untold value.

The case was one that would widen Brandon's
reputation as a good law enforcement officer.

On Tuesday, June 22, Brandon returned to
Zwolle from Odessa, Texas, with enough evidence
against five persons to go into the fall term of District
Court.

The Index story stated, "With only a meager
description of the get away car to go on, Brandon
began to methodically investigate and build his case
piece by small piece. He has been working on the case
constantly and has been led into a number of states
thousands of miles away and has had many a sleepless
night."

At the time the story appeared, three suspects
were still in custody and two had been released on
bond. All five were ex-convicts. They included
Herschel Baker Wesson and Frank Burt, both parolees
from Texas State Prison in Huntsville; B. L. Brock,
Huntsville; and Clifton Paul Gravier and Charles
Wilson, both of Shreveport.

In an interview, Brandon expressed appreciation
for the assistance given to him by the state police,
sheriff's department and other law enforcement
agencies in Louisiana and Texas.

Paul Ebarb, the store's owner, congratulated
Brandon and other officers for their efficient work in
solving the case.

Chapter 22

A Night in the Zwolle Jail

"Write, write, write me a letter.
Send that letter by mail.
Send that letter in care of
The Old Zwolle Jail."
—from Old Folk Song

Danny Ebarb now lives in Hemphill, Texas. Back in 1966 he was sixteen and lived in a two-room shack down on the Sabine River. One winter's afternoon, he and his cousin James Michael Ebarb, told his parents, Mr. and Mrs. Rex Hessie Ebarb, they were going to Zwolle to see what they could get into. Little did they know what they would be into before the night was over.

"We didn't know much about Zwolle, but we were eager to learn," Danny Ebarb commented. "We rode around awhile, then my old car quit. We later learned we were behind the Zwolle jail. We kept trying, but the car wouldn't crank. Finally we decided to sleep in the car."

He continued, "We had not been drinking, but you would not have known it from our behavior. Someone in that jail kept hollering foul things at us and we kept yelling back for the nut to shut up. As the night wore on, we kept hoping the car would start, but it didn't. We kept getting colder and colder."

Somewhere along the line Marshal Brandon heard the racket and came to see what it was about. Ebarb said, "He started questioning us and wanted to know what we were doing."

Ebarb related, "He asked if we were cold and we told him we were. He said he had a motel where we could be more comfortable than in the cold car. We were thrilled until he drove around to the front of the

119

building and we determined he was going to put us in jail. But we weren't about to argue about it under the circumstances."

The two awoke the next morning bright and early. "We started to try to escape," he stated. "We managed to pick the lock to our cell with a piece of wire we found. But there was still another door and as we attempted to pick it, the wire broke off in the key hole."

"We knew we were in trouble," Ebarb said. "Mr. Brandon was mad and gave us a good chewing out. He told us we were trying to act like tough guys. He asked if we knew a man in Hemphill and called his name. We told him we did. He said the man thought he was tough until he met him. I found out later that the man had broken into some houses on the Sabine River and stolen a shotgun."

Ebarb continued, "Mr. Brandon had pistol whipped him after he put up a fight. The man managed to swim the Sabine River, but Sheriff Blan Greer was waiting on the Texas side to arrest him. He returned him to Mr. Brandon. The man was a pretty tough guy with a long line of jailbreaks and crimes of different sorts. But, I'm sure he learned to respect Mr. Brandon after their run-in."

In closing, Ebarb stated, "Mr. Brandon probably did the right thing by locking us up, because we could have frozen to death or something else bad could have happened to us. He let us out the next day, but not before calling Sheriff Greer to see if he wanted us, since I had Texas tags on the car. My old battery was down, and Mr. Brandon was good enough to jump start my car."

And in conclusion, Ebarb remarked, "And the nut who was in the jail cell next to us wouldn't let us have any sleep after he got us locked up. He kept us awake most of the night. I can't forget that."

Chapter 23

Running for Sheriff

"Quinton didn't need to be Sheriff.
He'd try to fix everything and he just couldn't."
—*Mrs. Nannie Brandon*

Any American as red-blooded as Quinton Brandon wanted to move up life's ladder and better himself. He always tried to follow that practice. He believed strongly in America and improving one's status was the American dream.

As spring turned into the summer of 1967, running for sheriff weighed heavily on Brandon's mind. He thought about the possibilities for a long time. He talked to his friends to find out what kind of support he had. The support he was receiving all seemed very good. He made up his mind he would toss his hat into the ring.

Popular Sheriff Phillips was retiring at the end of his term. He had served twenty-four years. Brandon thought it a good time to run.

On Monday morning, July 16, Brandon put on his best suit and tie and that ever present Stetson hat and headed for *The Sabine Index* office in Many to have his picture taken and an announcement put in the paper. He gave his qualifications in the announcement and then said if elected "...he will seek to enforce the laws like he believes the people of the parish want and deserve."

Brandon proposed a deputy in each of the parish's ten wards. He said this would provide a closer working relationship with the people. He also stated he would like to see constables recognized fully with the authority vested in them.

In his first ad in the September 14 *Index* Brandon apologized for being unable to see everyone, although

121

he had been trying. He said a combination of factors, including sickness and death in the family, plus the fact that he worked a minimum of eight hours a day had prevented him from doing so.

Apparently the rumor mill had been working, saying that he had been fired from the state police. Brandon said that he had resigned as a trooper after Zwolle city officials solicited him as marshal.

In closing the ad, he wrote, "I am an independent candidate dedicated to law enforcement as a lifetime profession. I am in no way obligated to any individual or groups and I'll be the sheriff for all the people."

His next three ads were alike and ran in the October 19 and 26 and November 2 *Index*. The advertisement was headed, "Let's Make Sabine Parish a Better Place to Live" and included ten pledges, as follows:

1. Stop illegal sale of liquor to minors.
2. Cut down on high rate of highway accidents by strict enforcement of safety laws.
3. Put a stop to drag racing, speeding and other notorious law violations.
4. Promptly investigate every report of crime.
5. Inaugurate a program to teach young people to have respect for and knowledge of law enforcement.
6. See that sheriff's cars, paid for by the taxpayers, will be used exclusively for law enforcement.
7. Modernize the sheriff's office and work for economy.
8. Inaugurate a program of crime prevention.
9. Enforce all laws, impartially, without fear or favor.
10. Encourage closer cooperation among federal, state, parish and local law agencies in order to make Sabine a better place to live and rear families.

The election was held Saturday, November 4, and Sheriff's Deputy Harold Sandel led the field of six candidates with 2,625 votes. Many Marshal George R. Cook came in second with 1,917. Max Teasley ran third with 1,316, followed closely by Brandon with 1,259. Rounding out the field were perennial candidates Floyd Peterson with 424 and Joseph Brune Flores with 193.

In the run-off Saturday, December 16, Sandel polled 3,607 votes to defeat Cook, who garnered 3,058. Sandel had won by 549 votes. Outgoing Sheriff Phillips had come through for Sandel, endorsing him in an ad in *The Index* the week of the election.

In the November 16 *Index*, Brandon, being a gentleman, ran an ad thanking those who supported him, and "...especially the folks of Wards five, eight, and ten for their tremendous vote of confidence."

Even though the race was over, the rumor mill was still operating. In the November 23 *Index*, Zwolle physician Dr. J. Lane Sauls ran an ad defending Brandon. The ad stated: "In the recent election, an erroneous charge was made by one of the candidates that should be corrected. Brandon was accused of 'throwing a man in jail and letting him die.' Since I treated the man when this occurred over ten years ago, I am glad to say the man had medical care before, during and after his stay in jail. He died in the hospital despite our best efforts. To my knowledge he was not abused, mistreated or neglected." Floyd Peterson had made the charge, which Dr. Sauls addressed.

In a full-page ad in the July 8, 1971, *Index* there was a picture of Brandon and others endorsing Sandel for re-election. Brandon's part read, "I have served as deputy sheriff under Sandel and it has been a pleasure the entire four years. The cooperation between me as marshal of Zwolle and the sheriff's department has been excellent the entire four years and I am sure this cooperation can exist another four years in peace and harmony."

Cook beat Sandel this time around. While things might have been good between Brandon and Sandel, some say Cook never forgot that Brandon was not for him and relations between the two were strained until Cook's death in June, 1978. W. F. Jeter, Jr., who worked for both Brandon and Cook, said that this is not true; that relations between the two were good.

Jeter is probably right, because a story in the July 31, 1975, *Index* stated Cook and Brandon announced the opening of a sheriff's sub-station at the Zwolle police department.

The story quoted Brandon, "My department and the sheriff's department will work as one unit in serving the people. I'm very proud of this development because it gives us a chance to get calls answered in the Zwolle area much quicker."

Brandon concluded, "Any warrants and other work that need to get to the sheriff's department can be left at my office and it will be taken care of immediately."

Roger Lopez commented that Brandon took pride in the vote he got in Wards five and eight. "That was in the days of vote buying," Lopez stated. "Quinton carried both wards and he liked to brag that he never spent a penny."

Brandon's first attempt at running for office was for Ward eight constable in the December 5, 1959, democratic primary. Roy Sibley led the field of four with 324, S. L. Campbell came in second with 246, Brandon ran third with 216 and George Laroux rounded it out with 92. Campbell was elected in the January 9, 1960 run-off.

Trying his hand again, Brandon led the field of the same four in the December 7, 1963, primary. He polled 335, Sibley had 271, Campbell had 246 and Laroux ran last with 117. In the January 11, 1964 run-off, the tide turned and Sibley was elected with 362, as was Campbell with 289. Brandon ran third with 235 and Laroux again ran last with 110.

Other Brandons could not quite get into the

winning column either. His brother Howard Brandon ran for Ward five police juror in 1975 and 1979 and lost both times. Earl Brandon, a nephew, was defeated for Ward five justice of the peace in 1967.

Brandon had been defeated as sheriff, but he was always proud that he carried Wards eight, five and ten by healthy majorities. In later years he was glad to point this out when the opportunity arose.

One good thing did come out of it all. Whereas previous sheriffs had used Brandon when needed in the Zwolle area without a badge, commission and pay, Sandel saw the political advantage to himself to have the lawman on his side. So, he gave Brandon a commission and badge and placed him on the payroll. As long as Brandon lived, all other sheriffs followed suit.

Chapter 24

Integration

"Professor, don't you worry.
I won't tolerate any disturbances."
—Brandon to Professor Samuel Cross

The Sabine Parish School Board passed a resolution in 1967 that schools would be integrated. The Federal Government had spoken. Because the Federal Government controlled the people's purse strings, everyone listened. Integration was the law of the land and it would be enforced.

Samuel D. Cross, who was principal of the Zwolle Intermediate School at the time, recalled, "When the proclamation was issued to integrate schools, Mr. Brandon called me to his office. He said, 'Professor, don't you worry. I will not tolerate any disturbances.'"

Cross continued, "He did not allow any problems and the transition went very smoothly for our schools." Cross later went on to serve on the Sabine School Board himself.

Dr. George D. Brandon stated, "I do not know a lot of details of his law enforcement career, except that in the eyes of his fellow officers he was known for his dedication to the law. I do know and am proud that he regarded law enforcement without regard to status or race. The era of his career coincided with a time of racial strife in our state and nation, and racial and hate crimes were called as such by him and he would arrest a white man as readily as a black. As such, I believe he was equally respected by all."

Eddie Gaither, of Beaumont, Texas, remembered growing up with her grandmother Ann McClanahan in 1960 in Zwolle.

Said she, "He was a very nice man to all people, no matter what your race. Everyone was equal in his eyes. He would go to the quarters and check on my grandmother. If she needed any groceries or needed to go some place, he would see that it was done."

Ms. Gaither recalled one time when she left her lunch money at home. She explained, "Mr. Brandon saw to it I ate that day. If there was anyone else who did not have money for food, he would see that they ate."

She concluded, "We were not allowed to walk to school and if we missed the bus, he would take us to school at no charge. He believed that every child had a right to get a good education and grow up to be whatever he or she dreamed to be. Everyone had the utmost respect for him."

Alice Faye Holden Ward grew up in Zwolle in the 1950's and lives near Converse. She is also a granddaughter of Ms. McClanahan, who ran a cafe called the Blue Moon in the Hale Quarters. She remembered, "We had law and order back then. Mr. Brandon was a big, tall, handsome man. People listened when he talked. He was firm and out-spoken."

Ms. Ward continued, "When he was called to the Blue Moon for a disturbance, most of the time he would give the person a good talking to. Some others he had to take to jail. He would get to the root of a problem. He was well respected by most; disliked by others."

"Our family has talked about this man," she recalled. "We could sleep with our windows and doors open. We knew we had one of the best lawmen in Sabine Parish."

Ms. Ward concluded, "I was living in Dallas and came to Zwolle for a visit. I went by to see him. He was very ill and was in a wheel chair. It was hard for me to see him like that, when I knew him in good health. God knows that was one white man my family liked, and those of us who are still living remember and miss him."

Brad Falcon has lived in Zwolle since he was fourteen years old. He was sixty-five in December,

1998. Brandon hired him as a patrolman in 1969; he stayed fourteen years. He was the second black officer that Brandon hired.

Falcon said that Claude Shelby was the first black hired, but he stayed only a couple of months.

He continued, "I had applied earlier, but he didn't hire me. I think it was because I only weighed one hundred forty pounds. I think he thought I was too small. Shelby weighed about two hundred forty pounds. After Shelby left, I went back to him and he hired me. He called me his 'Top Man.' He said I was honest and he could trust me."

Falcon called Brandon "...a top law enforcement officer." He added, "He was always fair. Some people thought he was mean by his attitude and the way he talked. People thought he was mad. That's just the way he was."

Chapter 25

Double Murder, Then Suicide

*"That's just long enough to get
the law and come back."*
—Leroy West

Before the day was over on Friday, March 21, 1968, two persons had been murdered in Zwolle and a third had committed suicide. Marshal Quinton Brandon was the first to arrive at the scene.

He found that at about 10:40 a.m., Leroy West had killed his wife and daughter, Earline, eighteen years old, and then turned the gun on himself. He shot his wife three times with a .22 pistol, then turned on their daughter and shot her three times. After that West went outside to his car, got a .16 gauge shotgun, came near the house and blew his heart out.

The couple's three sons, ages ten, twelve, and thirteen and a daughter, about sixteen, witnessed the tragic event.

Deputy Sheriff Alfice Brumley, who investigated along with Deputy Truitt Walden, said that the children told the following account of the shootings.

The couple had been arguing most of the morning. They said that West did not want Earline to go to work at a cafe in Florien, where she had been employed six days. Margie Meshell, Earline's sister, is said to have told Earline if her daddy would not take her to work she would. Ms. Meshell and a girl friend and three of the West children left to go to the washateria in Zwolle. One of the children told her father that they would be back in ten minutes.

The children said that as soon as Margie left, West told the family, "That's just long enough to get the law and come back." He then started shooting.

The family had been having trouble for

131

sometime. A month prior to the incident, West brought a wanted notice and a picture of Earline, who was missing, to *The Index* to be printed. He later found Earline in Shreveport and canceled the notice.

Chapter 26

The Shooting of Jimmy Ray Pleasant

"I've got a little job to do."
—Quinton Brandon to Jimmy Ray Pleasant

Sheriff's Deputy Jimmy Ray Pleasant had been shot. His partner Deputy Jack Brown was speeding along the road leading into Zwolle in an attempt to get him to the Sabine Clinic. His life was at stake. Brown knew that every minute counted. "Jack, I ain't gonna make it," Pleasant kept saying.

Brown had radioed the sheriff's department and told them of the crisis. Deputy Walter Schulthorpe had called the clinic. Dr. Richard J. Oosta and Dr. J. Lane Sauls were on duty at the clinic. Pleasant said that he was getting where he could not see, but he could still hear and he knew what was taking place.

"Quinton was waiting at the clinic when we got there," Pleasant said. "He came up to the patrol car, opened the door and took me in his arms. I couldn't see and could barely hear, but I'll never forget his voice. He took me in and laid me on the operating table. Dr. Lloyd Murdock was there. He asked Dr. Murdock if there was anything else he needed him for. Dr. Murdock replied, "No."

Quinton said, "I've got a little job to do." And he turned around and left.

The day was Thanksgiving Day 1968. Pleasant and Brown were on duty and at about 11:10 p.m. they noted the driver of a pickup being erratic on the Garcie Loop, about five miles west of Zwolle.

The truck turned into a driveway on the Blue Lake Road, with the patrol car behind it. Brown went to the driver's side and got Herbert Ebarb out and arrested him for drunk driving. He was taking Ebarb to the patrol car and had just gotten to the back of the pickup when he heard a shot.

"I looked around and saw Jimmy laying on his back about ten feet from the rearof the pickup," Brown told *The Sabine Index*. "At the same time, he told me 'Jack, I've been shot.'"

Brown turned Ebarb loose and told him to hit the ground. Brown immediately drew his revolver and fired two shots at the passenger in the truck. Seeing the bullets would not go through the truck's cab, Brown started to the patrol car to get a shotgun.

He further related, "Jimmy fell at my feet and said, 'Jack, I been shot bad.'" Brown got the shotgun and was going to shoot Larry Parrie, seventeen, of Zwolle, the passenger in the truck. "I didn't know but what he was going to shoot me next," Brown said.

Brown raised the shotgun, but as he started to shoot, he saw Parrie's wife standing between him and Parrie. He learned later they were at Parrie's home. Pleasant at this point told Brown, "Jack, you better get me somewhere quick; I'm bleeding bad."

In being interviewed for this book, Pleasant recalled that night: "I had an old five cell flashlight and it rolled under the seat when Jack stopped behind the truck. I was trying to get it out as Jack went to the truck. When I got the flashlight, I went to the passenger's side. I opened the door and this boy was hunkered down and he shot me. I didn't even see him."

Pleasant had been shot at close range, in the stomach, with a .410 shotgun. He pulled through, but doctors at the time gave him a one in one thousand chance of recovery.

When Brandon left the clinic, he headed for Parrie's house. He took with him his deputy, W. F. Jeter, Jr., Brown, and State Trooper George Elliott joined them.

When they got there, they told Parrie to come out of the house. He ran to the fence and squatted down by the gate. He had a big hunting knife in his hand and later said that he intended to cut the first one he could get his hands on. Parrie's wife and daddy came out of the house and she managed to get the knife away from him. Parrie was arrested, handcuffed, and taken to jail.

Jeter said that when they got there, Parrie had his arms and legs stretched out like an eagle. He continued, "Quinton had a shotgun aimed at him through the picket fence. He could have shot him if he had wanted to. He told him, 'Drop that knife and come out and I won't kill you.'"

Pleasant, in an interview for this book stated, "Later Quinton told me, 'Jim, I went out there to kill the son-of-a-b——.' When I got out there, he and his pregnant wife were all hugged up and I just couldn't shoot a pregnant woman."

As an added twist, Sheriff Guffey Lynn Pattison said that Parrie thought he was shooting Brandon when he shot Pleasant.

Chapter 27

The Matchmaker

*"We are going to find you a good man in Zwolle
because I can see you are a good person and are
working hard to support those four children."*
—Quinton Brandon to Evelyn Hopkins

The situation is hard to image Quinton Brandon,
with his loud, gruff voice, standing six feet, one inch
tall, weighing two hundred pounds and the epitome of
"a macho man" playing cupid. However, Mrs. Evelyn
Hopkins, a retired employee at *The Sabine Index*, told
the following story:

"In the summer of 1969, I came to Zwolle as a
saleslady for the Liddell Candy Company of
Shreveport. I was scared to death because of
everything I heard about the little town of Zwolle. My
first stop was the restaurant on the corner of Highway
171 and Port Arthur Street, where E.B.'s Tamales is
now. I introduced myself to the owner and told her I
was there instead of their regular salesman. She gave
me a cup of coffee and as I tried to put the cup to my
lips, I spilled it because I was still a little scared to be
in this town.

"A man in a uniform came in and introduced
himself as the Chief of Police of Zwolle. His name was
Quinton Brandon. I said, 'If you are the chief of police
where is your gun?' His reply, 'I don't need one, I have
a big stick.'

"That voice was the sexiest, gruffiest voice I ever
heard and I began to feel better just knowing this man
wearing a uniform and carrying a big stick was now
my friend. If he could be an officer in Zwolle and not
have to carry a gun, the town was much better than I
had heard.

"I made the trip to Zwolle weekly, always on

Friday, and I always stopped at the restaurant to get an order and have a cup of coffee with Brandon. After a few weeks, he began to ask me questions because he saw I did not wear a wedding ring. After finding out I was a divorced woman with four children to support, he said, 'We are going to find you a good man here in Zwolle because I can see you are a good person working hard to support those four children. We need you in Zwolle.'

"Oh no," I said, "I will not live here, I have heard too many bad things about this town and although I have met many nice people here, I do not want to live here and I certainly don't want to raise my children in Zwolle.

" 'But you just wait, I have and will continue to make Zwolle a good place to live,' said Brandon. When he looked at you straight in the eye with that stern expression, you knew he was telling the truth.

"The next Friday I again went into the restaurant and Brandon was having a cup of coffee and motioned for me to join him. He told me, 'J.O. Kimbrell (a businessman in Zwolle and a very fine man) and I have decided Bill Hopkins who works at Lefkovits, is the man for you. You have four children and Bill has four children, you can be known as the 'Brady Bunch' of Zwolle.' He started to laugh in that big, gruff voice of his and I had to join in with him although I was thinking, 'Not me and Bill Hopkins. He is much too quiet and serious for me.'

"But guess what? On October 25, 1969, Bill called me at my home in Shreveport and asked me to go to dinner with him to help him celebrate his birthday. I went and had a great time. He was a very different man away from his place of business. Once again Brandon was right and in December, 1969, I accepted an engagement ring from Bill.

"The Friday after I got my ring I went into the restaurant and saw Brandon sitting at a table. I held up my left hand and when he saw the engagement ring, he jumped sky high, came over and hugged my neck. 'I knew we could find you a good man and we did it,' Brandon said. 'But most of all I think Mr. Bill will get a good wife and mother for his children. I know that to be the truth so hurry and move on down here in this good old Town of Zwolle.'

" 'Miss Evelyn, if you ever have a problem or you need help, or you just plain need to talk to someone you know how to find me,' he said. 'I also want you to meet my family. They will love you too.'

"From that day I knew I had a friend. I married Bill and moved to Zwolle in June, 1970. Marriage is always an adjustment and it took time and patience for me to feel I fit into the Lefkovits family and the family I married into. When I was worried or depressed, I would go talk to Brandon.

"Once when I was in city court covering the news for *The Index*, Brandon asked me to wait after court because he wanted to talk to me.

"Many times during court, the chief would have everyone laughing by stating something comical. Court was always interesting. However, during this court session one of the men Brandon had arrested and was trying in court, decided to break and run away. When he broke and ran, he shoved my daughter, Andrea, who was in the back of the courtroom holding her two-week-old baby. Brandon moved faster than lightning and caught this fellow and slapped him saying, 'You don't hurt a woman in my court, and especially one that is holding a little baby. You apologize to her now.' The man did so immediately.

"I did stay after court and talked to Brandon. He stated that he did not want me to put in the paper that he was being ugly in court, but if it took that to handle those who become convicts, so be it. He also said, 'Miss Evelyn, I don't feel like I'm gonna live too much longer, I feel like I need to talk to someone.' He went on to say he had spent most of his life in the City Hall building and when he died, 'I want my body to be brought here with a flag over my coffin for people to come and view me for the last time. I promise I won't jump out and scare anyone.' He gave that big, gruff laugh again.

"After this, I never failed to talk to Brandon at least once a week, mostly about something that happened and I needed a story on it for *The Index*. By this time I had met many of his children and his lovely wife, Nannie. Brandon was like a Daddy to me and I knew he loved his family. When he had his stroke, I never failed to ask the Good Lord to let him get well and come back to being the 'Sheriff that tamed Zwolle.'

"When Brandon passed away, I think the lights went out in Zwolle. There will never be anyone else like him. Everyone knows that."

Chapter 28

Out as Marshal?

"Some campaigned on replacing Quinton.
They were mad at him for one reason or another."
—W. F. Jeter, Jr.

As 1969 turned into 1970, Quinton Brandon heard rumors that he did not like. He had always taken pride in having the support of the mayor and the town council. This had always been a big part of his success. He realized he could only be successful if he and the other officials worked together as a team.

The rumors he had been hearing were that a new group of men were seeking election to the Zwolle Town Council on a platform to get rid of him.

When the results of the April 2, 1970, election came in, Brandon's old friend Elmer C. Marshal had been beaten as mayor. The new man was Ray S. Spurlock, who polled 390 to Marshal's 192. A third candidate, Wiley Hawkins, had received 129.

Elected to the town council were Fred Roberson, Jr., Bob E. Asseff, Roger Lopez, John Henry Procell, and James E. (Buddy) Veuleman. Procell was the only incumbent re-elected.

Others who ran but were defeated were Jack O. Napier, Hoyt Maxey, Garrett H. Walsh, Max Brown, and David Peterson.

Lopez recalled, "Some of us campaigned on getting rid of Quinton. John Henry and I were going to vote against Quinton. Buddy Veuleman was supposed to, but he changed his mind."

Lopez said that the reason he was mad at Brandon was that his father, George Lopez, ran a store in the Zwolle city limits. The store was in Ward five, which had voted beer legal in 1967. The elder Lopez took the position that beer was legal in Ward five and he could sell it. Brandon took the position Zwolle was

141

dry and kept arresting Lopez. "This is what I was mad at him about," Lopez said.

The pressure on Brandon kept getting stronger. In the May 4 issue of *The Sabine Index*, Ward five Justice of the Peace Fred Rivers issued an opinion from State Attorney General Jack P. F. Gremillion about whether the marshal could be removed from office by the new mayor and council which was to take office on June 1.

Gremillion said that his office obtained a copy of the Special Charter for Zwolle, which was adopted in June of 1898.

PHOTO BY THE SABINE INDEX

Brandon in August 1970, after being re-appointed Zwolle marshal.

The Attorney General wrote: "You will note the marshal is elected by the mayor and council. The power to appoint is incidental to the power to remove and when the new council takes office June 1 they alone are vested with the authority to appoint a new marshal. Upon removal of the present marshal, there would be no authority for payment to him of any monies, regardless of the fact that the past administration passed an ordinance authorizing payment of additional salaries beyond June 1."

The new council held its first meeting July 2 and voted to take applications for marshal. They voted to retain Brandon for thirty days while applications were being taken.

Spurlock said that there were about seventy-five people present at the meeting and there was a question-answer session with most questions being about the marshal's post.

Concerning who would be selected by the council, Spurlock told *The Index*, "The best qualified man will be selected, we hope."

So in that thirty-day period, each side had its work cut out. Petitions started circulating in support of Brandon. Lopez said that they were at the Pelican Drug Store, owned by Roberson, and Nichols Department Store, where Veuleman was manager.

One person, who asked not to be identified, said a member of the council approached him and asked him to apply for the marshal's job. The person, who was a close friend of Brandon's, said his reply was, "No."

When the council met on the evening of July 30, Brandon was re-appointed without discussion. Roberson made the motion and it was carried unanimously. There were no other applicants for the job.

This was a trying period for Brandon. For a while it looked as if he was not going to be able to retain his job.

In the August 6 issue of *The Index*, Brandon stated, "The people came to my aid when I needed them. They let the council know they wanted me as marshal. I want to thank the people of all races and religions for what they've done for me for so many years."

In the article, Brandon pointed out that each time he had been appointed by the council, it had been unanimous. He pointed out he had attended the State Police Academy, had taken basic and advanced courses in law enforcement, and had completed a finger print course. "I did these things to better qualify myself to give the people of Zwolle the law enforcement they deserve," he said.

Index Publisher Robert Gentry, who always was a supporter of Brandon, wrote in his August 6 column Observations: "We would like to offer our congratulations to Mayor Spurlock and members of the council for re-appointing Brandon. It's a very wise decision.

"As a lawman, Quinton can't be beat. He is dedicated to law enforcement, and the work he has done in Zwolle proves this. Right now, while working short-handed, Brandon is putting in about seventeen hours a day, seven days a week. There are few who would be so dedicated."

Spurlock told the writers of this book, "Our intention was not to get rid of him when we decided to take applications. It was never our intention at all to get rid of him."

After the wrangle with Brandon, the mayor and council decided that such an event would never happen again. In the 1972 Legislative Session, at the request of Spurlock and the council, State Representative H. M. (Mutt) Fowler offered a bill, which passed, to change the marshal's title to chief of police and make the position elective rather than appointive. The bill provided the chief would be elected at the same time as the other Zwolle officials.

Brandon had made it through the crisis and he felt good. He appreciated the support of his friends. The endorsement meant a lot to him. He knew if he was to be elected by his friends and neighbors that he would be in good shape.

Chapter 29

The Murder of Dick Maxey

"He told me what was so unusual is
Corley came to his house the night of the murder."
—Pete Abington

Richard (Dick) Maxey of Zwolle was only forty-three years of age when he was murdered the night of July 21, 1970. He was a brother-in-law to Quinton Brandon. Maxey's body was found at 1:00 p.m. the next day just off the Hot Wells Road, two miles west of Noble. James A. Diamond of Mitchell, who was operating a motor grader on the road, found the body. Maxey had been shot in the left side by a .22 magnum Derringer pistol.

Zwolle Barber William J. (Bill) Corley was charged with the murder. Sheriff Harold W. Sandel said that the two had been together at several lounges earlier during the day of the murder. He said that they got into an argument, which turned into a fight and later a murder.

Corley's truck ran off the road into a ditch on the Hot Wells Road and he walked to a house in the area. Maxey's body was dragged into the woods a short way off the road.

A search party was organized the next day to find the pistol. Corley told Sheriff Sandel that he threw the pistol into the woods as he walked along the road. Corley was brought to the scene but could not find the pistol. Corley was returned to jail and law officers and volunteers combed the wooded area along the road.

When it seemed the gun might not be found, Brandon offered a $200 reward. At about 7:00 p.m. that day, Ben Benthall of Noble found the weapon and collected the reward.

Pete Abington, who operated the Ford dealership in Many at the time, adds an unusual twist to the story. He explained, "Quinton used to come to the dealership. He told me what was so unusual is Corley came to his house the night of the murder. He said he couldn't figure out why."

Abington continued, "When Quinton ran it all back and found out that Corley and Maxey had been together, then it became apparent to him that Corley had come to his house to try to establish an alibi. Corley was standing trial when he died from cancer."

PHOTO BY THE SABINE INDEX

Brandon offered and paid a $200 reward to the person who found the pistol used to murder his brother-in-law, Dick Maxey in July 1970.

Chapter 30

The Great Zwolle Train Wreck

"For I'm going to run her 'til she leaves the rail;
Or make it on time with the southbound mail."
——*from folksong, "Casey Jones"*

The night of Wednesday, September 23, 1970, would long be remembered around Zwolle. Quinton Brandon and his men worked throughout the night.

The time was 8:20 p.m. when the southbound KCS freight train rammed into the rear of a switcher train which was on the through track, near St. Joseph's Catholic Church. Two Shreveport trainmen were killed.

There was an explosion upon contact, setting fire to more than twenty-six thousand gallons of diesel fuel and causing some cars loaded with pulpwood on the switch train to catch fire.

Four engines were pulling one hundred forty-four cars on the southbound; several of them loaded with chemicals. The switcher engine was pulling about twenty-five cars; most of them loaded with pulpwood.

The caboose on the switcher was completely demolished. Three of the engines were knocked off the track and the other one landed on top of cars loaded with pulpwood. In addition four boxcars and one flat car of the mainline train were derailed.

Brandon said that the switcher train was standing still on the tracks near the Zwolle depot and the through train engineer did not see the other train in time to stop.

Some two hundred feet of track was ripped up. The KCS crews moved in immediately to repair the track and clean up the wreckage. Normal service was resumed shortly after noon the next day.

Those killed were Marion L. Harwell, sixty, the engineer, and Ross A. Hartwell, forty-nine, the brakeman.

Fire units from four different towns were summoned to the scene and with the aid of foam battled the blaze until the early morning hours.

Brandon and his men stayed on duty throughout the night keeping spectators back and escorting fire units and equipment.

Old timers in Sabine termed the calamity the worse train wreck that they had ever seen.

Chapter 31

The Shooting of Gordon Oxley

*"The shooting was justifiable on Quinton's part
and nothing ever came of it."*
—*Sheriff Guffey Lynn Patterson*

W. F. Jeter, Jr. was on duty at a basketball game at the Zwolle school the afternoon of December 18, 1970. Marshal Quinton Brandon was in Many testifying in a court case.

"Gordon Oxley from Negreet was drunk and had been causing problems," Jeter said. "I didn't have a car, so I called Quinton and told him he needed to come to the school. Oxley even got out on the floor and was trying to tell the referees how to call the game."

Mayor Roger Lopez, said he remembered the incident very well. "Mr. James Q. Salter was principal at the time. Integration was new and they were concerned about trouble between the whites and blacks," he said.

During this period, Lopez was a member of the Zwolle council and they held a hearing, which cleared Brandon. Lopez said that his information came from that hearing.

Lopez continued, "Mr. Brandon got to the game and it was almost over. He decided to leave Oxley alone, if he didn't cause any more trouble. When the game was over, Oxley and his girlfriend, Bebe Pruitt, started walking out. When they got to the concession stand, they ordered a few items and started to go back in the gym. At that point Mr. Brandon informed him to leave; that they had some complaints about his conduct."

"At that point, Mr. Oxley did not offer any resistance, but his girl friend did," Lopez stated. "She said they had paid money to see the game and felt they had a right to stay as long as they wanted to. Mr. Brandon informed Oxley he would either have to leave or be arrested."

Jeter stated, "I got on one side of him and Quinton got on the other and we took him to the patrol car."

"We got to city hall and I got out and Quinton opened the back door and Oxley started to fight him," Jeter recalled. "Quinton drew his pistol and was in the process of hitting Oxley with it. The gun accidentally discharged and the bullet went into Oxley's neck and head. We did not know he was hit at the time. When we got him inside, we found he had been shot. At that point, Quinton thought he had killed him. We called an ambulance and got him medical help right away."

Lopez added to the story, "When Mr. Brandon opened the door, Oxley came out fighting. He said there wasn't enough sons-of-b—— in Zwolle to put him in jail. Mr. Brandon did not have his blackjack. He had recently hired Brad Falcon as a deputy and had let him borrow it and had not had enough time to get a new one."

"Mr. Brandon pulled his pistol, as Oxley was fighting him, and hit the prisoner over the head," Lopez said. "The pistol went off and the bullet hit Oxley in the neck. Mr. Jeter ran around and got Oxley and they did not realize he was shot until he collapsed and fell down."

Lopez said that the council held a hearing because, "...the rumor had surfaced that Mr. Brandon wanted to kill Oxley." He stated, "The council had like a court session and we brought in witnesses from the school and other people. We felt after the hearing there was no truth to the rumor."

Concluding, Lopez said, "What really changed things between the council and Mr. Brandon was the shooting of Oxley. We stood behind him on that. I did it because I knew he was right. After that, we became close to Quinton and from then on, he would do anything we wanted."

Jimmy Ray Pleasant said Oxley was "...whooping and hollering at the game and had been drinking. Oxley was a big stout man. When Oxley jumped on Quinton at city hall, he used his gun for a black jack. His finger just slipped and hit the trigger and it went off. I've seen him use his gun before when he had to hit a man."

Retired State Trooper James Napier of Zwolle said that he remembered Brandon showing up in court on the matter without an attorney. "When that was made known, every attorney in the courtroom jumped up and offered to help him," he said.

On December 16, 1971, Oxley filed suit in Eleventh Judicial District Court against Brandon for $710,000. In the suit, Oxley claimed that Brandon was liable for the injuries and damages sustained and that he was liable for intentional and willful misconduct.

Judge Jack E. Burgess dismissed the suit April 28, 1977, on grounds of abandonment.

Sheriff Guffey Lynn Pattison said that Oxley lived over the shooting, but some years ago met his death while working overseas. According to unconfirmed reports, Oxley was working for an oil exploration firm in Scotland when he met his death. There are those who said that he died under mysterious circumstances.

Chapter 32

Shoot the Man Down

"He really didn't have a choice."
- - - John Henry Procell

In all his years of law enforcement, rumor had it Quinton Brandon had killed at least half a dozen men. The story is true that he had shot several, but he had killed only one.

The day was Wednesday, May 26, 1971, and Brandon was at his home on Obrie Street. Two persons came to his house looking for him and reported that a man was drunk, causing a disturbance and obstructing traffic on U.S. Highway 171 at Bert Rule's service station. He looked at his watch as he rushed out the front door. The time was 3:45 p.m.

By all accounts Stevie Sneed was a big man. Coroner Dr. Richard J. Oosta said that he weighed at least two hundred twenty-five pounds. Sneed was twenty-five years old; Brandon was almost fifty-four.

Brandon drove up and got out of his patrol car. Sneed was standing in the middle of the road, stopping cars, and asking the women to come with him. When he saw Brandon, Sneed made a running attack on him, almost knocking him down on the highway.

Brandon quickly drew his trusty Smith and Wesson and told Sneed that he had better get in the patrol car. Sneed obeyed.

Brandon started down Highway 171 toward city hall to put Sneed in jail. Brandon soon realized he was in big trouble. Sneed was like a wild animal in the back seat. He was cursing and trying to tear out the protective screen between himself and Brandon.

The marshal had never heard of anyone tearing out the screen, but he looked in his rear view mirror and realized Sneed was crazy. Brandon took the microphone of his radio and asked the Sabine Parish sheriff's department to send him some help and do it immediately. He knew he was in trouble. They promised to send him two men.

Deputy Jack Brown took the call at the sheriff's office in Many. Deputies Jimmy Ray Pleasant and Floyd Terrell, Jr. were upstairs in the courtroom. Brown sent them on the call.

In front of the Methodist Church, Brandon again looked into his rear view mirror. He shuddered at what he saw. Sneed had succeeded in tearing down the wire mesh, which protected Brandon.

"You G— damn son-of-a-b——, you're mine now," Sneed cursed as he succeeded in tearing the wire mesh down.

Brandon picked up the mike again and told the deputies to hurry. By now they were at the roadside park, a couple of miles south of town.

Sneed grabbed Brandon around the neck with one hand and grabbed his pistol with the other. Brandon had two major problems. First, he had to break Sneed's hold around his neck, and second he had to try to maintain control of the patrol car.

Brandon attempted to maintain control of the car and after what seemed like an eternity brought it under control in Roy Sibley's yard.

Sneed was successful in getting Brandon's gun. Brandon's first thoughts were of his wife, who was waiting for him at home. Then he thought about all the years he had devoted to law enforcement and wondered if it was going to end on the streets of Zwolle at the hand of a drunk. He had worked too hard; he had tried too hard. He was not going to let his life end this way.

Using both hands and every muscle in his body and every ounce of strength, Brandon fought to get his gun back. Brandon could feel the life going out of his body as Sneed retained his strangling choke hold. Sneed was hitting and squeezing Brandon. The marshal could feel his ribs cracking. He did not know

Brandon, shown at center, had just killed Stevie Sneed when this photo was taken the afternoon of May 26, 1971. In fact, Sneed's body is still in Brandon's patrol car, at right. To the left of Brandon is Dr. Richard J. Oosta, coroner. State Trooper C. J. Miller is shown at left. The late Reverend B. L. White, parish civil defense director, has back to camera at center right.

until the ordeal was all over that Sneed had succeeded in breaking three of those curved, bony cartileges.

It seemed like an eternity and he was almost losing consciousness, but Brandon managed to get his pistol back. He thought about all the hours he had given in the name of justice, duty, and honor. He prayed, "Please dear God, don't let it end this way. Let my life mean something more than this." He later told a reporter, "By the help of God, I got the gun in my left hand and fired one shot."

The sound of the pistol going off in the patrol car was almost deafening. It was a sound Brandon would never forget. He had hoped the bullet would hit Sneed in the right arm to break the near-death hold around his neck. When the revolver fired, Sneed fell backward and Brandon slumped forward. Brandon was alive, but the struggle had taken every ounce of energy he could muster. He was totally wiped out—drained. He wondered if Sneed was dead.

The bullet had gone through Sneed's arm, but the path continued and entered his chest. He died, almost instantly. He slumped in the back seat, kicking, and jerking. His blood was going everywhere.

In 1981, Brandon told *The Baton Rouge Morning Advocate*, "The bullet went into his arm, turned down, and went right through his heart, a lung, his stomach, all the way to his rear end. The coroner told me it cut through everything it could have to kill him." There was little regret in Brandon's voice, the reporter noted. "I know he would have killed me if I hadn't killed him," he said. "Even his own mother told me so."

Brandon took a deep, long breath. He was so glad to be alive. The threat of death had been close. Much too close. He picked up the microphone and radioed the sheriff's office to send the coroner. By now, Pleasant and Terrell were at the first red light in Zwolle. They had traveled at break-neck speeds, but were too late to help their friend. But, with God's help, the marshal had done the job.

The June 3, 1971, *Sabine Index* quoted Brandon

as saying, "It's a regrettable incident. It's happened to others, now it's happened to me."

Sneed, who lived on the Belmont Road near Zwolle, had a record of resisting law officers every time he was arrested, Brandon told *The Index*.

"I never went down there," Mrs. Brandon said of the incident. "He never wanted us to come where there was trouble. He was greatly disturbed about it when he came home. It was the first man he had to kill. He didn't mean to do it."

W. F. Jeter, Jr. said that he was waiting at a cafe downtown for Brandon to pick him up to go to work when it happened.

Said Jeter, "I didn't know about it until it was over. Sneed was big and stout. He weighed about two hundred twenty-five pounds. He was mean. If he saw a uniformed officer in town, he would just stare at you."

He continued, "After it happened, Quinton's ribs were blue and bloodshot where Sneed had squeezed him so hard. Also, I think his arms were too."

Brandon said that Sneed was wanted in Franklin, Louisiana for assault and had served time in the State Penitentiary at Angola for aggravated battery and also time in a reform school in Utah.

Glenwood Bullard and James Napier were young men at the time and rushed to the scene of the tragedy. Napier said, "I remember State Trooper C. J. Miller arriving at the scene, looking at Sneed and saying, 'Damn Quinton, he's a big one.'"

Bullard said, "In later years, Quinton and I talked about it. It scared him to death. Sneed was a huge guy and much younger. Quinton thought he was dead."

Continuing, Bullard stated, "A pretty big crowd gathered. It was a regrettable event, but the people were concerned that Quinton was okay. No one held any ill will toward him."

Dr. Oosta, who served as the coroner for fifteen years, was called to the scene. He commented, "How

Sneed jerked that welded screen down, I'll never know. He actually broke the welds."

"I was on the town council when it happened," John Henry Procell recalled. "I was at Willamette working when someone came and told me. I quit the job and went downtown. We called a special council meeting that night to look into the murder. We decided Quinton didn't do anything wrong. We stood behind Quinton. It was bad to kill a man, but he didn't have much choice." Ray Spurlock was mayor at the time and verified the council did meet and supported Brandon.

Roger Lopez remembered, "We found a boy, Jerry Sepulvado, who was driving behind the patrol car. He saw the fight and saw when the patrol car went into the yard. He did not know what went on in the patrol car. We did listen to the person who filed the complaint against Sneed. We determined Mr. Brandon was justified in what he had to do."

Lopez continued, "Mr. Procell and I, both of us weighed at least two hundred twenty pounds each, got in the patrol car and tried to spring the cage and could not do it. After the incident we had the cage welded. I do not know how one human had enough strength to do what Sneed did. We felt like he had to be on something high powered to have the super human strength to be able to break that cage loose with those safety latches and get to Mr. Brandon."

Even with the support of the council, Brandon was still feeling down and out that night when he got a call from a deputy sheriff in St. Mary Parish, Louisiana. The deputy was jubilant.

"It turned out Sneed was wanted in that parish and they hadn't been able to hold him," Brandon explained. "Here I was, feeling awful, when this coonass deputy calls me and tells me what a favor I've done him by putting that boy in a pine box. He was gonna send me some cigars and drinkin' whiskey. I told him to forget it."

"Quinton really hated it happened," Pleasant

recalled. "He wasn't trying to kill Sneed. He was just trying to get Sneed off him. Sneed was beating Quinton in the side with the gun. He broke three of Quinton's ribs."

A retired district judge, who asked not to be identified, related, "I think killing the man really bothered him. He talked about it every now and then, saying he didn't have a choice. If it didn't bother him, he wouldn't have talked about it."

And in an ironic twist to the story, Bullard said that he understood Brandon helped pay some of the funeral expenses to bury Sneed.

Chapter 33

Woman Hangs Self Using Panties

"When we took her to the Zwolle jail,
she was raving and screaming."
—Quinton Brandon

Despite the best efforts of Quinton Brandon, a Washington state black woman hanged herself after being arrested in Zwolle Saturday night, September 29, 1973.

Mary Cooper, thirty years of age, had been arrested for disturbing the peace and for being highly intoxicated.

"When we took her into the Zwolle jail, she was raving and screaming," Brandon said at the time. "I thought she should be examined, so I called Dr. Richard J. Oosta." He said that while he waited for Dr. Oosta everything got quiet.

He continued, "When he arrived, we went to the jail cell and saw she had tied a pair of long pants on a bar above the top bunk and had the pants tied around her neck. I jerked the door open and caught her as she leaped off the bunk. She kept saying she was going to kill herself and that she wanted to go to the graveyard."

Dr. Oosta said he told Brandon, "We can't leave her here. Let's put her in jail in Many." The marshal put a man in the cell to watch her while he made arrangements to take her to Many. "She had been a regular weekend customer in the Zwolle jail," he added. Her husband had relatives in Zwolle, and they had been visiting several weeks but were planning to return home soon.

At 8:00 p.m. she was put in the drunk tank in Many. Dr. Oosta said that they had taken everything off her except her panties. At 8:10 p.m. a trustee, Terry

Beardon, went to check on her and found her hanging from the cell door.

Sheriff George Cook said that she had removed her wig and had placed it on a bench before her suicide. The woman had tied her panties to the top horizontal bar, then climbed up the other horizontal bars, looped her head through the panties and jumped. Parish Coroner Dr. W. E. Poimboeuf confirmed her death later that night.

"Despite our best efforts, she was successful," Dr. Oosta concluded.

Chapter 34

Walking Tall

"The spirit of rugged individualism that built America was alive and well with Quinton Brandon."
—A thought

In 1973, the movie screens exploded with the story of McNary County, Tennessee Sheriff Buford Pusser entitled Walking Tall. But folks in the northwest Louisiana area knew that Marshal Quinton Brandon had been walking tall long before that.

Pusser's wife was actually ambushed and killed in 1967. Pusser served three two-year terms as sheriff, from 1964-1970. Pusser was beaten up in 1957 in a brawl in a casino over money he himself had lost. That made him want to clean up the criminal element in his home county.

The movie proved so successful that a Walking Tall Part 2 was released in 1975.

When the movie became so popular, people began comparing Brandon to Pusser. But long before Pusser, Brandon had symbolized American democracy, with a strong sense of right and wrong, of virtue and justice. Brandon had early on set his own style of justice. To him it was perfect, simple, right, and swift. If you did the crime, you did the time.

The actual Pusser was a six-foot, six-inch former professional wrestler. He had been shot eight times and knifed seven. Brandon unfortunately never enjoyed any physical domination over the rest of the folks. He was six-foot, one-inch and weighed one hundred eighty pounds. In a story published in the August 10, 1978, Shreveport Journal, Brandon said, "I often came out on the short end of the stick with regard to size. I'm much smaller than a lot of the men I've taken on."

Sheriff Guffey Lynn Pattison was a deputy at the time. He said, "When Walking Tall came out and became so popular, everyone started comparing Quinton to Pusser. In the movie, Pusser carried a big stick. I went out and whittled Quinton a big hickory stick and gave it to him. He really liked it. It stayed at the city hall for a long time."

Rocky Brandon said that he remembered his father meeting Pusser at a law enforcement convention, but does not remember any details.

In addition, Brandon has been compared to Wyatt Earp and Matt Dillon because of their likenesses and to the characters played by John Wayne.

Even after all these years, when folks who knew him either personally or by reputation talk about Brandon, there is one thing that will always come out in the conversation: "He walked tall."

Chapter 35

Just Trying to Help

*"We will continue to help people in need,
but no more beer joints."*
—Quinton Brandon

The call came in to the Sabine Parish sheriff's department on Saturday afternoon, February 9, 1974, that an accident with a firearm had happened in the woods near Zwolle.

Quinton Brandon was the closest officer to the scene, and he rushed there to pick up Johnny Ray Meshell and take him to the hospital in Many. Also in the patrol car were Meshell's sister and her husband, Mr. and Mrs. Willie Malmay.

Brandon said that as he was traveling south on Highway 171, about a mile out of Zwolle, he came behind a car, driven by Mrs. Barbara Sepulvado, which had stopped and had the blinkers on to make a left turn.

He said that Mrs. Sepulvado apparently did not see his flashing lights or hear his siren until he was attempting to pass her on the right shoulder of the highway. As he started to go around her, he said that she saw or heard the emergency signals and immediately put her car in gear and pulled onto the right shoulder. As she did, Brandon said that he had no other choice but to hit her car because as she pulled over, she blocked both the highway and shoulder.

Mr. and Mrs. Malmay were taken to the Many hospital and treated. Meshell was treated in Many and transferred to a Shreveport hospital.

The patrol car was a total loss. The smashup would not be the last patrol car wreck Brandon would have to face. A year later, he was again troubled by wrecked patrol cars.

At the January 2, 1975, meeting of the Zwolle council, the low bid of Hanna-Abington Ford of Many for $4,789.45 was accepted for a 1975 Ford LTD. Brandon told the council, "No one regrets more than I do about the patrol car being in a wreck. There was an emergency and our boys were trying to get some boys who had been shot to the hospital. We can blame this one on rain-slick roads and fog. The car was a total loss. But I will promise this—we will continue to help people in need, but no more beer joints. They will have to wait for an ambulance, because this is twice in one year this has happened to us."

Chapter 36

Who Had the Best Rabbit Dogs?

"Rivers left the bar, went to his vehicle, and returned with a shotgun and shot Procell."
—*The Sabine Index*

The fifty-four year old father of two Zwolle men who were involved in a bar room shooting spree two weeks prior, was shot and killed March 1, 1974, by a brother of one of two men his sons were accused of shooting. Sheriff George R. Cook said that officers could not definitely make the conclusion the two shootings were connected.

The dead man was identified as Villice Procell of Zwolle. He died instantly of a blast from a .12 gauge shotgun loaded with buckshot. He was shot one time from about fifteen feet.

The shooting took place about 4:15 p.m. at Club 482, located a mile from the Zwolle city limits on the Ebarb Road, according to Quinton Brandon, who investigated. Mrs. Arlene Fry owned the bar.

Charged with murder was Danny Rivers, twenty-two, of Shreveport and a native of the Zwolle area. Charged with attempted murder were his companions, David Wayne Peacock and Chris Lewis.

Witnesses told the officers, Procell was playing pool with Clifton Sepulvado. Procell went to the rest room and Peacock and Lewis followed him and an argument erupted. The argument ended and when they came out, they shook hands and Procell went back to playing pool.

Rivers left the bar, witnesses said, went to his vehicle, and returned with the shotgun to shoot Procell. They said that no words were spoken between Rivers and Procell.

After the murder, all three left the scene but

called officers to let them know where they were. About eight to ten persons were in the bar when the shooting happened.

On February 15, Benny Rivers and Clellie Lee Batson, twenty-six, of Noble were hospitalized with wounds sustained when they were allegedly shot by Huey Procell, thirty-one, during an argument in the same bar.

At that time, Rivers and Batson became involved with Huey and his brother, Frank, twenty, over who had the best rabbit dogs.

Brandon is shown with the double barrel shotgun allegedly used to kill Villice Procell March 1, 1974.

Huey reportedly wounded Batson first and shot Rivers as he dived under a pool table.

A picture of Brandon was carried on the front page of *The Sabine Index* showing him holding the double-barrel shotgun that was allegedly used to kill Villice Procell.

Rocky Brandon said, "Chris Lewis told me he was wanted for questioning about the murder, and he had his mother call Daddy to pick him up. Daddy told his mother, Shirley, he would bring him home as soon as the sheriff's department was through questioning him. When they finished, he was told he would have to go to jail. Dad had given his word to Mrs. Lewis and told them they were both going to be locked up or he was taking Chris home. Needless to say, he took Chris home. Daddy's word was law and he would not back down under any circumstance."

As the day came to a close, Brandon thought back on the events and pondered. It was all just another day in the life of a law enforcement officer.

Chapter 37

Running for Chief

"I need no introduction to you.
Your children all know me by my first name."
—*Quinton Brandon*

Quinton Brandon wasted no time in offering his formal announcement for Chief of Police for the March 23, 1974, election.

The November 8, 1973, issue of *The Sabine Index* carried a picture of Brandon, showing a miniature American flag sewn over his right pocket and his announcement on the front page.

"As you know, I have served as your city marshal to the best of my ability for twenty-four years," he wrote. "I promise no miracles, but I will promise to work day and night, if necessary, to keep our town clean and peaceable to the best of my ability. This will be the first open primary election for marshal ever to be held in Zwolle. I have no ill feelings toward any of my opponents. I am not running for anyone's job. I am merely running for the job I have held for twenty-four years."

He continued, "I am running on my own merits; you all have known me during my entire police career. I have no intentions to enter into a dirty, underhanded political 'mud slinging' contest. If the citizens cannot elect me on my merits as a law enforcement officer, then I don't deserve the job. However, if I am attacked with any abusive mud slinging, I shall retaliate with honest facts. I am asking for this office for one more term, at which time I will be eligible for retirement and at that time, at my age, I feel that a man should accept retirement. I need this one term to qualify me under this new retirement system."

When the deadline for qualifying ended at 5:00

p.m. January 22, Brandon had drawn as an opponent his old nemesis, George Laroux, Jr. Running for mayor was the incumbent Ray Spurlock, Fred (Billy) Rivers, and Raymond Walraven. Seeking the five council posts were three incumbents, Vernon Mitchell, John Henry Procell, and Fred Roberson, Jr. and Thomas Joe Cassell, Samuel D. Cross, David Ebarb, Wiley Hawkins, William S. Hopkins, W. F. Jeter, Sr., Elmer C. Marshall, James J. Procell, and Bert C. Rule.

In an ad in the January 24 *Index*, Brandon stated that he had been marshal, twenty-two years, not the twenty-four used in his announcement. He said, "I promise to render you the same honest, clean and hard work that I have given you in the past. I think you all know that I believe in law enforcement 'straight across the board,' regardless of race or religion and I do not believe that prejudice of any type has any place whatsoever in law enforcement."

He continued, "If re-elected as your chief, I will give you full time employment. I have no other interests or employment and, as you all know, have given my life to law enforcement, which I have enjoyed to the full extent."

Brandon's ad concluded, "I ask you to elect me as your chief of police to serve you for the next four years. I will then be sixty years old and eligible for my retirement and at such time will retire."

One other ad was run by Brandon in *The Index* in the January 24 issue, titled, "A Letter of Thanks." In it Brandon thanked several law enforcement officials and agencies for "...the wonderful cooperation and assistance during 1973." He singled out Sheriff George Cook and his department, the Louisiana State Police, Chief Alfice Brumley and the Many police department, Converse Marshal Guy Snelling, Noble Marshal Willis Webb, Florien Marshal Cliff Davis, and Pleasant Hill Marshal Otha Gregory.

Brandon stated, "I thank you, gentlemen, from the bottom of my heart for your assistance in handling parades, funerals, ball games, and other activities relative to law enforcement. Without this manner of cooperation, small police departments can not exist. I am looking forward to another year of the same wonderful cooperation in law enforcement in 1974."

His ad concluded, "May God's blessings prevail over us in 1974 in our efforts to curb crime in Sabine Parish."

When the results came in, a landslide elected Brandon. He polled a whopping eighty-two percent of the vote. Of the nine hundred seventy-five votes cast, Brandon received eight hundred and one to LaRoux's one hundred seventy-four.

Walraven was elected and the five councilmen elected were Cross, Mitchell, Roberson, Procell, and Hopkins.

Brandon officially took office as chief July 1. On July 2, he held a ceremony to administer the oath of office to his force, Assistant Chief Wayne Ebarb and Patrolmen Glen Ebarb, and Brad Falcon.

As July, 1977, approached, Brandon had changed his mind about not seeking another term. In the July 14 issue of *The Index*, he stated that he was getting an early start on things and said that he would seek re-election.

He said, "I will definitely run again for chief of police. I am not going to retire as I had said I would. I love my job and am devoted to it."

As the deadline for qualifying passed in early February, 1978, Brandon was returned to office without opposition. Gentry wrote in his Observations column in *The Index*, "This will be the last roundup for him, as he does not plan to run again after this term, he told us Tuesday."

In a formal statement later in the month in *The Index*, Brandon thanked the people of Zwolle for "...showing enough confidence in me by allowing me to return to office without opposition."

He continued, "This has shown me that you have placed the utmost confidence in me and I shall continue to do the best job I can in keeping Zwolle a law-abiding town."

The story stated, "Brandon, who has been in law enforcement some thirty-eight years, came to Zwolle years ago, when women or blacks couldn't walk the streets without fear of being harassed. Since then, Brandon has cleaned up Zwolle and kept it a safe town. Citizens respect this 'man behind the badge' and admire him for the job he has done."

Brandon concluded, "I want the public to know I am thankful for the chance to serve them for another four years. I'll do my best, and always be on hand to help the people of Zwolle."

Chapter 38

Visiting A Friend

"Mr. Everhart had cancer, so Quinton
went to see him."
—*Mrs. Nannie Brandon*

The May 8, 1975, edition of The Richmond Virginia News Leader carried a picture of Quinton Brandon and a story headed, "Wartime Friends Recall V-E Day."

Brandon had gone there to visit Marcel Everhart, whom he had not seen since they parted after the end of hostilities in Europe in 1945 during World War II. Thirty years ago on that May 8 date, the Germans had surrendered unconditionally to the Allies; it was V-E Day. The guns were silent in Europe.

Mrs. Nannie Brandon recalled when her husband and Everhart parted at the end of the war, they promised to stay in touch. "Mr. Everhart had cancer, so Quinton went to see him," she remembered. "He flew by himself to Richmond and stayed three or four days. Mr. Everhart was up and around during Quinton's visit, but before that May was out, he died."

The two friends met during that week in 1975 to relive the invasion of Europe, in which both participated, the defeat of the Germans, and their close brush with death.

Brandon told the newspaper he had "grabbed a plane" to Richmond that prior Monday to visit Everhart.

"I would have known him anywhere, even if I had seen him on the streets of Zwolle," Brandon told The News Leader.

"We stayed in touch," Everhart said, "and every Christmas Eve one of us would call the other."

Both were U.S. Army enlisted men and members

173

of the amphibious unit charged with patrolling the English Channel and several French rivers. Their boat was named for Brandon's daughter Doris Lorene.

"We were on different types of patrol duty and rescue work," said Everhart, who was sales and advertising manager for Coca-Cola in Richmond.

On the night of the invasion of Europe—D-Day—Brandon, Everhart, and the rest of the crew left the English port of Southampton. But heavy fog rolled in and they were lost for a time.

"We stayed offshore," Everhart said, "and watched the invasion of Utah and Omaha beaches on the French Coast."

"There was a big bluff on Omaha," he said, "and those German concrete gun emplacements opened up in a cross-fire," which accounted for heavy allied casualties.

"The coast was bombed and shelled so that I thought nothing would be alive, but the Germans were dug in there," Brandon said.

The Germans fired at their boat and crewmembers returned fire at strafing planes.

"I don't know whether we scored or not; we didn't have time to think about it," Brandon remarked.

After a beachhead had been established and the front moved eastward, Brandon and Everhart were due to take part in the invasion of northern Japan "from southern Siberia," Everhart said.

They were returned to the United States for a month's leave and then transferred to Camp Pendleton, California; however, the atomic bombs were dropped on Hiroshima and Nagasaki and the war in the Pacific ended before they were shipped out.

But they remembered the celebration of V-E Day in Europe.

"We all got pretty well drunked up," Brandon said.

"On three-star Hennessey," Everhart concluded.

Chapter 39

The Death of a Son
and Grandson

*"When he died, his wife and I dug it up and
brought it here, so he'd always have shade."*
—*Quinton Brandon*

Quinton Brandon was known as one of the
roughest, toughest men that ever lived. He was
fearless against guns, knives, or fists, but the death of
his oldest son brought him to his knees and literally
took away his will to live for years thereafter.

Jerry Lee came into the world as the Brandon's
second child and first boy. He was an adorable little
man with blond hair and blue eyes. He was always full
of energy and very mischievous. He grew into a fine
young man and a gifted athlete.

He graduated from Zwolle High School in May,
1968, and will always be remembered for his
accomplishments as a member of the Hawks basketball
team. His basketball jersey, number thirty-one, was
retired on April 29, 1977, after his younger brother,
Rocky, wore it during his high school basketball years.

He was named to the Louisiana All-State team for
two consecutive years, 1967 and 1968. This
accomplishment had been achieved previously by only
one other athlete in Louisiana.

Headlines around the state read "Brandon's
Brilliant Performance Sends Zwolle to B Title." The
Zwolle Hawks came home with the winner's trophy in
1968-Brandon's senior year. During the first half of
that championship game, Brandon made fifteen of
twenty-six shots from the field and grabbed ten
rebounds. His athletic ability gained him the title of
Most Valuable Contender in the 1968 Top Twenty
Tournament.

He averaged 20.7 points per game and made 50.9

percent of field goals attempted. Jerry was unanimously named by the Louisiana Sports Writers Association and the Louisiana High School Athletic Association to All-State teams in 1968.

Jerry Brandon of Zwolle and Terry Veuleman of the Many High School were named Honorable Mention, All-American Prep Basketball and received certificates of award. They were two of five hundred youths throughout the United States to receive this honor. Players were selected in a competition in which one hundred thousand high school basketball players were eligible and polling coaches and sportswriters in the fifty states made selections.

Under Coach Sherman Tatum, Jerry was the only Zwolle student to ever be named to the Prep All-American Basketball team by the Coach and Athlete Magazine. He received the honor in 1968 but did not stop his pursuit of improving his ability and sharing it with others.

After graduation from high school, Jerry attended Louisiana Tech University in Ruston, Louisiana, on a basketball scholarship and remained a student there until his graduation in May, 1973. He received the coaching position at Glenbrook Academy in Minden, Louisiana, in the fall of 1972, but continued to work on a degree in physical education.

He gave of himself fully to his team and he also participated in the Minden City Recreation League, an independent basketball team. His ability led the team to the semi-finals in the state in 1974.

The former Zwolle High School basketball star and Glenbrook Academy coach died at Schumpert Memorial Hospital in Shreveport on Saturday, July 12, 1975, at 5:40 p.m. from injuries received in an automobile accident. The accident occurred on Louisiana Highway 137, two miles west of the Bossier-Webster line on Friday, July 11. The truck in which Brandon was a passenger dropped off the pavement causing the driver to lose control.

The July 17, 1975, edition of *The Sabine Index*,

Jerry Brandon, seated center, is shown signing to play basketball for the Louisiana Tech Bulldogs at Ruston in 1968. He had been a standout for the Zwolle Hawks. Seated at left is Zwolle Coach Sherman Tatum and at right is Tech Coach Scotty Robertson. Standing are Zwolle High Principal Woodrow Salter, Mrs. Nannie Brandon, Lorene Jones, Quinton Brandon, Becky Brandon, Bonnie Brandon, and Rocky Brandon.

Number 31, the green and gold basketball jersey worn by Jerry Brandon during his days as a Zwolle Hawk was retired in ceremonies at the school April 29, 1977. Jerry had lost his life as the result of an auto accident July 12, 1975. Members of the family shown at the bittersweet affair were, left to right, Mr. and Mrs. Rocky Brandon, Mrs. Jerry Brandon, Mrs. Calvin Jones, Mrs. Nannie Brandon, and Quinton Brandon. Rocky also wore the number 31 jersey when he played basketball.

stated "......hundreds of local citizens, friends, and relatives gathered at the First Baptist Church of Zwolle, in what was believed to be one of the largest attendances at a funeral in the parish, to pay their last respects to Jerry Lee Brandon."

Services were held in Zwolle on Monday, July 14, at 3:00 p.m. with the Reverend J. D. Wagnon and the Reverend Lee Dickson officiating. Burial was in the Zwolle Cemetery under the direction of Warren Meadows Funeral Home of Many.

Pallbearers were Sherman Tatum, Cecil Ross, Captain Tomlinson, Don Roberts, Charles Corley, and members of the basketball team of Glenbrook Academy in Minden, where Jerry was coach.

Larry Burgess, a student at Louisiana College in Pineville at the time of Jerry's death, wrote an editorial about him, which ran in the July 31, 1975, edition of *The Index*. "He took young lives and trained them in the many facets of athletics," Burgess wrote. "He not only produced athletes; he produced men. Men who had pride in their team, their school, their ability, their coach, and most of all, in themselves. He taught us that manhood is not about who is bigger or stronger but a giving of all you have, all of the time, and giving unselfishly to benefit others no matter what the cost."

Jerry was only twenty-five years old at the time of his death. He and his wife, the former Beverly Felknor of Plain Dealing, Louisiana, had one son, Dustin, age ten months, and another child on the way. Beverly was seven months pregnant with Jerry Lynn at the time of Jerry's death.

Throughout the years Beverly and the two boys were as close to the Brandon family as they would have been if Jerry had not died. When Beverly did remarry, she did so with the blessing of the Brandon family. Her husband, Clay Bohanon, is close to the family, also. When one sees either of the two boys, it is just as if one is seeing Jerry again because they look so much like him.

DeLane Christianson said, "The loss of Quinton's oldest son probably impacted on him the most of anything in his life. It damn near killed him. He never got over it. He'd say, 'The Lord wouldn't give me anything I couldn't handle.' "

"He never could talk about Jerry without crying, especially after his stroke because he was more emotional," Christianson continued. "We love all of our children, but we have one that we dote on and that was the way Brandon was about Jerry."

W.F. Jeter, Jr. said, "Jerry was his life, his pride and joy. It like to have killed Quinton when Jerry died; he never got over it."

Jimmy Ray Pleasant stated, "Jerry's death was always on Quinton's mind. Never a day went by that he didn't refer to it in some way."

"The death of his son almost 'broke' him," Roger Lopez said.

The Reverend Lee Dickson, former pastor of the Zwolle Baptist Church from 1970-1978 said, "I preached Jerry's funeral. In fact I have returned to Zwolle to preach a lot of Brandon funerals. Quinton and I got pretty close during Jerry's death. After I learned of Jerry's death, I was with the family as soon as I could get there. Quinton was in total shock and disbelief. He went into a state of depression and for a while he did not want to live. His world just caved in."

"After his son was killed, Quinton used to meet Jerry's wife in Mansfield to get and return the grandchildren," Don English, Mansfield, Louisiana, chief of police, said. "He loved his family. They would meet at the Dairy Queen and he'd always call me to meet him there."

Near one end of the Zwolle Cemetery, a black granite tombstone that says "Brandon" marks Jerry's grave. A small oak tree grows near the marker. Quinton planted it there. He said, "My boy was out hunting one day, and he ran across that little tree. He took it home and he and his wife planted it next to the front door of their home. When he died, his wife and I dug it up and brought it here, so he'd always have shade. In some strange way it comforts me to know it's there with him."

To make bad matters worse, the Brandon family lost Jason Douglas, the son of Bonnie Brandon and Joe Rivers, her husband at the time. The accident happened Saturday, April 14, 1979, in a log truck at about 3:00 p.m. on a little dirt road just off the Old Firetower Road near Naborton in DeSoto Parish.

Rivers remembered it was Holy Saturday, the day before Easter, and they had gone to work cutting and hauling timber. They left the woods early in order to go to confession.

Larry Rivers, Joe's brother, was driving the truck. In the truck with Joe were his two sons, Jason, six years old, and Roddy, who was five at the time, and a brother-in-law, Randy Lewis.

"Jason had been begging all week to go to work with me," Rivers stated. "He loved to ride with me on the tractor. I thought it would be slow that Saturday, so I took him with me and let him ride."

Rivers continued, "At the time of the accident, we came to a curve. When Larry tried to turn the steering wheel the truck went straight. For some reason, the fifth wheel wouldn't turn. We were in loose gravel also, and when Larry tried to turn, the wheels just slid on the gravel."

He stated, "We were loaded with logs and the truck centered a pine tree about eighteen inches in diameter. That sheared a pin on the fifth wheel and it all came in on the cab. Roddy was in my lap and Jason was beside me. When I saw we were going to hit the tree, I held Roddy and reached for Jason. I couldn't catch him; the load came in on us. We stayed pinned in the wreckage for three hours. The doctors told us if we had stayed in there five more minutes, none of us would have made it. I lost hope. I closed my eyes and was just about ready to let go."

The story of the series of events that caused him not to let go is most interesting and incredible.

Rivers continued, "No one traveled this little road. There was no one to find us. As bad as the situation was, I told them all to say a prayer of contrition. I said in my prayers, 'If there's a God, let someone come through here.' At that point, I heard gravel hitting the body of a vehicle that was coming toward us. It so happened it was a man who worked for the telephone company. It also happened he had a telephone with him that would plug into the boxes along the line. And it so happened there was a box right where we had wrecked."

There are more strange occurrences in connection with the wreck. Rusty Williams had been listening to his scanner and heard the news of the event. He was the only person in the area who would have the equipment big enough to help.

"He had a 'cherry picker' and came and got the load off us," Rivers remembered. "They had the jaws of life there. They had to cut us out."

On a sad note, Rivers remembered, "I heard Jason when he took his last breath. It was about thirty minutes after the wreck happened. I didn't tell anybody at the time, but I knew he was dead. Just before we went around the curve, Jason looked up at me and smiled. It was just so pleasant."

Rivers said that Brandon consoled him a lot during this time of tragedy. Rivers concluded, "He was an extra tough old man, but he helped me a lot. Jason's death really did a number on him, too." Jason was buried in the St. Joseph's Catholic Cemetery in Zwolle.

Chapter 40

Zwolle Mayor's Court

"Oh yea, oh yea, the honorable Court,
Town of Zwolle, State of Louisiana
Is now in session. Order is demanded
In the name of the law."
—-Bailiff's call to open Mayor's Court

If anybody ever told Quinton Brandon he was not in charge of the Zwolle Mayor's Court, he never listened. Not only did he serve as the arresting officer, but at times as the prosecuting attorney. More often then not, Brandon seemed to be more in control of Mayor's Court than the mayor.

Mayor's Court was usually held once a month, at night, and had from twenty to sixty cases. If you attended a session, there was never any doubt about who was in charge.

Retired State Trooper James Napier told the story about a case Brandon handled when Raymond Walraven was mayor. He said, "Quinton acted as the district attorney. He would call the cases and swear the witnesses in and then question them. There was a woman testifying. She told her story and Quinton jumped up and said, 'That's a damn lie.' "

Napier continued, "She replied, 'I'm telling the truth.' Quinton told her, 'If you're gonna sit there and lie, we ain't gonna listen to you.' He then added, 'I think we've heard enough.' Then looking at Walraven, he asked, 'Haven't we heard enough?' "

According to Napier, Walraven replied, "Yes," as he rapped his gavel and announced, "Guilty."

The following are a group of the more interesting cases that Brandon presented in Mayor's Court. They are taken from the files of *The Sabine Index* and were written by Mrs. Evelyn Hopkins, who covered court for the newspaper.

MAY 26, 1976: Thaddis D. Edmunson, charged with disturbing the peace, plead not guilty.

Brandon asked Edmunson to take the witness stand and then spoke to the spectators in court. He told them, "While this case is being tried, there will be some very dirty language used so if you ladies would like to step out while this is going on, you may do so and then return later."

He called Calvin Jones (who filed the charges) and asked him to tell why he had filed the charges.

Jones told the court on Sunday, May 16, he, his wife, and children went to Joy's Drive In in Zwolle. When he got out of the van, he heard some loud profanity coming from the car by his van. (This language had to be repeated in court at this time— only one lady chose to leave the courtroom.) My little girl who was about thirteen years old got out of the van about this time and one of the men in the car said quite loud and I quote, 'Give me my god d— f———— glass,' and this was more than I could take," Jones continued. "I went over to the car and shook my finger at the man and told him to cut the ugly talking. Edmunson then got out of the car and I thought he was coming around after me. I asked my wife to call Mr. Brandon, which she did, and I filed the charges." Jones went on to say when his wife went to get Brandon, Edmunson got back in his car and drove off.

Brandon said, "In other words when you asked Edmunson to watch his language he came around his car in a fighting manner, right?" Jones nodded, yes.

Edmunson then called his witness, Joann Hilmes. She was sworn in and told her story.

Joann said she, Edmunson, and others were at the drive-in enjoying themselves when one of the men in the car with them said, "Give me my d— glass," and the first thing she knew "some white dude" came up to the car and was shaking his finger at them. She went on to say, "That is when I told Thaddis to crank up the car and let's get out of here. There were three carloads

184

of us."

She was dismissed from the stand without any questioning.

Edmunson was sworn in and the following is his story:

He said, "We came to Zwolle to see if we could get a group together to play ball and then we came to Joy's Drive In to get some refreshments. While we were parked there, one of the men in the car said, "Give me my d—— glass, and the first thing I knew, this man came up to the car and pointed his finger at me. I got out of the car to see what he wanted and that is when Joann said we better get going. We were picked up by a state trooper down around Florien and brought back to Many and then to Zwolle. Charges were filed and I posted bond and here I am."

Brandon said, "You admit there was some very foul language used then, do you?"

Edmunson answered, "Yes."

Brandon said, "We have made one terrible mistake, all in the car should have been fined, but he does admit the terrible language was used."

Mayor Walraven said, "Guilty as charged" and fined him one hundred dollars.

MAY 26, 1976: Raymond Holt, charged with disturbing the peace by Alice Staten. Holt pleaded "Not guilty."

Again Brandon warned the spectators of the language that would be used in this case, but no one left. He called Alice to the stand and asked her to tell what happened.

Alice said, "I was walking down the road and saw Raymond and Jimmy sitting in a truck. I went to the truck and told Jimmy I wanted to talk to him and Raymond got out of the truck and told me to get my mother f—— face out of his and he then threw a can of beer in my face. I wasn't talking to Raymond, although I was on his side of the truck but I was trying to talk to Jimmy. As mean as he is, I was scared of him so I left."

Three witnesses were called to the stand, one for

Alice and two for Holt. They all told similar stories except the cursing and profanity got worse with each witness.

Holt then was sworn in and told his story. He said Alice stuck her face in his and started cursing Jimmy and "all I said was get your big black a— out of here and I poured a can of beer in her face."

Brandon said, "In other words both of you were cursing, were you not, but she filed charges and you didn't?"

Holt nodded in a 'yes' manner.

Mayor Walraven said, "I find you guilty as charged and fine you thirty five dollars."

JULY 28, 1976: Marie and Norman Compton charged with disturbing the peace by using profanity by Mrs. Bob Meshell. They plead not guilty.

Mrs. Meshell was brought forward and put on the stand to tell her story.

She said, "I was out in the yard minding my own business when Mrs. Compton came over and accused me of stealing her chickens. I have lived here a long time and don't bother no one because I stay in the hospital more than I stay out."

Brandon told Mrs. Meshell he did not want to know about the stealing of chickens, he wanted to know if Mrs. Compton cursed her or used profane language to her.

She replied, "No, but her husband walked out and looked at his watch and gave me three minutes to get back in the house. I ain't going to go back in the house because he told me to. He accused me of stealing and selling his chickens too."

Again, Brandon replied, "Mrs. Meshell, we do not want to hear about chickens, did the man curse you or use profanity to you?"

She again replied, "No, but he accused me of stealing his chickens."

Brandon said, "That is all, Mrs. Meshell."

Her husband was called to the stand and also stated he did not hear profanity used by either Mr. or

Mrs. Compton.

The Comptons were found not guilty.

MAY 11, 1977: Alberta Frazier and M.T. Frazier, charged with disturbing the peace by cursing. The couple appeared with their attorney, James B. O'Neill at the April 27 court and plead not guilty.

Glen Ebarb, policeman, was called to the stand and told the following:

"I was taking Brad Falcon, police officer, home about 2:00 a.m. on April 3, and as I was coming down Camille Street a car was parked and we stopped to investigate. When we got out of the car we heard a lot of loud, profane language coming from the house in front of us, so we decided to investigate. When we went up to the house we asked Alberta and M.T. to quit this ugly talking. Alberta continued to use loud, abusive language and even cursed me. She was holding a bottle of vodka and there was not much left in the bottle. When they didn't quit we arrested them, brought them in and booked them and let them go on their own bond that they would be in court."

Attorney O'Neill asked, "You arrested them in their own home?"

Ebarb answered, "I did."

O'Neill asked, "Without a warrant?"

Ebarb replied, "I didn't need a warrant."

O'Neill said, "No more questions."

Brandon called Falcon to the stand and after he was sworn in asked him to tell what happened.

Falcon repeated the same story as Ebarb.

Chief Brandon asked Falcon if he had any prejudice toward M.T.

Falcon replied, "No sir, in fact I've taken him home and put him in bed two or three times when he was too drunk to walk."

O'Neill asked, "Did you arrest M.T. and Alberta in their home?"

Falcon replied, "Yes, we did."

O'Neill, "Without a warrant?"

Falcon stated, "We did not need one."

"No further questions," replied O'Neill.

O'Neill called Frazier to the stand to testify in his own case.

O'Neill said, "M.T., you have heard the testimony of these two officers now tell your side of the story."

Frazier said, "It was about 10:00 p.m. and I was laying on the floor watching T.V. I turned around and asked Alberta for some money and she told me I had spent enough money but there wasn't no cursing."

O'Neill said, "Were you arrested inside of your own home without a warrant?"

Frazier replied, "Yes."

O'Neill, "No further questions."

Brandon said, "M.T. were you and your wife arguing?"

Frazier said, "Oh, I had asked her for money and she said I had already spent too much, but we weren't using no bad language."

Brandon said, "M.T. you said it was 10:00 o'clock when this happened and are you sure it was just 10:00 o'clock?"

"Object to this question," O'Neill replied, "You know you don't have the right to ask this question."

Brandon replied, "I do have the right."

O'Neill, "You do not and you know it."

Mayor Walraven said, "Objection overruled."

O'Neill called Alberta to the stand and asked her to tell her side of the story.

Alberta said, "I was home sitting on my couch when these two policemen came up to the door and said we were under arrest."

"Were you drinking?" O'Neill replied.

"Oh, I had a bottle and had just taken one drink from it," she replied.

"Were you arrested in your own home?" said O'Neill.

"Yes, sir, I was," said Alberta.

Brandon asked, "Alberta, what time was this?"

Alberta replied, "About ten or eleven, something like that."

Brandon called Wayne Ebarb to the stand and asked him to tell the court exactly what time it was when all of this happened.

He told the court that he got off at 1:30 a.m. and the arrest of Alberta and M.T. had not taken place at that time. Also that Brad Falcon did not get off until 2:00 a.m. and Glen usually took him home at that time.

Brandon then stood and read from the criminal code of Louisiana the definition for an arrest without a warrant and then stated, "The evidence is correct according to the book."

Mayor Walraven called Alberta and M.T. forward and said, "I find you both guilty as charged and fine each of you forty five dollars plus ten dollars court costs."

O'Neill then presented an appeal.

Brandon said, "We must have a three hundred dollar appeal bond and have your appeal papers ready within ten days."

O'Neill nodded and left the court with his clients.

JUNE 22, 1977: Sandra Ebarb, charged with aggravated assault, was in court and plead not guilty.

Connie Woodle, who had filed the charges, was called forward and sworn in before telling her story.

Brandon said, "Connie, what happened on the night of June 9?"

Connie said, "We were up at the washateria and Sandra drove up with a young boy in her car and pulled a gun on me and Patricia Spurlock."

"Can you describe the gun?" asked Brandon.

"Yes, it was a black pistol with a white handle," she said.

Brandon then asked Sandra if she wished to ask Connie any questions?

Sandra said, "Connie, where did I get the gun from?"

"You took it from the glove compartment of your car," said Connie.

"What did I do with it after I was suppose to have pulled it on you?" asked Sandra.

"Well, you probably stuck it—I guess I better not say it," said Connie?

Patricia Spurlock and Carolyn Leone were called to the stand and both told the same story.

Brandon asked Wayne Ebarb to go to the office and get the gun. When Ebarb brought the gun in the courtroom, all three girls identified it as the one Sandra Ebarb pulled on them.

Brandon told the court that Miss Ebarb had been brought to the court before for pulling a gun and it was time this feud stopped. Sandra was found guilty and fined one hundred ten dollars.

JUNE 28, 1978: Ruthie Jean Epps, charged with disturbing the peace and resisting an officer, was not in court last month and a bench warrant was issued. She failed to appear this time.

Brandon said he had gone to the quarters and Miss Epps' mother said she was in the hospital. He said he had proof she had been in a fight around noon and at 5:00 p.m. was still in the quarters.

"It is time we put a stop to those who are trying to make a spectacle of this court," Brandon said. "I am asking that you put the highest bond on her and make it cash only."

Walraven set a one hundred seventy dollar cash bond and said if she didn't have it, put her in jail.

JULY 26, 1978: Leslie Frazier, charged with disturbing the peace by fighting. Plead not guilty. Betty Jean Frazier the former wife of Leslie who filed the charges was called to the stand.

After being sworn in, Betty Jean stated she was visiting a friend's house when her ex-husband came in and said he wanted to talk to her. She let him in and after talking for a while, she went into the kitchen to get some ice for her water. Betty Jean said he followed her and started choking her and she started hollering. She went on to say her friend came after Leslie with a chain and beat him and he went through the back door without opening it, tearing the screen off.

Lynn, the friend, was called to the stand and she

told the same story, but Leslie said he did not do that.

Lynn said, "You old skunk, you know you did."

Falcon, came to the stand and said after Betty Jean filed the charges, he went after Leslie, who ran, but Brandon caught him, and brought him to jail in a drunken condition.

Frazier was found guilty, fined sixty dollars and thirty days and if he could not pay the sixty dollars then another thirty days.

Frazier was also charged with simple damage to property and plead not guilty. He was also found guilty of this charge and fined sixty dollars or thirty days.

JULY 26, 1978: Lana Lee, charged with disturbing the peace, plead not guilty. Glen Staten, Jr. filed the charges and took the stand. He said he went to Lana's house and told her to stay out of his business, and Lana started cursing him.

Chief Brandon said, "Staten, did you say you went to Lana's house or inside her yard?"

Staten said, "I didn't go inside her yard, I was outside her yard. Lana is always messing in my business and I am tired of it."

Lana then took the stand and told the court Staten came inside her yard and started cursing her because she was talking to the men who had cut his water and electricity off. She said Staten thought she was telling them about how he was turning his utilities back on after they were being cut off.

After much discussion back and forth, Lana Lee was found not guilty.

JUNE 27, 1979: James Anderson charged Shirley Scott with theft. She pleaded not guilty.

"Are you ready to be tried?" said Brandon.

"I am," replied Shirley, and she was sworn in.

Anderson who had filed the charges was called to the desk and sworn in to tell his side of the story.

Anderson said that he bought a quart of beer and went home to drink it and take a nap. He said, "Someone knocked on my door and I looked up and it was Shirley and she asked me to buy her a quart of beer and I said, 'o.k.' I gave her a ten dollar bill and she was to bring me back the change, but instead of doing that, when she came back she took my billfold with approximately forty four dollars in it. "

Anderson went on to say he told her to put his billfold and money back where she got it, but she would not. "So I came up here and filed charges on her," he said.

James Earl Jackson was sworn in as a witness for Anderson.

Brandon said, "James Earl tell us what you know and saw concerning this matter."

Jackson said, "I went to Anderson's home and he and Shirley were sitting on the side of the bed. Anderson had two ten dollar bills in his hand and Shirley was sitting next to him, so I decided there was something going on and I shouldn't be there. That's all I know about this."

"What did you think was going on?" said Brandon.

"Oh!, you know, I don't want to say it out loud because you know what goes on when a man has money in his hand and a woman is sitting next to him, especially on a bed," Jackson said.

Brandon asked Shirley if she wanted to ask James Earl anything and she said, "No."

Shirley then took the stand to tell her side of the story. She said that she and a group of friends had been drinking all day and she was in the café when she saw Anderson.

She said that Anderson told her to come up to his house, that he had some money for her; so she went.

She went on to say, "Anderson gave me a ten dollar bill to go buy us some beer and I did. I told him when I came back that I was going to keep the change because I think I deserved it. I did not take his billfold or his money."

"Shirley, you went to this man's house for something besides beer, did you not?" asked Brandon.

192

"What do you mean Mr. Brandon?" said Shirley.

"You know what I mean Shirley, did you go to this man's house to make 'whoopee' with him, yes or no? " stated Brandon.

"Yes, sir," stated Shirley in a low voice.

"Say that louder for the court to hear," said Brandon.

"How many times have you been charged with this? " said Brandon.

Shirley said, "Two times."

"Did he pay you to make 'whoopee' with him? " said Brandon.

"Yes, sir," replied Shirley.

"I've told you Shirley, time and time again, that you cannot make 'whoopee' and charge for it because this is illegal, do you understand?" asked Brandon.

Shirley nodded 'yes'.

Shirley was then called before the mayor and found not guilty because of lack of witnesses to the theft.

NOVEMBER 29, 1979: Brandon told those in the courtroom he wanted it known that he and Walraven would not put up with any disturbance at the school gym during the basketball games or anything else going on there or in Zwolle.

"This is a place for family sportsmanship and a place for one to go and enjoy a good evening of clean fun and sportsmanship," Brandon said. "And I will not put up with this type of disturbance."

MARCH 26, 1980: Jerry Taylor, Jr., charged with aggravated assault and plead not guilty. He stated he was ready for trial.

James D. Remedies, who had filed the charges against Taylor, come forward and was sworn in.

After hearing the testimony from David Remedies and also the story from James D. Remedies, Brandon found this was a feud that had been going on for two years between two young boys and he asked that court be dismissed for fifteen minutes. After being granted this permission he took the two boys in his chambers and talked to them. When Brandon returned, he asked that the charges be dismissed against both boys.

Mayor Walraven agreed to this and court continued.

MARCH 26, 1980: Richard McCullough, an eighth grade teacher for the Zwolle Intermediate school, was in court and plead not guilty to disturbing the peace. This charge was made by Mrs. Nola Hamm, the mother of a student he taught.

His job while at school was to see that no child left the grounds without the written permission of his parents or by a telephone call from the parents. He said he noticed three boys (one of them being the son of Mrs. Hamm) were across the street talking to Mrs. Hamm, and he asked the boys to return to the school grounds. He said he then asked Mrs. Hamm if she could talk to him for a few minutes and that he wanted to be friends with her.

Mrs. Hamm was called to the stand. She stated as she was leaving the home of the Jessie Knights that she was talking to her son and two other boys when McCullough came over raving and wanting the boys on the school ground, and also he said, "I want to talk to you, Mrs. Hamm; I want to be your friend."

Mrs. Hamm said, "I cannot talk to you or any other teacher and you know it. I'm under a peace bond." She went on to say he then hit her child because she would not talk to him.

Brandon asked McCullough, "Did you hit her son?"

McCullough answered, "No sir, I did not hit her son. All I did was whisk him on the 'hiney' and say, 'Get on the school ground.'"

Knight was called to the stand and stated the same as Mrs. Hamm. He said that McCullough did not do any cursing as far as he knew; he did not hear him, but he saw the teacher hit Mrs. Hamm's son.

Many character witnesses were called to the stand on behalf of McCullough from the Zwolle

Intermediate School. These included Principal H.D. Garner, and Marguerite Ferguson, Carroll Leggett, Rebecca Stevens, and David Hall, all teachers. Each stated McCullough was a very likable teacher and was well loved by all the students.

Brandon then asked McCullough to repeat to the court for the record what the boy had called him after his mother left.

The name that McCullough repeated was very obscene.

McCullough was called by Mayor Walraven and found not guilty and was also released from his peace bond.

MAY 28, 1980: Janis and Tom Montgomery, charged with disturbing the peace by fighting. The case was heard in court during April and sentencing was postponed so the mayor and Brandon could study this case. The couple was in court every month for the same problem and most of the time, one would not show up. Both were found guilty as charged, fined one hundred ten dollars each and thirty days in jail or in lieu of that to serve six months in jail. The sentence was suspended, provided they did not show up in court again for six months.

SEPTEMBER 3, 1981: Clinton Staton, Jr. plead not guilty to theft by shoplifting.

Ellzy Anderson, owner of White's Auto in Zwolle, was called to the stand and sworn in. His statement was as follows:

"On this certain Friday, at about 4:00 p.m. I received a phone call that Clinton Staton, Jr. had stolen a radio and cassette player from the store. After talking to the person, who wishes to remain unknown, I called the police station and gave them the story. After they went to the home and arrested Staton and brought the radio to the station, I came over and identified it by the serial number. I keep everything I order on microfilm and the article came from my store."

When Wayne Ebarb was put on the stand, he

stated when he and Glen Ebarb went to the home of Staton, he came to the door with the radio in his hand playing. They advised him of his rights and booked him.

Staton was then put on the stand and stated: "I did not go near White's Store on that day. I have never been in that store. Some white dude came along to my house and sold me this radio."

Chief Brandon said, "What did this white dude look like, Staton?"

"I don't know except he had long hair and a long beard," Staton said. "They all look alike to me."

After reading a statement taken from the informer, Mayor Fred Roberson found Staton guilty and fined him one hundred seventeen dollars and fifty cents and thirty days in jail.

Brandon held his last mayor's court session Wednesday, August 27, 1981, with sixty cases being heard. He retired September 1 after serving the town of Zwolle as chief of police for thirty-five years. The men who worked under his supervision, Glen Ebarb, Wayne Ebarb, Brad Falcon and Daniel Meshell presented him with a beautiful plaque which stated: "Chief Brandon for outstanding law enforcement work 1946-1981," followed by "An old soldier never dies, he just fades away." A reception was held at the home of Wayne Ebarb immediately following court.

Brandon conducting court has been compared to a father disciplining his children, a king presiding over his kingdom, or a "Godfather" keeping order in his "family." No matter what the comparison, court with Brandon was never dull or boring.

Chapter 41

The Practical Joker

"When one pulled a stunt on the other,
there was just one thought—-to get even.
—-James Q. Salter

James Q. Salter, retired Zwolle principal, said, "During my years in Zwolle I have known some individuals who were just as colorful and interesting as anyone can read about anywhere. The exploits of Quinton Brandon, Zwolle's equivalent to Matt Dillon, have been well documented. Many, however, might not know about his penchant for practical jokes."

He went on to say, "Brandon had a special friend, one of Zwolle's school bus drivers, Luther (Luke) Litton, who is now deceased, and who was best known for his friendliness and generosity. Visitors to the Litton household usually left with some fresh garden vegetables, a sample of fresh ribbon cane syrup, or some 'goodies' from Mrs. Litton's kitchen depending upon the season."

Apparently Brandon and Litton had a "thing" going for years in the way of practical jokes. When one pulled a stunt on the other, there was just one thought—to get even. There was a mystique—a peculiar bond—between the two.

Salter told the following stories:

The Handcuff Episode

On a number of occasions Quinton actually handcuffed Luke and even went so far as to lock him in city jail just to get even for a stunt. One day while the KCS freight train was stopped at the depot, the crew walked across the tracks to a restaurant for lunch. Quinton told the engineer he had a man handcuffed to the handrail on one of the boxcars. "I'll meet you out at Loring pond when you stop for water and get him off," he said.

Sure enough, there was Luke, standing on the bottom rung of the ladder, handcuffed to the handrail on one of the boxcars. Someone else might have thought about filing suit against the KCS, the town of Zwolle or Brandon, but not Luke—he had only one thought and that was to get even.

As promised, Quinton met the train out at Loring pond and released his "prisoner."

One day Quinton handcuffed Luke to a utility pole in downtown Zwolle. Finally, after a number of folks walked by, a little girl came along. Luke asked her if she had a bobby pin he could borrow. Luke picked the lock on the cuffs and for the rest of his life carried a bobby pin in his pocket.

The Preacher Episode

Luke stopped by the barbershop very early one morning. There sat Quinton's pastor getting a haircut. Luke dialed the Brandon residence. When Mrs. Brandon answered, she told Luke that Quinton had been out all night on the job and really needed to sleep. "Nannie, this is an emergency. I've got to talk to him," said Luke.

When Mrs. Brandon woke Quinton and handed him the phone, Luke really "let him have it" with a classic prank phone call.

Handing the receiver to the preacher, Luke said, "Preacher, here is a fellow who wants to talk to you."

That preacher held the receiver away from his ear for a while in disbelief as Quinton blasted away, telling him what a lowdown, sorry sneak he was, with some choice expletives thrown in—thinking he was talking to Luke.

After he had heard enough (actually too much), the preacher identified himself as "your pastor."

Quinton immediately knew Luke had "got" him again and apologized profusely to his pastor.

No doubt, as Brandon hung up that phone he was thinking of a way to get back at Luke.

The Cornstalk Fiddle

For one of his pranks on Quinton, Luke made a "cornstalk fiddle" and wrapped it neatly to look like a genuine present and mailed it from Alexandria. It was just a little gag gift that Luke had fashioned from the stalk of a corn plant. Quinton received the nicely wrapped present and just could not wait to see what someone sent him.

When he opened that box, there was the "fiddle" and some unflattering words written to the tune "Home Sweet Home."

Very shortly thereafter (probably the next time Luke went to town) Quinton handcuffed Luke and actually put him in cell number three in the city jail. Quinton really enjoyed taking several folks over to city hall, telling them he had something he wanted to show them. While Luke watched disconsolately, Quinton would "play" that "fiddle". After a sufficient number of folks had enjoyed the event, Quinton released his "prisoner."

Salter said, "There are hundreds of these stories. Brandon and Litton will be long remembered in and around Zwolle. They had a unique sense of humor, with a strong bond of friendship uniting them. They were special."

Chapter 42

The Found Interview

"I would paint my face black, go in the quarters and
buy whiskey from the bootleggers."
—Marshal Quinton Brandon

Just days before this book was to be sent to the printer, Police Chief Marvin Frazier of Zwolle called and said that he found a document in his office about Quinton Brandon and it may be of interest.

The document was dated March 25, 1977, and is fourteen typed legal pages. It is not known who conducted the interview, which was taken from a tape recording. It is not known why the interview took place. The interview took place in Brandon's office and the interviewer said, "Anything we publish would meet with your approval, whether we do it in fiction or as an event."

Instead of weaving the information in this document into existing chapters, the authors decided to let it stand alone as a chapter. Some editing has taken place to get rid of wordiness, but the information in the document stands.

"When I got out of the service in November, 1945, I couldn't help but notice Zwolle had very poor law enforcement. I made the statement after seeing a soldier walk the street and knock down several men and there wasn't anything done about it, that the town of Zwolle needed a marshal.

"I was asked by a councilman if I would be interested in the job and I started working here in November, 1946. When I first went to work, I didn't have an automobile. I walked and policed Zwolle, including the Mansfield Hardwood Quarters and Sabine Quarters. I had quiet a bit of gambling and bootlegging—it was dry in this area at the time.

"I immediately went to work on that and shut it down. I would paint my face black and go in the quarters. I would stay back in the dark and buy whiskey from the bootleggers myself.

"I was here two years and the mayor and I had a little difference. I couldn't get the backing in city court I thought I should have. I resigned and went to work for the state police. I worked with them three and one-half years and then Zwolle elected a new administration. They encouraged me to quit the state police and take the marshal's job and I did.

"It was still the rough town I had encountered when I first went to work before. On several weekends I would have to fight all weekend to stay here, when I first went to work. I had several scuffles. I would arrest four or five men at a time and have to fight all of them. I later got where I used my own car and the town would put gas in it. I worked for a little salary.

"A colored man working in the quarters and having to go across to the Sabine Quarters, would be afraid to walk down the front street. He'd go around the darn railroad track. I had to work to see the colored community was treated right and got justice under the law the same as the whites. I've been very fortunate. I've never had any racial trouble here. I had a few things start, which I broke up immediately, and I have good relations with the colored community. I have on several occasions been involved in violence that I felt, at the time, and still feel, was justified in the action I took.

"Understand, I didn't go clean. I got scratched up and got some black eyes myself during all of this. I won all my fights, but there were some of them that I came out with some bruises.

"I remember the first person I ever shot, a boy named King, who was wanted in Texas for armed robbery and escape. Two deputies found him and he ran away. We got the bloodhounds on him and I was riding a horse following them through the woods. He got to his mother's house and barricaded himself in.

His mother went out back and told us he had a gun. He came out on the front porch and all the other officers took cover. I was riding my horse and kept riding down on him. I was telling him all the time we didn't have anything against him. I told him he was wanted by Texas authorities and would have to surrender because we had to take him.

"He kept cursing me and telling me, 'You're going to have to come and get me.' He told me, 'You son-of-a-b——, you've got to come and get me.' And I said, 'Son, I'm on my way.' I kept pressing him, trying to determine what kind of gun he had. I made it out to be a single barrel shotgun. I kept trying to get him to fire it because I was out of range of squirrel shot, which I figured he had in the gun. The horse I was on, I knew what he would do. He would go on that porch and ride that fellow down.

"I was using all precaution to try to avoid killing the man. I didn't want to kill him and I certainly didn't want to get killed. So, I got so close I knew he could hurt my horse if he shot. I got off my horse and made him leave. I had me an old tree picked out that I could get behind just in case I needed to. By that time, I had pulled my gun. I carry a .357 magnum and the man was standing on the edge of the porch.

"I pulled my gun and told him, 'Lay that gun down and come out of there.' He told me, 'You son-of-a-b——, you got to come and get me.' And I said, 'Well, I'm on my way.' I had my gun aimed at his chest and he came up with his shotgun. I moved my sight over and caught him in the right arm and squeezed the trigger at the right time. The bullet hit him in the right arm and he dropped the shotgun outside. We picked it up and unbreeched it and it was empty. That boy, during interrogation, told us he was in so much trouble he was trying to make us kill him. I was thankful I didn't kill him after this showed up.

"I had many, many encounters with disorderly people. Sometime it was just fisticuffs, but I always got my man. One time we had a burglary that was very

203

interesting. It happened in a heavy rain one night and the night watchman didn't make his rounds. They broke into Mr. Paul Ebarb's Store and busted the safe. I worked on the case three months. I got two men out of Buffalo, Wyoming, one out of Kansas, and two out of Shreveport. I was very proud of that accomplishment. They were all escapees and wanted in other states. I am very proud at this time there is not one outstanding burglary in Zwolle. There are some petty thefts outstanding, but not one outstanding burglary.

"My next real case of violence is when I had to hit a man with my gun and the gun went off and I had no intention to shoot him. This Oxley boy, I had known all of his life. He was a man who weighed about two hundred sixty pounds and was a very stout man; and a man who prior to that had run roughshod quite a bit. He was causing a disturbance up at the school at a basketball game. I always watch very closely any activities at our schools and churches, because that's where our women and children are and I want them protected.

"I was called up there and I went and asked him to leave. He said, 'Well, god d— you.' I arrested him and was attacked by his girl friend. I got loose from her and put him in the car and brought him to the jail, along with Mr. W. F. Jeter, Jr., who was working for me at the time. He attacked me in front of city hall and I hit him with my gun and it went off and shot him. As a result, the grand jury found a no bill against me, but a true bill against him and his girl friend after it investigated me. I was also sued for that.

"On one other occasion, I arrested a boy by the name of Sneed. It was north of Zwolle on Highway 171. He had set a roadblock up, standing in the middle of the road and in a drunken condition. He saw my car and when I got there, two ladies were locking their doors and they kept driving to get around him. He jumped over on the windshield and gave them an obscene sign with his finger—he 'shot them the bird.'

"I drove up and arrested him and we got into a

scuffle there and I got a good one laid on me. Well, I got him in the car and started to town. He broke the screen down between the back seat and front seat—the protective screen—and attacked me. By the time I got the car stopped, he had the gun in his hand—my gun in his hand. I was trying to turn the gun from my chest. Someway, with the help of the Good Lord, I got the gun out of his hand and told him to get back or I'd shoot. He told me, 'You god d—- son-of-a-b——, I'm going to kill you.'

"He had me almost choked to death. I pointed the gun, just guessing, at his right arm and pulled the trigger, shooting right back toward him and me together. I knew I had to do something or I'd get killed. And the bullet went into his right arm and into his chest and killed him instantly. The sheriff's department and the city council investigated and nothing was ever filed on it. I never went before the grand jury. The FBI did not investigate this one, but did investigate the Oxley one. This is the only man I ever killed in the line of duty.

"Seven years ago, a new administration was elected and they gave me a hard time and tried to fire me. The council appointed me and the people refused to let them do that. I worked under handicapped conditions for four years and I asked Representative H. M. (Mutt) Fowler to put a bill in the legislature making my position elected and not appointive. My title was changed from marshal to chief of police. I had one opponent and I got eighty-two per cent of the vote. And the people, which I'm very proud of, voted like free folks and voted one hundred per cent of the qualified voters in Zwolle that day. I obtained eighty-two per cent of the vote. George Laroux ran against me. Since the election, working conditions have been much better. We elected another mayor and council at the same time and we all ran on the ticket together. What made me feel real good—there were older people who knew what Zwolle was like before I became marshal; they came down here in wheel chairs and on walkers and told me, 'I came especially to vote for you.'

"Family disputes are the biggest headache in my work. I believe the biggest percent of law officers are killed answering calls in family disputes. They drive up, get out of the car, and are down before they know what's going on. I have many times acted as marriage counselor and sometimes I preached a little bit.

"It happens many times a kid would get in trouble with the law or get pregnant. Many times I have helped juveniles. One of the things I'm proudest of is the work I've done with juvenile delinquents, but it is the most heartbreaking work that an officer can do. Just a few days ago a seventeen-year-old came and told me she was pregnant and didn't have anyone to go to. She said she couldn't talk to her daddy and she needed help. The boy who got her pregnant had married another girl, after she was pregnant, and denied the child was his. Since she was over seventeen that knocked out the carnal knowledge law. I assisted her in getting welfare assistance until the child was born. That happened this week. I just got a call.

"The background on this girl is she has an alcoholic father. He draws a veteran's disability and is about fifty-six or fifty-seven years old. Her mother seems to be good, but hasn't had a chance. She's raised a bunch of children under those conditions and she hasn't had a chance at anything. It's a pitiful situation. Neither of the parents had a high school education. He was in the service and I think he has a mental disability. He got married out of service and the mother was two or three years younger and they have six or seven children. The boys in the family have been arrested quite a few times on misdemeanor offenses. They get drunk, fight, careless and reckless driving, and drunk driving.

"The girl didn't seem to have any other problems. She seemed to be a pretty nice little girl. She'd been going with the boy a couple of years and she thought he was going to marry her. She dropped out of high school. I don't know what grade she was in. She didn't have a job; she was just living at home. The boy that got her pregnant, dropped out of school, but was working. He was working in the logwoods running a power saw. He'd already been going with somebody else when she came up pregnant and she cried and told me there was no other boy who had touched her and she knew it was his child.

"When I would go to investigate someone at their home and they would have their gun drawn, sometime I would draw mine, but at other times I wouldn't. It depended on the circumstances. If he had the drop on me, I knew if I pulled my gun, he'd shoot. I would rely on conversation and draw his attention away from me as much as I could. I would get close enough to the gun to charge him and hit him—get his gun. This is what I did in this particular case.

"I would tell him he was fixing to get into trouble and I would tell him things like, 'If you shoot me, you'll go to the electric chair.' And he'd say, 'I don't give a d—- where I go.' I would just keep talking to keep him occupied as I kept easing up closer to him. I would get close enough to grab his gun and throw it up and the gun would fire. I would use any means I had at that time to knock the person out and get my handcuffs on him. That night I grabbed the shotgun out of his hand and hit him up side the head with it. I gave him an army-trained butt stroke with his own gun.

"George Laroux, the man who opposed me in the last election, is approximately fifty years old now. He worked for me as a deputy and committed some offenses that were unbecoming a police officer. I'd rather not go into detail. Well, let's put it this way, he was guilty of some law violations and some offenses that were unbecoming a police officer and I fired him. I'd rather not say anymore.

"As far as I know, there's no prostitution. They don't run a house, but if you show them the money, well, they're ready to go. If somebody comes along with money or groceries or what have you, they're ready to go. That's been my experience and my knowledge. The law says if they commit an essential act with intent to gain, it is a violation in prostitution. This includes married and unmarried ones.

"There are many instances in this case. I had a colored man report a colored woman had stolen his billfold. This happens very often. On my investigation, I learned she was at his house and he had given her a ten dollar bill to go to bed with him. While they were in the act and he was excited, she got the billfold. That is a very common practice among them. She does not give him a chance to go to sleep and then get the billfold. She's in a hurry and won't even let him undress. While he's at his most excited stage, she gets that billfold. She then gets up and gets out, and she's gone before he misses it. That was at a bachelor's house.

"I had another occasion where two hundred forty dollars was taken. This colored girl made a date with this colored man and told him where to meet her. He was a married man, so when he went in the old house where they were supposed to meet, her brother was there and they took two hundred forty dollars off him. It was a case of simple robbery. They overpowered him and took it. There wasn't any gun involved in this case. He reported it to me. I investigated, got admissions and got all the money back.

"In this case, the man hit her up and she said she would for twenty dollars. He paid her twenty dollars and she told him where to go meet her. She had seen he had a wad of money on him, so she told him she'd be down there in a few minutes. So she made a circle around and got her brother and they went on to the place and got in the house. When he walked in, the girl put her arms around him and got his billfold and his money. They'd thought he'd be too embarrassed to report it. That is the case with a lot of whites. I've had it reported to me in whites that the same type thing would happen with a white woman. He'd probably be a married man and not report it.

"I never carry a blackjack. I use my gun for a club. With just a blackjack, a slap, you can't render the blow you can with a gun. It doesn't have the same effect. If you can hit a man with a heavy gun, at the right time and in the right place, it's effective. Now, if you slapped him up side of the head with a flyswatter, it's a different thing. If you don't hit him in the right place, then you had better be careful.

"Well, I was raised on a farm. I always wanted to be a police officer. My daddy was before me. I competed in rodeos when I was a youngster. I produced several rodeos. Back then I was six foot two, weighed one hundred fifty-six pounds and was all man, too. I'll be sixty in October. I was about twenty-seven when I first went to work here.

"One of the biggest problems I have now is the abuse of drugs. I guess it's nationwide. I have mostly misuse of marijuana. I have some hard stuff, but very little. It's marijuana and it's getting among our juveniles in our schools. I'm working on it. I'm catching some. In fact, I have three bills before the grand jury now.

"I work on the distributor to the juveniles, which I have is mostly black. Some whites are putting it out, but most blacks are letting these juvenile boys have it and then in turn will go sell some. They sell it out by the cigarette at school. They get one dollar for a cigarette—a 'joint' they call it. The children of some of the best families in Zwolle smoke it. In other words, there's no set pattern on what type children use it. In fact, I believe seventy-five percent of our teenagers today have tried dope, one way or the other. I'm not saying they stayed with it; I'm saying they tried it. I'm doing research on it all the time. I'm after it all the time.

"Every time I get a boy or girl in here, I talk to them about it. I get their confidence and I get information from them. There are lots of children who tell me, 'Yes, I smoke it.' I go into detail and do research as to why they want to do it. They tell me it's just something to do to see what it's all about. Usually their friends have suggested they try it. We're talking about as low as twelve years old. The average user is fifteen to eighteen and then they usually graduate to the hard stuff or they get off it.

"Lots of kids do what they call 'throw it'. That means to quit it. But if they don't quit it, they go to stronger stuff. They commit criminal acts in order to get money to buy the stuff and that goes for adults too. The older people who get on the hard stuff, most of the money they buy it with comes from stolen property.

"We don't have any regular red light districts, any prostitution, or any big time gambling. They play a little blackjack or penny ante poker or something like that. I know that goes on, but I don't allow it in a public place. If they want to go to someone's house and play, I don't pay that any attention. One of the reasons we don't have any more of a red light problem is because there are some clubs out on the lake where they can go and find somebody they can.

"I've made arrests before for gambling. There have been times when it's been reported to me there was big gambling going on at a certain house. Usually someone who had lost some money would be the one who would report it. I would raid the place and arrest the operator—the man who had the box sitting there and was cutting the game. I would arrest him and release the others. I'd confiscate the money.

"I worked about ten or twelve years by myself. I didn't have any deputies. I have a force of three men now, and they are very efficient. I have one of the best little police departments in the state.

"Here is a story about the type of scuffle you get into. I was easing around this house and couldn't find the door. I knew if I knocked, they'd have everything out of sight when I got in. I found a window that I could get up right quick. I pulled that window up and just jumped in. I landed right in the middle of the table. Well, there were two or three that grabbed me and I flipped over on my back with that gun in my hand and they fell back. I had my gun in my hand when I jumped in. There were about twenty people in the game. The reason I raided the house was because I knew there was a law violation going on. I knew there was gambling going on. They had a regular room set up for gambling.

"Mostly colored people ran this kind of game. This particular time the man was around sixty years of age. There was beer and whiskey, but he wasn't selling it. He was running straight gambling. There were all black participants. You would need a warrant now to get into a place like that, but back then you didn't have to have a warrant.

"Way back when I first became marshal, there was a white man who did quite a bit of drinking. He had been to college and had a wife and two very sweet little girls. He came to me and was very broken hearted that his wife and little girls had left him. I talked with him until way into the night. I told him to go home, go to bed, and the next morning I would talk to his wife.

"He told me if she would come back he would go to work and quit his drinking and stuff. I went to see his wife and it took me about half a day to talk her into the notion of coming back. I did get her and brought her and the girls back with me. Incidentally, it was very rewarding in that the little girls are grown ladies now and married. They came to see me awhile back and their daddy did quit drinking for awhile and went to work and did real good. But, he did go on another drunk and wrecked his car and cut his wife's face. She was a beautiful woman and her face was cut and scarred real bad. She quit him and I haven't seen her since. She never came back. He's in an insane asylum now.

"I don't remember too much about the wreck he had when he cut up his wife. He was drunk at the time and driving. She told me when I went and brought her home that she was leaving and would never come back. She said she appreciated my interest in them, but she couldn't live with him anymore. That was after he cut up her face.

"She knew and had caught him several times and told me he was bootlegging whiskey and had quit his job. He asked her to go some place with him that night. He went and got a load of bootlegged liquor and was drunk when he had the wreck. The children were around five and seven. He would slap them around, too.

"It was 1948 when I got her back and she stayed about six months. He would beat her up when he was drinking. That's the reason she left him to begin with. He'd stay out late at night and come in drunk and wake her and the children up just 'raising cane' in general. He'd beat her up and accuse her of things she wasn't guilty of, just as an excuse to beat her up. I've seen her with both eyes swollen closed. I arrested him on several occasions for doing that.

"I had to get him one night when he had his shotgun after his mother. I believe if I hadn't got there when I did, he'd have gone completely crazy. This was after his wife left him. He was after his mother with a shotgun and I believe he would have killed her.

"His aunt called me and told me they were having trouble. When I got to the house, I just busted on in. She told me all the details. The mother was out back and he walked around the house with the shotgun—a .12 gauge Remington pump. He told me if I didn't get out of the house he'd kill me and I told him I wasn't leaving. I kept talking to him and got close enough to grab the barrel of the gun and turn it up. He tried to follow the gun, but I blocked the firing of it and arrested him. I charged him with aggravated assault on a police officer and he was convicted of it."

Chapter 43

Quinton Saves the Day

"About that time I heard, 'You people back up.
What's up here?' It was Quinton."
—*James Napier*

State Trooper James Napier thought it was just a routine investigation that October 15, 1977, when he answered the call to a wreck on Highway 482, the Ebarb Road.

When he got there, he found that Mrs. Carmen L. Smith, sixty-six, of Zwolle, had become the parish's eleventh fatality of the year. She was a passenger in a car driven by Sharon F. Ezernack, also of Zwolle.

Napier said that a vehicle driven by Larry D. Malmay, eighteen, also of Zwolle, struck from behind their station wagon. Glen P. Meshell, nineteen, of Noble and a juvenile were passengers with Malmay.

Upon investigation of the accident, Napier found that drinking had been involved. Malmay was charged with driving while intoxicated and resisting arrest.

Napier recalls, "We found Malmay's vehicle about a quarter mile from the scene. When we got there, Malmay was intoxicated and belligerent. Malmay's friends started gathering. Back then, it sometimes took the coroner a long time to arrive at the scene."

Continuing, Napier said, "Malmay and I broke out in a fight. More of Malmay's friends started arriving at the scene. Malmay and I were down in the ditch fighting. William H. Malmay, a bystander, tried to help Larry and he was charged with interfering with a police officer and resisting arrest. Glenwood Bullard was working with the Attorney General's Office and went with me. No one knew Glenwood, so he didn't get into it. I was in a mess and didn't know

Brandon and State Trooper Hurshel Davis are shown transferring Larry D. Malmay and William H. Malmay to the parish jail following an accident which left a Zwolle woman dead on October 15, 1977.

what I was going to do."

Concluding, Napier said, "About that time, I heard, 'You people back up. What's up here?' It was Quinton Brandon. Even the guy who was fighting me quit. 'You want some of this?' Quinton asked them. We handcuffed the two that had been fighting me and put them in the car. Quinton had saved the day."

Chapter 44

Pelican Bank Robbery

"Even so, no one told Mr. Brandon what to do."
—-Bill Leslie

February 5, 1979, just did not turn out to be a very good day for Quinton Brandon. The Pelican State Bank in neighboring DeSoto Parish had been robbed that morning. Two masked men with a sawed-off shotgun and a pistol held up the bank shortly after 11:00 a.m. They made off with $7,333.

DeSoto officials quickly put out an all points bulletin and as was his nature, Brandon was one of the first to offer his assistance.

Robert Davidson, now a sheriff's investigator in DeSoto, said that he remembered Brandon was told to set up a roadblock at the Old Davidson Store on Highway 175 because it was felt the robbers were headed that way.

Davidson related, "After so many hours, we lost hope of finding the robbers and called the manhunt off. Our mistake was that we failed to notify Quinton. Later some of us drove to Sabine Parish only to find Quinton still at this roadblock."

If that was not bad enough, Sabine deputy sheriff Bill Leslie told another story about the same event.

He said, "We were assisting DeSoto Parish and I returned to the office to work the radio and declared the radio to be off limits to all traffic until the chase was over. Mr. Brandon came on the radio and I told him to get off the air. Not over fifteen minutes later, he was in the office in Many and told me in no uncertain terms that no one told him what to do. Bear in mind, we were fellow police officers, as well as personal friends. Even so, no one told Mr. Brandon what to do.

Chapter 45

The Man

"He had a very sensitive side. Those close knew he cared very much for his fellow man."
—-Many Chief of Police Dean Lambert

In his glory years, Quinton Brandon stood six feet one and one-half inches tall and weighed one hundred eighty to one hundred ninety pounds. His hair, which had started thinning, was light brown and his eyes were blue.

Most of the time he was in uniform. He always wore that Stetson hat. He believed a lawman should always be dressed properly and that he should wear a hat. He was "from the old school" and he was proud of his conservative beliefs.

He was a smoker, up until the end. He drank some back in his younger days, but Mrs. Brandon said that her husband was not a drinker and "never drank at home."

Brandon was a member of the First Baptist Church at Zwolle. "He did not attend church regularly," Mrs. Brandon said, "because when he was physically able he worked so much, and after he had his stroke he was physically unable to sit for long periods of time." In a 1978 interview with the Morning Advocate, Brandon described himself as "A true Christian."

Did he have any bad habits? Mrs. Brandon, thought a minute, then said, "Yes, he was bull-headed. He was determined."

What aggravated him? "Anyone who mistreated old folks or babies," Mrs. Brandon said. "That was the wrong thing to do. You got in bad with him very quickly when you did that."

What traits did he like in a person? Mrs.

Brandon said, "Number one—honesty. If you told him something, then do it. He liked a person of his word."

Among his favorite foods was a good steak cooked rare, fried fish, and barbecued goat. For his drink, his favorites were coffee and ice tea. His hobbies were fishing (more so in his younger years), hunting, and the rodeo. He loved gospel music and some country and western, especially Hank Williams. He had no favorite saying or slogans that his family could remember, but he did start his sentences many times by referring to the person as "son."

When Brandon started his career in 1946, his firearm was a Smith and Wesson .357 magnum on a .44 frame. The gun had a pair of white and brown stag grips. Brandon used it in two ways: as a pistol and as a club, if need be. In later years, he switched to a lighter, easier to handle Smith and Wesson Chief's Special Airweight .38, but kept the .357.

Rocky Brandon said his father always instilled in him a deep respect and love for America and the flag. "I once got into a fight with someone because they disrespected the flag in my presence," he said.

Brandon always stood ready to help people in need. He was usually the first one there to assist. Remembered W. F. Jeter, Jr., "He would help them. I've seen him buy food for the hungry. If someone needed to go to the doctor in Shreveport and didn't have the gas, he'd fill their vehicle for them and pay the bill. People have the opinion he was rough and tough, but he was very softhearted. You could get to him."

An announcement was reported in the June 19, 1980, issue of *The Index* that Brandon had started a fund for Edna Williamson, seventy-seven, a lifelong resident, whose house was burned by arsonists. "She lost everything she had," Brandon said. "We think all the citizens of Zwolle should help her."

Dr. George D. Brandon remembered once when Quinton was hospitalized, that his former fellow officer, retired Trooper Andy Anders died. Upon getting out of the hospital, Quinton got Anders' brother to carry him to the grave to pay his last respects to the trooper.

In another story, Dr. Brandon told, "A few years ago, Quinton drove my dad Victor to Leesville and they brought a pig that had a hernia for me to operate on. On the way back home, Quinton, knowing my dad was unable to drive, carried him by the old cemetery, where their little sister, Lorene, was buried along with other relatives. It meant a lot to my dad and he still talks of the time they were able to reminisce."

Many Chief of Police Dean Lambert remembered as a young officer when he was fortunate enough to work with Brandon. "I can remember driving through the parish and nearly every house, curve, bridge or person we came across, had a story," Lambert said. "He did the talking and I did the listening. Even when we got to a meeting, it seemed everyone knew Quinton and he did his share of the talking there also."

Lambert continued, "One thing that stood out was when we stopped at a cafe to get coffee, it was not beyond Quinton, when the coffee was a little hot, to pour the coffee onto the saucer, if one was handy, and sip the hot coffee from the saucer. Now Quinton's sip was more than a sip, it was a rather loud slurp and usually caused glances from way across the restaurant." Sheriff Guffey Lynn Pattison also remembers Brandon's slurping and added, "You could hear him all over the place."

In continuing his discussion about Brandon, Lambert said, "Being a fellow chief and being around Quinton, I did find that even though he had a reputation as a hard nose, tough lawman, he also had a very sensitive side. Those close to Quinton knew very well he cared very much for his fellowman and carried many of their burdens on his shoulders."

Mrs. Brandon said that her husband always thought a lot of Sheriff Phillips, Paul Ebarb, Louis Lefkovits, and Oliver Elliott. All are now deceased.

"He said at times he needed to talk to someone about what he was doing or something," Mrs. Brandon related. "He would always talk to them for advice, if he wasn't sure of what he was doing." She remembered that Sheriff Phillips loved her coconut pie. She said, "He was allergic to coconut, but he would eat it anyway."

One of Brandon's passions in life was hunting with friends. "He loved to go deer hunting," Bob Key, son-in-law of Mr. and Mrs. Max Brown who lived next door to the Brandon's house, remembered, "It wasn't unusual to see fifty people gathered up at his house to go out hunting. It was the collecting point."

Howard Brandon spoke of his brother's love for hunting deer, squirrel, rabbit, and anything else that was in season. "There was a lot of competition concerning who had the best dog every year," he said. "One year Quinton had a dog named Sue, and he was so proud of it. Sue was always the first to pick up the scent, and always ran the animal the longest. Sue was especially adept at running deer. If you took Sue to the woods, the only way you would miss killing a deer was if you didn't hit it when you shot at it."

Howard continued, "It was deer season and Quinton had a bunch of men from all over running dogs that day. He wanted to show Sue off. He didn't know that younger brother, Bob, had whittled some deer feet out of wood, and he went up the road and very carefully made it look like a deer had crossed."

Continuing, Howard tells, "Quinton let Sue out of the back of his truck and led her by the leash up the road to the deer tracks. All the men came to see Sue in action. Sue just walked right past the tracks as if they weren't there. Bob said the look on Quinton's face was priceless and it was all Bob and the other brothers could do to keep from falling out on the ground with laughter. None of the other men were in on the joke, so for about ten minutes Sue and Quinton sure looked bad. Bob said Quinton was about to take his gun out and shoot Sue, so he finally confessed. His brothers teased Quinton about this for the rest of his life. It was always a part of any stories told around the deer camp."

After his stroke, Brandon had a swivel chair with an armrest made especially so he could take it to the woods during deer and squirrel season. Howard stated, "He was able to kill a lot of game this way. He left it in the woods one time and someone got it. It took about six months, but he finally found out who got it, and made them bring it back to him."

Roscoe Rains of Leesville, who worked with Brandon as a state trooper in the late 1940's and early 1950's, said they were close friends and had a lot of fun in those days.

He related, "One day State Trooper Andy Anders and I carried Brandon fishing at Bull Sneed's private pond. Brandon didn't have a rod and reel and Andy loaned him an old bait casting reel that was no account. Every cast Brandon made wasn't over about ten feet, and that old reel would backlash into the biggest bird's nest you have ever seen. Brandon would patiently unravel it, and every time he would reel in, he would have a big bass. He wound up catching more than both of us together."

"I carried him quail hunting once," Rains recalled, "Back then I had some dogs, and quail were in abundance. We had a fine hunt, and Brandon was impressed with those pointer bird dogs. He had never been around dogs like that. When we got back from the hunt, he insisted we go by the Troop H office to brag about our hunt. He got so involved in telling the story, he even got down on his hands and knees to show the other troopers how those dogs worked."

How would Quinton like to be remembered? Mrs. Brandon replied, "He was a man who loved his country, family, town, and community, and wanted everyone to have the best."

Chapter 46

Awards and Recognition

"Give me the roses while I live,
trying to cheer me along.
Useless the flowers that you give,
after I'm dead and gone."
—Old Hymn

Nannie Brandon, Quinton's wife said, "Quinton didn't like publicity—especially if it was about him and his job. He tried to stay out of the limelight and just do his job, but people wouldn't let him do that."

"Doing his job" many times required him to attend church or civic functions to present or accept awards. One could spot his brown Stetson hat or hear that gruff, deep voice at just about any social event that took place.

He attended numerous "ribbon cuttings" and "grand openings" and participated or hosted "kickoff suppers" for various political campaigns.

OCTOBER 1947 - When a post of the American Legion was organized in Zwolle, he was vice-commander.

MARCH 1955 - Brandon was named chairman of the March of Dimes for Zwolle. Under his direction $943.40 was raised and in 1955 this was a great amount of money.

AUGUST 1966 – The Louisiana Municipal Review devoted several pages and photographs to the town of Zwolle. In the editorial it stated, "Marshal Brandon has achieved prominence in state law enforcement circles as an outstanding example of small town police efficiency."

MARCH 2, 1972 – *The Index* carried a picture of Brandon on the front page, recognizing his twenty

Robert Davidson presented a plaque of appreciation in July 1979 from the Mansfield Jaycees for Brandon's assistance in law enforcement.

Brandon spoke about patriotism at the 1975 meeting of the Many Pilot Club. Mrs. Catherine Davis was patriotism chairman for the club.

straight years serving as marshal. The article stated, "Hats off to you for a job well done."

DECEMBER 20, 1974 – Awards were presented by Brandon to Willamette Industries employees. He also gave a talk about being dedicated to your job and looking out for the good of your fellowman.

JANUARY 16, 1975 - He spoke on patriotism and service to America at a meeting of the Many Pilot Club.

MAY 1975 – Brandon presented trophies to Zwolle intermediate school boys' cross-country track winners.

JANUARY 20, 1978 – The Community Service Award was presented to Brandon by the Zwolle Jaycees at their annual banquet. Making the presentation was Gary Bridges.

MARCH 27, 1978 – *The Shreveport Times* ran a very flattering article titled "Chief Quinton Brandon-He Tamed Zwolle." In the article he was praised for his dedication to the town and his outstanding reputation statewide as a top law enforcement officer.

OCTOBER 5, 1978 - He spoke to TAP students at Zwolle Elementary. He told them about the "Duties of a Law Enforcement Officer." He told the children anytime they needed help, to feel free to call on him because he was their friend. He said he had devoted much of his life to God, his country, and his fellowman.

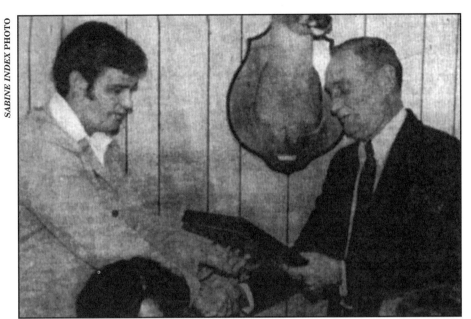

The Zwolle Jaycees honored Brandon on January 25, 1979, upon his thirty years of service to law enforcement. He in turn presented State Trooper James Napier a plaque naming him Outstanding Young Law Enforcement Officer.

He asked the children to be good citizens and to be thankful for this great county. He also told them, "Remember policemen are here to keep you safe."

JANUARY 1979 – He was presented a beautiful plaque for his thirty years of service to law enforcement at the Zwolle Jaycee Week Awards Banquet. The presentation was made by State Trooper James Napier. Brandon was affectionately known as "the papa of law enforcement in Sabine Parish," and he later presented the Outstanding Young Law Enforcement Officer Award to Napier.

As he presented the award to Napier he said, "I am glad to see good, young law enforcement officers coming on. A man must be dedicated to be a good law enforcement officer."

JULY 31, 1979 – A plaque of appreciation was presented by the Mansfield Jaycees to Brandon for his assistance to the city of Mansfield in law enforcement. It was presented by Robert Davidson.

JANUARY 31, 1980 - Brandon was presented the award for Outstanding Law Enforcement Officer by the Zwolle Jaycees at the Annual Outstanding Service Awards Banquet. His daughter, Becky Loupe, was named Outstanding Woman that year.

OCTOBER 1984 – Brandon was named King of the Zwolle Tamale fiesta.

The town of Zwolle celebrated its seventy fifth anniversary in 1973, and on June 7, *The Index* published a special tabloid dedicated to that event. On the cover was featured a picture of Brandon.

Inside, an editorial titled, "Quinton Brandon, Zwolle's Unsung Hero," praised the marshal. The editorial stated, "*The Index* feels Brandon is one of Zwolle's unsung heros. He has stood courageously for law enforcement in Zwolle, many times probably misunderstood. But, you could always count on him to stand up."

The editorial continued, "He has put in many hours for Zwolle and the work he loves so well. Probably the number of hours and the amount of worry this man has gone through is known only to God."

"As former Sabine Parish Sheriff Phillips said, 'Brandon served as Marshal when probably no other man could have held the job. And he stayed with it through thick and thin. He wasn't a quitter.'

"And as the seventy fifth anniversary of Zwolle approaches, *The Index* feels it is time, maybe past time, to honor Brandon for his efforts on behalf of Zwolle.

"We think he is a fine man. We feel he has done a great job for Zwolle.

"Quinton, from the bottom of our hearts, 'We appreciate you.' "

In an ad in the special edition, Brandon stated, "I am proud to be a part of Zwolle. I am proud to serve my town, and have served for twenty one years straight, and most of all I am proud of my country and the American flag."

In March, 1981, the first edition of *Louisiana Life*

hit the newsstands with a very complimentary story about Brandon, entitled, "The Sheriff who Tamed Zwolle." He was compared to Bufford Pusser in the hit book and movie, Walking Tall.

"Having people read about me hasn't made me any different," Brandon stated. "I'm going to do my job anyway. Let them write good or bad. I'll always be the same as I am now."

Throughout his entire life these words proved to be true. No matter how much praise or how many awards he was presented all Brandon wanted was to do his job in the way he felt it should be done.

Chapter 47

The Stroke

"It seems the stroke is the only thing
ever to get the better of Quinton Brandon."
—Louisiana Life, March, 1981

The day was Friday, March 16, 1979. Quinton Brandon usually went home to take a nap in the early afternoon if his work allowed him to. Mrs. Brandon, at the time, was employed as a teacher's aide at the Zwolle school.

The phone rang at the office of Palmer-Jones Timber Company in Zwolle. Bill and Edith Palmer and Calvin and Lorene Brandon Jones owned the company. Mrs. Jones is the Brandon's daughter.

Mrs. Palmer answered and at first, she could not figure out what the conversation was about. She did understand that Brandon was in some kind of trouble and she immediately left to go to his house, as she knew he was there alone.

Mr. and Mrs. Jones were building a new home just off Highway 171, north of Zwolle, and Mrs. Jones was coming from there when she passed her parent's house and notice Mrs. Palmer's car there. She stopped to see what was wrong.

They found Brandon had suffered a stroke. About this time Sheriff's Deputy Andrew Leone arrived at the house to give Brandon some legal papers to serve. They immediately took Brandon to the hospital in Many. Someone came to the school and got Mrs. Brandon and took her to the hospital.

In the March 29, 1979, issue of *The Index*, publisher Robert Gentry wrote in his "Observations" column: "Brandon was released from Fraser Hospital March 26. He is now recuperating at home from a mild stroke. Best wishes for a speedy recovery are

229

extended to Chief Brandon."

The April 12 edition carried this note in "Observations:" "Word has reached *The Index* Brandon is back behind his desk at Zwolle. That just goes to show you can't keep a good man down."

The May 24 newspaper said, "The surgery on Brandon May 21 at Schumpert Hospital in Shreveport was a great success." The May 31 *Index* stated, "Brandon returned home May 28 after being a patient for over a week."

Brandon was on Ann Bebee Wilson's program on KSLA-TV July 9. *The Index's* Zwolle correspondent Evelyn Hopkins wrote, "Although I was working and did not get to see him, those who did said he was great. He is looking better all the time. Keep on keeping on, Quinton. We love you."

On the night of July 12, Brandon was among those attending a barbecue for State Representative H. M. (Mutt) Fowler on Toledo Bend Lake. Evelyn Hopkins, Zwolle reporter, wrote in *The Index*, "It was a joy to see him at the barbecue, walking around slowly and shaking hands with everyone."

In the July 19 "Observations" column by Gentry said, "Brandon was in the intensive care unit at Schumpert following major surgery July 16." The column continued, "A family spokesman stated the surgery was successful and he is doing well. Our best wishes for a speedy recovery are extended." In her July 9 news, Mrs. Hopkins wrote, "I have just talked to Quinton and he tells me he is entering the hospital again on Sunday for more surgery and after that will be good as new. We know you will Quinton and our prayers for a quick and complete recovery go with you."

In her news on August 9, Mrs. Hopkins wrote that Brandon had been a patient at Fraser Hospital in Many for a few days.

As fall was winding down, Mrs. Hopkins wrote on October 25: "Say, have you noticed? That chief of police we have for Zwolle is doing great. You can't keep a good man down, can you, Quinton? Boy is he doing good. We are so proud of you. That is what will and determination, along with all the prayers, can do."

Mrs. Brandon said that at first, after the stroke, her husband was confined to a hospital bed, then a wheel chair, then a walker, and then he got to the point that he could use a walking stick. She said Many physical therapists Keith Broussard "...brought him to the point that he could walk and then he just took off."

After the stroke, Mrs. Brandon said her husband was plagued with medical problems for the remainder of his life.

"The arteries in his neck were unrepairable," she stated. "He was advised to let the doctors bore a hole in his skull and connect it to an artery in his brain. He did this on one side and then a month later on the other side. It worked and Quinton kept his right mind until the end."

In addition, he later had a bleeding ulcer and he had a colostomy for about two or three months before he was able to have it reversed.

Mrs. Hopkins' Zwolle column of January 28, 1980, stated: "And by the way, Mr. Brandon looks better all the time. He is really getting around these days. You talk about 'get up and go,' he sure has it. Keep on keeping on, Quinton."

Mrs. Brandon said of the stroke, "He was down for awhile. But he said, 'I'm going to walk again.' It got him at first. He couldn't do anything but lay in the hospital bed. However, he never lost faith and remained in good spirits. He learned to walk again with sheer will power."

Delane Christianson stated, "The stroke had a tremendous effect on him mentally. He was so proud of his physical abilities. In spite of the stroke, he still tried to do what he could to accommodate the public and our group when we came from Omaha to visit. Everyone we brought thought the world of him."

Christianson said his 1979 visit almost coincided with Brandon's stroke. "He had one of his officers meet us at the Shreveport airport. We went directly to the hospital in Many to see him. The stroke changed him a lot. He was a very proud person. It took him some time, but he did work after the stroke. He carried a cane and I heard he wasn't above jabbing a person a little bit with it, just to get their attention."

Pete McCormick, said, "At first he was despondent over it. As time went by and he got better, he started to be his old self again. Along at the last he would drive up to the post office and if he didn't feel good, he'd get somebody to go in and get his mail."

Mrs. Edith J. Palmer remembers, "He would come to the post office every day. Some days he didn't feel like getting out of his truck. He would ask someone to get his mail. If it were me, he would always say, 'Give me a sugar and get my mail.'"

I admired the way he handled his disability," Ms. Palmer said. "He was totally a macho man."

"He was an avid sportsman," John Patton remembers. "He was one of the best deer hunters I've ever seen. When I never saw a deer, he could go and kill one. After his stroke, he had a special chair he would set up out in the woods and continued to deer hunt."

"Quinton was tough," Dr. Brandon said. "After his debilitating stroke that left his left arm and leg with paresis, he was still determined to enjoy life. He continued to hunt and had a special chair constructed with a rifle rest. Since he wasn't able to load and unload it, he would often leave it along side the road and it was stolen one day. Yet, he was not to be outdone. He had another one constructed and had the biggest log chain and lock on it I've ever seen."

Wayne Ebarb, who served under Brandon and became Chief when he retired, said, "The stroke put him down a long time. I'd go and get him every day and bring him to the office and ride him around town."

"He just couldn't do the job as Chief anymore," Ebarb said. "He decided to try it by himself, but he had some close calls in different kinds of scrapes. He just couldn't do it anymore, so he decided to retire at the end of August 1981.

"After he retired, he'd still come down to the office," Ebarb recalled. "He'd ride out to see me on Toledo Lake. He liked the Opelousas catfish that I'd catch and I'd give him some."

Ebarb continued, "He also had that goat farm and he would go out there. He had a radio put in his truck so he could keep in touch. He'd report things to us that he was aware of. One time he was at the goat ranch and fell down and couldn't get up. He managed to crawl to the truck and radio me. I went out and helped him."

W. F. Jeter Jr. said, "He never talked about the stroke to me. We kept a relationship after he retired. He'd come out and visit me."

In an article in *Louisiana Life* in March, 1981, Brandon said that he was hanging up his badge because of the stroke, which left him partially paralyzed on his left side, not from any real desire to quit. It continued, "He carried a huge walking stick, inviting comparisons with a club-carrying Tennessee Sheriff, Buford Pusser of Walking Tall fame."

An article in the October 15, 1981, *Index*, stated Brandon "...was still a patient at Fraser Hospital. He had served as Grand Marshal for the Tamale Fiesta parade and then was hospitalized Sunday night, October 10."

The stroke knocked him down and came close to stomping him. But it could not kill his determination, his desire, his strong will, or his spirit. He would rise above it as best he could. There was only one thing that could take him out and that was death. It would be sixteen long years before he felt its cold, icy hand.

Chapter 48

The *Louisiana Life* Article

"I never was hurt by something I didn't say."
—Calvin Coolidge

In March-April 1981 the first edition of the slick magazine *Louisiana Life* reached the newsstands. In that premier issue was a nice story about Quinton Brandon, entitled, "The Sheriff Who Tamed Zwolle."

The magazine had sent writer Steve Smith and photographer Andy Sharp to do the story. The feature was three pages and included three pictures.

Brandon was quoted in the article as saying Toledo Bend Lake, created in 1968, had "...brought us two things, legal liquor and trashy people."

The Sabine Index reprinted the article in its March 12 edition and when folks in the lake area read it, criticism for Brandon started coming.

The March 19 edition of *The Index* carried two letters critical of Brandon. One was from the Reverend Hoy N. Leach, who was pastor of Toledo Baptist Church.

"First I want to make it clear that I appreciate the years of dedication by Mr. Brandon to make Zwolle a better community in which to live," the Reverend Leach started.

Then he wrote, "This remark stunned me. I have known Mr. Brandon for several years and I can not believe he would make such a statement. I want to apologize to the many wonderful people who this may have offended."

Continuing, the Reverend Leach wrote, "The term 'trashy people' is what really got to me. Maybe if he got off his throne and rode down to the lake and met some of these people he calls 'trashy' his attitude would change."

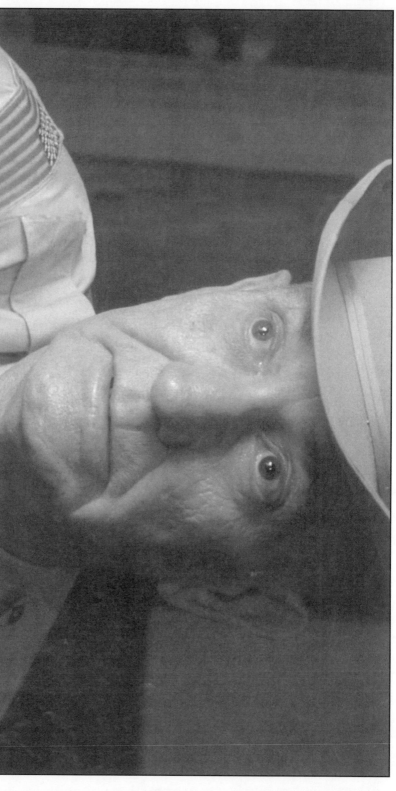

Brandon is shown in this photo featured in the premier edition of *Louisiana Life* in the spring of 1981.

He concluded, "I can say also without a doubt, I have not found one person on the lake who would fall into the category Mr. Brandon put them into. It has been completely the opposite. They are 'The cream of the crop' as far as I am concerned. They are my friends and I resent very much anyone calling these wonderful people 'trashy.' "

If that was not enough for Brandon to mull over, Mrs. Jack H. Green, who signed her letter, 'Lake Area Resident and Proud of It,' not only took him to task, but also *Index* publisher Gentry.

She wrote, "I cannot believe you would print something so insulting to the people who have chosen to make their homes here. We are law-abiding, tax-paying citizens. We came here because we loved the area and the friendliness of the people, who for the most part do not share 'Lawman Brandon's' narrow mindedness."

Mrs. Green concluded, "A law officer, supposedly a leader in his community, who makes insulting remarks about people he doesn't even know should have been retired thirty-five years ago. Zwolle can only be better after September. It is bad enough to think these things; to print them in a community newspaper, bought and read by all, is unbelievable. We are waiting for an apology."

In the March 26 edition of *The Index*, Brandon issued a front-page statement saying he had been misquoted in the article.

The article stated, "That one statement has created more controversy for the Zwolle Chief than anything else in recent years."

In the same issue of *The Index*, Brandon wrote a letter to Gentry, which offered an explanation and apology.

Brandon wrote, "First I want to say I appreciate the article written about me and to be able to appear in a news magazine makes me feel mighty good, but as you have known me over all these years you have been around, I do not like to talk to the press because I feel

Quinton and Nannie Brandon on the porch of their home on Obrie Street in Zwolle, as pictured in the March-April 1981 edition of *Louisiana Life*.

Brandon proudly holds a copy of the premier edition of *Louisiana Life* in 1981, which carried a nice feature about him titled, "The Sheriff Who Tamed Zwolle." But, that was before the storm hit.

they sometimes misquote statements people say. Now don't get me wrong, I am not talking about you, for I know you believe 'right is right, and wrong is wrong' and you have always tried to print the news like it is. So let me go on record as saying that what I said to the man who interviewed me for this magazine was, 'The lake brought in legalized liquor and a few trashy people.' You can bet your bottom dollar most of the people on the lake are good honest Christian people and I love them all, but there are some good and bad in everything and everywhere. You know that as well as I do."

He continued, "Yes, Robert, I have dedicated myself for many years as a law abiding marshal that one would love and not forget after he was gone. I am dedicated to the town of Zwolle, its people, the lake and all of Sabine Parish. I am proud to be a native of the parish; I have raised my family here; and God knows I would not want to hurt anyone intentionally. If I have hurt anyone, and according to the letters appearing in the paper and the phone calls, I have, please let me APOLOGIZE. Yes, I mean, I want to APOLOGIZE for the statement in the magazine that was untrue and in my opinion, I know WHAT I SAID, and I did not say it like it was printed. But since this article and statement is already printed, there is nothing I can say but, 'I'm sorry.' WHAT MORE CAN I SAY!!!!!"

He added a postscript to the letter: "Mrs. Green, how could I have been talking about you when I don't know you and you don't know me?"

Dr. George D. Brandon stated, "I believe he regretted that remark more than anything in his life, but I also believe what he was trying to articulate, was he was afraid that development meant an increase in bars and nightclubs which would increase crime, accidents, and other undesirable elements."

Also in the same edition of *The Index* was a letter from Stephen L. Hanna of Zwolle, which defended Brandon's position. He wrote, "Brandon was giving an honest opinion without any intention of provoking those on the lake into civil unrest.   Besides, I have been told the entire quote was not published. The quote contained a word, which could have vanquished the lake people's ill feelings, released by the article. The word was 'few.' "

Hanna went on to write that reporter Smith could have well left off the word and it could have been a human oversight, and really was not that important.

He continued, "Brandon is outspoken, as everyone knows. A veteran of the force he is prone to criticism of others; he just gave the interviewer what was asked for: honesty and straightforward personal views. He has never been one, as far as I know, to hold back his thoughts and feelings toward his fellowman. If he thinks a person is not worth his weight in salt, he'll tell him so.   Honesty and integrity are the backbone of this man and still there are these people who would like to string him up. To me, you people are pathetic! You people, who would be swimming in a sea of illegal narcotics and inhuman hate if it were not for

Brandon is shown inside his office at City Hall in this picture which was carried in the March-April 1981 edition of Louisiana Life.

him, have the audacity to accuse Brandon of slander and demand an apology. You deserve nothing!"

Hanna concluded, "I'm new here myself, but have known Brandon long before my residence was made permanent. I know, since I am new here, I am trash! Well, I'm nowhere near being what many of you people are! And to those people who have taken grave offense to the statement, then you certainly know who you are, don't you?"

Chapter 49

A Look at the Cases He Worked

"He didn't bring his work home with him too much."
—-Nannie Brandon

During his lifetime, Quinton Brandon made literally hundreds of arrests, served hundreds of legal documents, and investigated hundreds of cases. It would be impossible to study everything he did, but below are a sampling of the cases he worked, as taken from the pages of *The Sabine Index*.

JUNE 19, 1953: Sam Craig, J. Martinez, Earl Garcie, Lou Leone, and Cedric Ezernack plead guilty to possessing untaxed liquor.

JULY 16, 1955: At 4:00 p.m. Emmett Ebarb was shot by his brother-in-law, Buddy Laroux, on the streets of Zwolle. Laroux was charged with aggravated battery. He fired two shots from a .32 pistol, one went wild going through the clothing of bystander Lee Meshell, and the other struck Ebarb in the chest.

NOVEMBER 7, 1956: Carl W. Rivers, twenty-six, was killed this afternoon when a load of logs shifted on a truck bed and crushed him in a lumberyard in Zwolle. Brandon said Rivers loosened the binders on the load and two logs at the top rolled off, striking him on the head.

NOVEMBER 18, 1965: Bryne Sepulvado, sixteen, was charged with the murder of Joseph Steve Ebarb, twenty-three, and Vernon Ebarb, a witness to the shotgun shooting, was charged with murder. After the shooting, Sepulvado came to Zwolle and reported the incident to Brandon.

JANUARY 11, 1966: Three juveniles who burglarized Lonnie Martinez's Grocery were rounded up with the aid of Brandon and Sheriff George Cook's bloodhounds. They had stolen about one hundred dollars worth of goods.

JUNE 30, 1966: Two prisoners escaped the Zwolle jail. Brandon said at 6:00 p.m. three men drove into J. O. Kimbrell's Station and wanted a flat fixed. Kimbrell told the men his help was gone and they cursed Kimbrell, who called Brandon. Two of the three were jailed and after dark, the one who remained free pried a window open, entered the courtroom, got a key, and let the pair out of jail.

JULY 13, 1966: Brandon had to call Sheriff George R. Cook's famous bloodhounds in to catch Glen Perry, nineteen, a mental patient. He was apprehended and taken to Sabine Parish jail, where he set himself on fire that afternoon.

AUGUST 10, 1966: Thomas B. Upton, of Texarkana, USA and Apple Valley, Calif. was arrested by Brandon for cashing a fifteen dollar worthless check. He said Upton was an ex-convict, and had served six or seven terms for burglary and writing hot checks. Brandon said Upton was a professional check artist, and had many check books in his possession when arrested.

AUGUST 12, 1966: A nineteen year old man was charged with attempted rape and aggravated assault on a thirteen year old girl about 1:30 p.m. Brandon said five young girls were going down the road near the edge of the woods to pick grapes. They saw Joseph Earl Leone standing down the road with a rifle and became frightened. The girls went in the woods to avoid Leone, but he ran and headed them off. He grabbed one of the girls and threatened to shoot the others. He made the four leave, took the one into the bushes and attempted to rape her. She resisted, screamed and finally scared the man away.

FEBRUARY 2, 1968: Hoyt Maxey called Brandon to Zwolle Feed and Grocery to report four hundred dollars had been taken from his cash register. He said two black men had come to his place, looked around,

Brandon with a new patrol car, about 1968.

and left. They came back and one ordered some meat. While Maxey and the man went to the back to get the meat, the other took the money.

SEPTEMBER 12, 1968: James Laroux was charged with murder following the shooting of Claude Sepulvado about midnight at Sepulvado's Store on the Ebarb Road in Ward five. Brandon said Laroux and Jesse Clastic got into a scuffle and Sepulvado got his gun to separate them. The ruction moved outside and Sepulvado put Laroux in his car and told him to leave. Sepulvado was then having trouble with Hollis Manshack. Laroux got out of his car with a .22 automatic pistol and shot Sepulvado four times.

JANUARY 17, 1969: Raymond Dennis Utz, twenty-four, of Shreveport was charged with armed robbery and aggravated battery and Emmitt Joseph Parrie, Jr., eighteen, of Zwolle was charged with armed robbery of Britt's Store in the Bethsadia community. Owner A. J. Britt had been pistol whipped by Utz. Brandon arrested Utz, just north of the Zwolle cemetery.

SEPTEMBER 17, 1969: Brandon was called to investigate a T. C. Morrow Drilling Company truck and trailer which ran into Buddy Laroux's service station. The driver, Thurman D. Stewart of Fisher, said he left the vehicle out of gear and it rolled into the store.

JANUARY 1, 1970: Fred Douglas Kauffman, nineteen, of Shelbyville, Texas was killed at 10:25 p.m. when a KCS train hit his car. Brandon said the car, which was traveling at seventeen miles per hour, had not been running long enough and the windshield was fogged up, in addition to it being a foggy night.

JANUARY 28, 1970: Gary Primm, twenty-three, of Many was killed at 9:00 p.m. when his car left the road in a curve on the overpass on Highway 171 near Noble and hit some trees. Primm had come through Zwolle at a high rate of speed and Brandon had turned his car around to follow him. Trooper Joe Byles said Primm was traveling so fast he probably did not know anyone was following him. The officers did not see the wreck and went all the way to Converse before turning around.

JUNE 4, 1970: Hal W. Gatti, seventeen, of Shreveport was lucky to be alive after he outran a state trooper, ran through two road blocks, and hit a china berry tree in Zwolle at 11:30 p.m. Trooper Jerry Rains pursued the car at speeds up to one hundred twenty miles per hour. Brandon charged Gatti with reckless operation.

JULY 10, 1970: Nine persons were injured in a two-car collision at 11:30 p.m. on Highway 171 north. They were passengers in a station wagon driven by a Mr. McGinnis of Leesville. A car driven by Joseph C. Sepulvado turned in front of it, according to Brandon.

JULY 26, 1970: Aggravated battery charges were filed against Fred Scott and his common law wife, Rosa Lee Carter, following the cutting of Lesie Frazier in Sabine Quarters. Brandon said Frazier was in serious condition and the Carter woman received wounds where Scott accidentally cut her during the affray.

MAY 31, 1971: A murder charge was lodged

244

against Alice M. Webb, operator of Alice's Lounge, Highway 171 North at 4:45 a.m. Dead was Woodrow Wilson Reeder, fifty-four, of Bernice, Louisiana. Brandon, who assisted in the investigation, said Reeder was shot five times in the head and chest with a .38. Lt. Alfice Brumley of the sheriff's office said the shooting started with an argument.

JUNE 17, 1971: Brandon reported counterfeit twenty dollar bills being circulated in Zwolle, Many and Converse. All bills had the same serial number, K29705698B. They were 1969 series, with face plate number fifty-two, and back plate number eighty-three.

JULY 19, 1971: Ola T. Homes, forty-five, of Pleasant Hill, was killed in a collision on Highway 120, one and one-half miles east of Zwolle, according to Brandon. Negligent homicide charges were filed against Kenneth Ray Bison.

MAY 30, 1972: Brandon said it was a miracle. He received a call at 9:30 p.m. that a child had been drowned at Hide-A-Way Park Subdivision, ten miles from Zwolle. When he arrived he found that Chris Barousse, six-year-old son of Mr. and Mrs. Albert Barousse, had fallen off a boat ramp into Toledo Bend Lake. Mrs. Barousse told Brandon when she discovered the child was missing; she started looking for him, and found him floating face down. She retrieved him, and the child had no life. She gave him mouth-to-mouth resuscitation and revived him. Brandon said Mrs. Barousse stayed calm until it was all over, then she panicked.

OCTOBER 3, 1972: Noble Neal had five thousand dollars stolen from him by a slender black man and a heavy-set white man. They were riding around in Neal's truck when it ran hot in Many. While he got out to look at it, the two took five thousand dollars from the glove compartment and replaced it with play money and also took his ignition key. Brandon brought another key to Neal, who would not give much information.

OCTOBER 28, 1972: Eddie Lee Castie, eighteen,

was crushed to death at 2:30 p.m. Brandon found out he had jacked up his car with a bumper jack and the car fell, crushing him underneath.

DECEMBER 19, 1972: Scotty Ray, fifteen, was killed by an accidental 20-gauge shotgun wound. Brandon and Sheriff's Deputy Travis Bennett found Wilmer Ray had left Scotty, and his two brothers, Wayne Phillips and Kenneth Ray, at home alone. Scotty was meddling around in the closet when the gun, which was propped in the corner, went off.

MARCH 24, 1973: Around midnight Helen Frazier, twenty-four, shot and killed her husband, Willie Frazier, thirty-one, after a family argument. Brandon, who made the arrest, said Fraser was shot in the heart with a "Saturday Night Special."

AUGUST 6, 1973: Albert Meshell and James Martinez were arrested following a scuffle at 8:30 a.m. Brandon charged them with unlawful shooting of firearms inside the city limits.

OCTOBER 14, 1973: Wilson Garcie, thirty-eight, died as the result of a gunshot wound. Mary Garcie, his wife and the only witness, at first told Brandon and other officers he had shot himself, but later said they were fighting near the parked car when he attempted to choke and hit her. She apparently grabbed the gun and shot him.

OCTOBER 23, 1974: Brandon told *The Index* if anyone in Zwolle lost any item of value last week to come to city hall. He said a valuable item had been turned over to him, and he would like to find the rightful owner. "I can't say what the item is because it would be easy to identify," he said.

APRIL 16, 1974: Steve Longora, seventeen, died from a self-inflicted gun shot wound at 7:00 p.m. Longora and his juvenile brother had been sought by the sheriff's office for their involvement in a motorcycle theft. They had also stolen items in Coushatta. As Brandon and other officers had them cornered near Hot Wells, Deputies Clarence Key and Wayne Ebarb were walking down a road, heard a noise and turned to see Longora raise up and say, "Ya'll never take me to jail anymore." He turned to his younger brother and said, "Lay down and cover your head," just before shooting himself.

OCTOBER 22, 1974: Sherman Odis Armstrong, thirty-one, was arrested by Brandon and Deputy Wayne Ebarb, at Harold Thames' Lounge for possession of marijuana and carrying a concealed weapon.

NOVEMBER 1, 1974: Charles Gossett, twenty-four, was charged with possession of marijuana with intent to

Brandon is shown behind the wheel of his patrol car in this 1973 photo.

distribute. Brandon said his department was continuing to investigate pushers in Zwolle. Brandon said they received information Gossett had gone to Houston and were waiting at the bus station for his return. They found he had one and one-half pounds of marijuana when he came back.

APRIL 26, 1975: One man died and several were injured in a two-car collision near the Zwolle Cemetery. Woodrow W. Austin, a passenger in Robert W. Singletary's sedan, was killed. They were from Haynesville, Louisiana, Mrs. Ima Cavanaugh of Frierson, Louisiana, drove the other vehicle. Brandon said a stop sign on Highway 120 had been torn down previous to the wreck. He said, "To the people who pull down our safety signs and destroy them just for pure meanness, I hope you will take notice of this wreck. If the stop sign had been in the proper place, perhaps the wreck might not have happened."

JULY 31, 1975: Brandon and Sheriff Cook announced a sub-station for the sheriff's department in the Zwolle police station. "My department and the sheriff's department will work as one unit in serving the people," Brandon said.

SEPTEMBER 10, 1975: Chester Terrell Durr, twenty-six, was charged with the murder of his wife, Martha Durr, and Sammy Mitchell, Jr., twenty-eight, at 8:30 p.m. Sheriff Cook and Brandon headed the investigation.

JANUARY 10, 1976: William H. Chambers, Jr., seven years old, escaped serious injury when he was struck by a car at 10:30 a.m. Brandon said several children, including Chambers, were playing on the shoulder of Highway 171, prior to the accident. A vehicle driven by Robert L. McClanahan was traveling south when the child darted into its path.

FEBRUARY 17, 1976: Nichols Dry Goods was burglarized during the night and Patrolman Glen Ebarb made the discovery prior to 2:00 a.m., while on routine patrol. Brandon said about three thousand five hundred dollars in goods was taken.

JUNE 26, 1977: Claudia Mullen, eighteen, Odessa Waites, twenty, and Sheryl Delores Lynch, nineteen, were arrested and charged with possession of marijuana. Brandon said the Lynch woman was also charged with having a concealed weapon, as she had an eight-inch butcher knife.

AUGUST 24, 1977: Jimmy Dyess, forty-nine, was killed during a family argument at his home in Sabine Quarters at 10:00 p.m. Brandon said his common-law wife allegedly fired the shot. Sheryl Delores Lynch, nineteen, was charged with first-degree murder.

OCTOBER 21, 1977: Jerry Perry, twenty-one, was shot and killed on Sabine Street. Brandon said the shooting, which occurred in front of the Julie Pittman residence, stemmed from a quarrel between Perry and his assailant, Howard Lee Booth, nineteen, of Many, who was charged with first degree murder.

OCTOBER 13, 1977: Mrs. Wayne Ray Hamm of

Belmont alleged her son, Wayne Ray Hamm, Jr., fourteen, was whipped with a paddle by teacher, Tim Leone. When asked about the matter, Brandon said, "No comment."

APRIL 13, 1978: Christopher A. Mitchell, seventeen, and Rick Pass, both of Many, were injured when Mitchell's motorcycle hit the railroad tracks too fast and both went airborne. Brandon said Mitchell suffered several injuries.

AUGUST 11, 1978: Big Star was burglarized of seven hundred twenty-five cartons of cigarettes valued at four thousand dollars and one thousand two hundred twenty five dollars in cash. Brandon said it looked like a professional job as the safe had been pried open. He said the burglary took several hours and several were involved in it.

NOVEMBER 26, 1978: When Raymond Walraven came to work at 7:00 a.m. he discovered his store had been broken into. By 11:00 a.m. that day, Brandon had arrested Leon Queen, twenty-five, and charged him with simple burglary. Brandon recovered one hundred fifty of the two hundred dollars which was stolen. A bit modest, Brandon chalked up a fine piece of police work to "just luck."

DECEMBER 8, 1978: Bessie Miller Brown, thirty-seven, was charged with homicide in the knifing death of her husband, Willie Brown. Brandon said the couple had been quarreling at their home in Sabine Quarters. Brown hit her with a chair. She ran to the back of the house; he chased her and at that point, she sliced his neck with a knife.

MARCH 11, 1979: James Earl Jackson, twenty-eight, was charged with felony theft in excess of $500. Brandon said Jackson was attending a party at the home of Samuel Aldredge the previous night and stole twenty-two one hundred dollar bills and an unknown amount of ten dollar bills and twenty dollar bills from Arthaniel Penegar.

APRIL 13, 1979: Metrice Paul Maxey was arrested for aggravated battery and disturbing the

Sheriff George R. Cook and Brandon are shown looking over a bale of marijuana confiscated in Zwolle in January, 1975.

peace during an incident at the home of Sandra Leone. Brandon said Maxey, who was wielding a knife, kicked Lynn Strickland in the stomach and grabbed her one-year-old child and left the house. Assistant Chief Wayne Ebarb said Maxey had the child in one arm and was still holding the knife when he was arrested.

APRIL 15, 1979: Eugene Frazier, Jr., seventeen, was charged with simple burglary of the home of retired teacher Marguerite Ferguson. Brandon said she was at church when Frazier entered her home and stole two hundred thirty dollars, which was an Easter offering collected at her church.

OCTOBER 12, 1979: Henry O'Banion called Brandon at 8:14 a.m. and told him he found a body entangled in a fence. The discovery led to the end of a four-day search for J. R. (Rhett) Paddie, fifty-one. He had been squirrel hunting and was crawling through a fence when he became entangled. He was using his .22 rifle for a prop to balance him when it went off, killing him.

The Baton Rouge, Louisiana Morning Advocate carried this picture and a story titled, "The Sheriff Who Tamed Zwolle," in it's March 26, 1978 edition.

NOVEMBER 18, 1979: In the early morning hours of this Sunday, Herman James and Willie Katherine James, who operate Herman James Place in the Sabine Quarters, were arrested for illegal liquor sales. "This is the first of a number of arrests in a crackdown which is now in progress," Brandon said. "They'll be hearing from us again."

NOVEMBER 19, 1979: Uncle Albert's Chicken was burglarized in the early morning hours. Brandon said one thousand dollars had been stolen from a hiding place in the restaurant.

APRIL 2, 1981: This issue of *The Index* carried an announcement from Brandon that he had arrested four men and charged them with the March 26 burglary of Acklin Saw Shop. He recovered the stolen saws.

APRIL 1, 1981: Alvin G. Pittman, twenty-four, was shot with a .22 pistol while horsing around with his friend, Wayne Mullens, twenty-four, in Sabine Quarters. The shooting was an accident, but Brandon charged Mullens with discharging a firearm in the city limits.

JUNE 14, 1980: Brandon ruled a shooting in Corley Quarters was accidental, even though Jimmy Ray Malmay, twenty-seven, was charged with illegally discharging an automatic weapon filled with buckshot. The shot traveled through some bushes and struck Sandra Richardson, who was treated in Many.

JUNE 24, 1980: Mrs. Odessa Boone Sullivan, fifty-two, of Houston, Texas, and her son, John Lane, died in a collision at the intersection of Highway 171 and Highway 120. Brandon said Mrs. Sullivan ran a stop sign and traveled into the path of a truck driven by Lonnie C. Cato, forty, of Shreveport. He said over a period of years, there have been at least four fatalities at the same intersection. The fatalities were the first in Zwolle in a number of years, Brandon said. He pointed out Mrs. Sullivan, who had attended the funeral of her mother in Coushatta, Louisiana, earlier in the day, was the wife of Tom Sullivan, Jr., who was raised in Zwolle. The Senior Sullivan was active in the early oil boom in Zwolle and Brandon said was a personal friend.

DECEMBER 1, 1980: Ray Charles Johnson, thirty-one, was charged with the second-degree murder of Randolph Davis. Brandon said Davis was visiting on the front porch of the Johnson home when an argument broke out between him and Ernie May McElroy, who was residing with Johnson. Davis struck the woman and Johnson, who was inside, came out shooting. He chased Davis through Sabine Quarters, firing shots from his .357 magnum pistol. After shooting Davis down, Johnson took him to the Fraser Clinic in Many, where he was arrested.

DECEMBER 22, 1980: Three men were in Zwolle shooting fireworks. Brandon said officers approached them and saw something being thrown from the truck. Upon investigation, it was found to be marijuana. They were arrested.

And so, there are some of Brandon's cases. Some were in the day; some at night. Whatever, whenever, he was always there. He was loyal and dedicated to his profession.

Chapter 50

Retirement and Thereafter

*"I'll never forget any of you and please
don't forget me."*
—Quinton Brandon

On the night of Thursday, August 6, 1981, Brandon, who had suffered a serious stroke two years prior, announced his retirement at a meeting of the Zwolle town council. It was not a happy time for him. He made the announcement with tears in his eyes. He submitted a letter of resignation to Mayor Raymond Walraven and the council members. It read as follows: "Gentlemen: After thirty-eight years and my sickness, I have decided to retire. I want to say it has been a pleasure working for the town of Zwolle. I have honestly loved my work and hope I have been of some benefit to the community. I have knowledge to know when I should give it up. I want to ask you to ratify my appointment of Henry Wayne Ebarb, my assistant chief. I know he is well qualified and know he will do the job well. Gentlemen, please make this effective August 31, 1981."

The decision to step down had not been an easy one for Brandon. Since his stroke he had struggled to get back on his feet and rule the town as he had in years past. Though hampered by the loss of the use of his left arm, he still struck a tough image to the townspeople. He was seen daily patrolling and taking care of matters. He never gave up and he continued to do his duty. He still had the respect of the people.

In the March 12, 1981, edition of *Louisiana Life* Brandon talked about his stroke and retirement. He said, "I had a warrant for a couple of old boys, and one of 'em goes to sassin' me and smartin' off. You know what bothers me the most? Not being able to whup that boy...and others like him. Something will happen and you want to run over to it, and you can't. When you've led as active a life as I have, it can't help but hurt." He said his only regret was that his career was nearing its end. "You've got to have it in your blood," he said. "It takes guts, and you won't get rich, but I can honestly say I've enjoyed every day I've spent as 'Sheriff of Zwolle.'"

A reception and open house was held to honor Brandon at Zwolle town hall, Sunday, August 30, 1981. It was a beautiful tribute. He was seated in his "old faithful chair" next to the podium that held the guest book. He shook hands and kissed and hugged over two hundred people who attended. Nannie, his wife, was by his side. A beautiful cake was made by Mrs. Katherine McCormick for the event. It had "Chief, 1946-1981" and had the insignia of the police department in the upper left-hand corner and was trimmed in gold and brown. Another smaller cake had "CHIEF, 1946-1981" and had one red rose as a symbol of the love and appreciation the people of Zwolle had for Brandon. At the serving table were his daughters, Bonnie Rivers, Lorene Jones, and Becky Loupe and his granddaughter, Miss Staci Jones.

Brandon was presented a plaque by the city inscribed: "Thirty-five years of faithful service from the Town of Zwolle." With tears in his eyes he said: "I want to thank you for this. I'll never forget any of you and please don't forget me. I've done my best and I'll still help as much as I can, whenever I can."

Brandon was featured in *The Shreveport Times* Sunday Magazine on October 18, 1981. Concerning retirement, he told reporter Calvin Gilbert, "I've got a bunch of grandkids that like to visit me. I want to spend more time with them. And I want to spend more time with my wife. Not once did she ever complain about me leaving in the middle of the night and staying gone all weekend."

After retirement Brandon had a special chair made that he could take to the woods during deer or

Sheriff Alfice Brumley shared a laugh at an open house honoring Brandon upon his retirement August 30, 1981.

Mr. and Mrs. Quinton Brandon are shown with the cake made by Mrs. Katherine McCormick for the open house August 30, 1981, honoring his retirement after thirty-five years in law enforcement.

squirrel season. It had a place to put his gun and it would swivel around so that he could shoot. He killed a lot of game from this chair. He enjoyed visiting his old friends and family and he especially enjoyed having time to be with his grandchildren.

In about 1970, Brandon had purchased thirty acres of land located near Hurricane Valley from Sam Busher. He raised a few goats, a butcher cow, and a few hogs. "He went out to the place every morning and afternoon, and sometime in between," Mrs. Brandon recalled.

His morning ritual was to go to the post office, visit with people, including his sisters in the nursing home, and to visit his farm.

"He went by himself as long as he was able," Mrs. Brandon said. "He loved his truck. She remembered that Steve Ezernack helped him a lot on the farm and in hunting. "Steve would set Quinton up on the deer stand," she said. "He also did some squirrel hunting. There were a few trees that he could drive close to and kill a few squirrels. But, Steve would squirrel hunt for him."

Rocky remembers that a year after his stroke, Brandon killed a ten point buck while deer hunting.

Joe Rivers, a former son-in-law, said one time after the stroke Brandon took his grandson Roddy Rivers deer hunting at the edge of his place near Hurricane Valley.

River continued, "Roddy heard the dogs coming and being inexperienced held the barrel of the gun on his shoe. The rifle went off and shot him in the foot."

"Roddy was a big ole boy," his daddy stated. "Quinton was able to pick him up and get him to the doctor. It was just the two of them and I don't see how he managed to do it."

Even with all of these activities he still missed his job. Jimmy Ray Pleasant recalled, "After Quinton retired, he'd call me every week or two. He just wanted to know what was going on. We'd talk politics. He just wanted to know what was happening and he

Grandpa Quinton Brandon was all smiles on Christmas Day, 1988, as he gave a $5 bill to all his grandchildren. Shown in the picture are Staci, Todd, Joe, Dustin, Roddy, Jerry, Erica, Cole, Jerry Lane, Lee, Seth, Cody, Erin, Amy, Rachel, Jeremy, Amanda and Meredith.

missed being a part of it."

Wayne Ebarb remembered, "After he retired he'd still come down to the office just to see what was going on or he'd ride out to see me on the lake. He liked Opelousas catfish and I'd catch some and give the fish to him. He also had that goat farm and would go out there. He had a police band radio in his truck so he could keep in touch. He'd report things to us that he would see or hear about. One time he was at the goat ranch and fell down and couldn't get back up. He managed to crawl to the truck and radioed me and I went out and helped him."

Mrs. Brandon told, "Anytime he'd hear a siren you could see him try to jump up out of his chair to get ready to go again. It was just a reflex action because he had done this for so many years. He just wasn't the kind of man who could sit around and watch television or read. He wanted to be a part of the action. Retirement was not something he wanted to do. His health forced him to retire."

Chapter 51

In at the Death

*"Doctors had been treating him, but they never
found the cancer. I don't know why."*
—*Mrs. Nannie Brandon*

Sunday, January 15, 1995, was a special day in the Brandon family. It was Mrs. Nannie Brandon's birthday and also the birthday of a daughter, Becky Loupe. Becky had invited her parents out for a birthday meal.

"Quinton told me to go ahead," Mrs. Brandon recalled. "He said he didn't feel like going. He had gotten where he couldn't walk very well. His legs were giving out."

Mrs. Brandon continued, "The next morning, he couldn't get up. We took him to the hospital in Many and he stayed two days. Dr. Jack Corley said there had to be something else wrong with him that he wasn't finding."

"We took him to Highland Hospital in Shreveport and he stayed there overnight, but we weren't satisfied with how they were handling him, so we took him to Schumpert," Mrs. Brandon said. "They did an MRI and found he had cancer. He had been treated by different doctors for a long time, so I don't know why they never found the cancer."

As it was diagnosed, Brandon had cancer just about all over his body. "He had severe back pain," Mrs. Brandon remembered. "He was operated on the next Saturday. The surgery was done to relieve some of his pain."

"The doctors said they didn't see how he could live day after day and not know he had cancer," Mrs. Brandon said. "He thought he had arthritis. I kept telling him I thought he was taking too much pain medicine toward the end and before he found out he had cancer."

Rocky Brandon said that he took his father to the hospital the day before he left to go back offshore to his job. "I was called to come help put him in the car," Rocky recalled. "I eventually had to pick him up. Daddy was always such a big man in my eyes that I was amazed at how he had dwindled down. I could lift him like a baby because he probably weighed one hundred fifty pounds or less."

Rocky said that he left to go to work, but was called back home. "I spent the night with him when he was in the hospital. He told me, 'Get me out of this bed and take me home.' "

"I was honored by the family to be allowed to sit with him the night before he passed away," Dr. George D. Brandon said. "I cannot find the words to express the emotions of that night. As he was at best only semi-conscious, I believe to this day, he sensed my presence and it was pleasing to him that I was there."

"We were all at the hospital with him toward the end," Mrs. Brandon said. "Jerry's two boys, Dustin and Jerry, were there and they were going to have to leave to go back to school. They didn't want to leave, but they had to."

They went to Quinton's bed and told him, "It's okay, Papaw. You did all you could for us." Rocky said Dustin told his grandfather, "Tell my daddy hello."

Mrs. Brandon said, "It was such a wonderful, touching moment. It seemed like that's what Quinton wanted or needed to hear. He seemed at ease and at peace with himself after that."

The two grandsons left but were called back in about fifteen minutes. Everyone knew the end was near.

It was Sunday, January 29, 1995, at 4:00 p.m. when the earthy life of Quinton Brandon came to an end. He had lived seventy-seven years, nine months, and fourteen days.

"We were all in the room with him when he breathed his last," Mrs. Brandon said. "He went easy."

Chapter 52

The Funeral

"He was not a perfect man, but none of us are. However, he was a good man, and by his confession to me, he was a Christian man, saved by the grace of God."
—*The Reverend Lee Dickson*

The earthly life of Quinton Brandon came to an end that January day, but it had been eighteen years earlier that he had made plans for his funeral. The Reverend Lee Dickson at the time was pastor of the Zwolle Baptist Church, a position he held from 1970-1978. He had taken twenty-eight young people on a trip to the Southern Baptist Camp in New Mexico. While there, he received word of the death of Clifford Bray, and flew back to Zwolle to conduct the services.

James Napier, who was a state trooper, met him at the airport in Shreveport. After the service, the Reverend Dickson said that Brandon wanted to take him back for the flight to New Mexico.

Said the Reverend Dickson, "That trip back to Shreveport impacted both of our lives. Before we reached Converse, Quinton asked me to conduct his funeral. I responded that I needed to know where he would spend eternity before I would make a commitment to do it."

During the next fifty miles, the Reverend Dickson said that Brandon poured out his soul, with much of the information falling into the area of confidential. Among items Brandon talked about were growing up as a boy in Hurricane Valley, his service in stopping Hitler in Europe in World War II, his years as a state trooper and chief of police, his duty as a husband and father, the man who shot at him while he hid behind a concrete water fountain on Zwolle's main street, the man who managed to get his gun in the patrol car and whom Brandon was forced to shoot, and the times he would get up at night to go break up a domestic dispute or arrest a drunk. Added the Reverend Dickson, "He said he would kiss his kids on the forehead and stop and ask God to take care of them if he did not get back."

The Reverend Dickson said, "About four times, as we drove along, he asked what I would charge him to do his funeral. Of course I responded as I always have, 'I do not charge to do funerals,' but that did not satisfy him."

The minister finally responded, "Okay, I will do your funeral for one more of those good barbecue goat dinners that you like to fix."

He continued, "That seemed to satisfy him, and upon returning from New Mexico the next week, I received a phone call that my wife Barbara and I were to be at his house for lunch the following Saturday. Guess what we ate? You are right. It was barbecued goat."

Ending the story, the minister said, "He often reminded me that I was to do his funeral and that it was already 'paid for.'"

And on Tuesday, January 31, the Reverend Dickson came back to Zwolle to fulfill that obligation. The service was held at 2:00 p.m. at the First Baptist Church. The Reverend Jerry Penfield and Monsignor Earl Provenza assisted him at the funeral.

At the funeral, the Reverend Dickson told the packed sanctuary, "Quinton Brandon was my friend. We talked many times about death and heaven. Especially after the death of Jerry, he really became homesick for Heaven."

In his message, the minister made three points: (1.) Heaven is a real place, prepared by God for every person, (2.) The only way to get there is through faith in Jesus Christ, and (3.) Are you ready to go to Heaven?

The Reverend Dickson concluded, "Mr. Brandon assured me as we traveled to Shreveport that he was ready to go anytime God was ready for him. By his own confession, Quinton was a sinner, but by faith, he had accepted Jesus as his Savior and had been forgiven of those sins and cleansed through His grace. Quinton was ready to meet God."

Today, the Reverend Dickson lives in Natchitoches and is Director of Missions for the Louisiana Baptist Convention.

The Reverend Dickson recalled that he used to ride on patrol with Brandon, and that he was pastoring in Zwolle when Jerry Brandon died, and had preached his funeral. "Jerry was the love of his life," he stated.

"I loved and respected the man," the Reverend Dickson said of Brandon. "After I left Zwolle, each time I got called back for a funeral or to supply, he was always there."

Serving as pallbearers were Kenny Dyess, Douglas Brandon, Darryl Dyess, Buddy Brandon, Wayne Brandon, and Stanley Brandon. They laid him to rest in the Zwolle city cemetery, which he had taken care of for so long.

In a story published in the August 10, 1978, *Shreveport Times*, Brandon told writer Gary Hines, "I always wear my hat. When I die, I want my hat in my casket. A good lawman never goes without his hat." Mrs. Brandon said that she was unaware of his request and Brandon was buried without his hat.

Roger Lopez said Brandon told him and others that he wanted his wake to be held at Zwolle city hall. "He loved that place, had worked so long there, and it meant so much to him," Lopez said. "I am sorry the wake was not held there." Mrs. Evelyn Hopkins said that Brandon also told her the same story.

So, peace had at last come to Quinton Brandon. He had lived a long life, full of turmoil, strife, stress, and worry. He was free at last. He would be missed. He would be remembered. And he was probably smiling as he was laid to rest by his beloved son Jerry.

Chapter 53

Town Elections, Interesting Facts and More

"The appointment didn't set well with the Zwolle Council."
—The Sabine Index

When Quinton Brandon took the job as Zwolle Marshal in 1946, the mayor and council he would work with had been elected in June of that year. Joe B. Parrott was mayor and aldermen were F. P. (Pete) McCormick, A. J. Rivers, M. L. Corley, Robert Smith, and H. M. Click.

In the July 18, 1950, runoff, C. B. Halbert unseated Mayor Parrott. A third candidate M. H. Burkhalter was eliminated in the June 13 first primary. Winning the five aldermen posts on June 13 were Max Brown, Louis Lefkovits, Clarence G. Bullard, William L. Gaul, and Hoyt Maxey. Also running were F. P. (Pete) McCormick, Roy Martinez, Walter Dans, R. L. Oakerson, and Arthur J. Rivers.

Nichols Dry Goods was the first building in Zwolle to be air conditioned in May, 1951. General Manager T. D. Nichols said all Nichols stores were now air-conditioned. A. D. Belisle of Many was the contractor.

Mayor C. B. Halbert, sixty-six, was claimed by a heart attack August 15, 1951, at his home. He had lived in Zwolle twenty-five years and was a native of Milam, Texas.

Effective September 10, 1951, M. H. Burkhalter was appointed mayor by Governor Earl K. Long to fill Halbert's unexpired term. He was agent for KCS in Zwolle and had lived there ten years.

On Saturday, October 10, 1952, a big crowd

turned out for the Trades Day in Zwolle. The merchants sponsored it. It was so successful that another was held November 8 and featured entertainment by the Many High School band and special bargains.

In an election Tuesday, June 24, 1954, Burkhalter was returned to office. Aldermen elected were Max Brown, C. G. Bullard, Louis Lefkovits, W. L. Gaul, and Hoyt Maxey.

Those running for mayor were M. L. Corley and Carl Willis. Others running for alderman were R. L. McComic, R. L. Bailes, R. T. Addington, and J. T. Elliott.

Work on blacktopping three miles of Zwolle streets was completed September 23, 1955. The State Highways Department did the work, with the town supplying the materials. After the work was finished, the town threw a barbecue with Senator R. S. Copeland and Representative J. M. Belisle being special guests.

J. W. Hale, seventy-three, a prominent Zwolle citizen, was burned to death about 3:00 a.m. Tuesday, December 25, 1956, when his home was destroyed by fire. The victim's daughter, Mrs. Ovie Bullard and her two young daughters, Jenell and Margaret Rose, barely escaped, but were unhurt. Brandon and Dr. Lloyd Murdock, coroner, investigated. The verdict of the coroner's jury was that Hale burned to death by fire of an undetermined cause.

Jim Darby, eighty-four, a pioneer citizen of Zwolle passed away December 25, 1956, following a lengthy illness. He was once Sabine sheriff and as far back as 1948 was the only man then living who signed the Zwolle Charter on June 12, 1898.

Burkhalter was re-elected mayor June 10, 1958. He won over W. C. Vickers. Elected, as council members were Max Brown, Louis Lefkovits, W. L. Gaul, Hoyt Maxey, and C. G. Bullard.

Governor Jimmie H. Davis appointed Ottis L. Salter as mayor effective January 24, 1962. He was to fill the unexpired term of Burkhalter, who retired after serving as mayor for ten years.

The appointment did not sit well with the Zwolle council. In a meeting, the council was critical of State Representative Cliff Ammons for having the appointment made without consulting them.

Elmer C. Marshall was elected mayor in the June 12, 1962, election. He defeated Ottis L. Salter, Williams S. Hopkins, and Wiley Hawkins. Elected as aldermen were Paul Ebarb, John O. Napier, Williams S. Gaul, Garrett Walsh, and Hoyt Maxey. Max Brown and Kenneth Dockens were defeated.

Marshal was re-elected in the May 14, 1966 runoff. He defeated J. C. Ferguson. In the first primary on April 9, Guy Wayne Maxey and W. H. Burkhalter were eliminated in the mayor's race. Elected as aldermen were John O. Napier, Hoyt Maxey, Max Brown, Paul Ebarb, and Garrett H. Walsh. John Henry Procell was eliminated.

The town of Zwolle had a full-page ad in the August, 1966 issue of The Louisiana Municipal Review entitled "The Welcome Mat is always out in the Town of Zwolle." The ad read, "Zwolle, situated in the heart of the famed Sabine timber forests and also a center of the growing oil industry, is moving ahead and wants YOU to join our March of Progress."

Brandon had always been against the sale of liquor, legally or illegally. More problems for him were looming on the horizon as the sale of beer was made legal in neighboring Ward five in a special election Saturday, June 17, 1967. Saloons started popping up in the area and so did trouble. There were a number of murders, shootings, cuttings, and fights until it all finally settled down sometime later. W. F. Jeter, Jr. said, "When liquor was voted in, we'd arrest ten to twelve every Friday and Saturday nights after the bars closed. Most of the time, it was people who didn't even live around here."

Ray S. Spurlock was elected mayor Saturday, April 2, 1970. He defeated Elmer C. Marshall and Wiley Hawkins. Elected to the council were Fred Roberson,

Jr., Bob E. Asseff, Roger Lopez, John Henry Procell, and James E. (Buddy) Veuleman. Also running were Jack O. Napier, Hoyt Maxey, Garrett H. Walsh, Max Brown, and David Peterson.

Census information released by Louisiana Tech University at Ruston showed Zwolle's population for 1970 at 2,098. This represented a gain of 58.2 percent over the 1960 population of 1,326.

A two-page article about Zwolle was featured in *The Louisiana Municipal Review* in the early 1970's. It called Zwolle "a typical American Town" and listed the population at 2,320. The article continued, "Police-wise, Zwolle has had a minimum of crime due largely to the work of Marshal Quinton Brandon. There is little juvenile delinquency in Zwolle and there has not been an unsolved burglary or other major crime in the past fourteen years."

Raymond Walraven was elected mayor in the March 22, 1974, primary, defeating Ray Spurlock and Fred (Billy) Rivers. Brandon was elected chief of police, defeating George Laroux, Jr. Elected to the council were Samuel Cross, Vernon Mitchell, Fred Roberson, Jr., John Henry Procell, and W. S. (Bill) Hopkins. Others in the running were Bert Rule, W. F. Jeter, Sr., James J. Procell, Elmer C. Marshall, Wiley Hawkins, Thomas Joe Cassell, and David Ebarb.

Walraven was re-elected mayor in the spring of 1978. He defeated Elmer C. Marshall and David Peterson. Brandon was returned to office without opposition. Elected to the council were Vernon Mitchell, Williams S. Hopkins, Samuel D. Cross, John Henry Procell, and Fred Roberson, Jr. Others running were Paul H. Sepulvado, Yvonne Sutton Myers, and James J. Procell.

When Brandon retired August 30, 1981, before the end of his terms, he had worked with nine different groups of mayor and council members. And during those years he saw a lot of changes take place and a lot of people come and go, but he stayed.

Chapter 54

The Family

"I am proud of the fact that on my salary I have been able to send three of my children to college. The others could have gone, but chose not to."
—Quinton Brandon

"I got one of the good ones," Quinton Brandon told *Louisiana Life* of his wife, Nannie, in March, 1981. "I've been knowing her since we were barefoot kids."

Of her life as a chief of police's wife, Mrs. Brandon told the magazine, "You just learn to accept it and to live with it. After a while I realized what was going to happen would, whether I was lying awake at night worrying about it or not."

The article went on to say, "Sharing her husband with a whole town didn't leave much time for family life. Brandon, sixty-three, still works seven days a week, but it isn't as bad as it used to be."

Brandon stated, "It isn't as bad as it used to be. Sometimes on the weekends I would just have time to come home and change into a new shirt. The old one would be covered with blood and gore. But we still raised five kids and sent all of them to college that wanted to go."

"He had a strong love for his family," Edith J. Palmer remembered. "He was involved with his children and grandchildren. The light of his life was those two boys. He never missed a basketball game they played in."

John Patton said, "I either coached or taught all his children. I never had a crossword with any of them. They were all well disciplined. They would say, 'Yes, sir' and 'No, sir.' We never had a minute's problem."

There were five of the Brandon children. Doris Lorene was born February 13, 1942, at Hurricane

Valley. She married Calvin Jones of Zwolle on May 31, 1963. They had two children: Staci Lynne, who was born March 30, 1964, and who died from a mysterious disease December 14, 1997. She was married to Todd Lafitte and they had two children, Robert Tyler, born June 8, 1992, and Ashley Lynne, born May 27, 1997. The Jones' son is Calvin Todd, born February 18, 1967. He is divorced and has a son, Calvin Patrick Jones.

Jerry Lee Brandon was born February 16, 1950. He was killed in a wreck July 12, 1975. He was married to Beverly Felknor of Plain Dealing and they were the parents of two sons. They are Dustin, born September 10, 1974, and Jerry Lee, born September 4, 1975, two months after his father's death.

Rebecca Ann Brandon was born January 15, 1953, and is married to Chris Loupe of Zwolle. They were married June 18, 1977. They have four daughters: Erica Ruth, born January 20, 1980; Erin Katherine, born August 14, 1984; Amy Elizabeth, born July 28, 1985; and Meredith Anne, born June 16, 1987.

The fourth child was Bonnie Gayle Brandon, born October 29, 1956. She is divorced from Joseph Rivers and to that union, four children were born. They are Jason Douglas, born December 13, 1972, and who died in a wreck in 1979 at the age of six; Roderick Blaine, born November 11, 1973; Brennan Cole, born July 29, 1980; and Joseph Seth, born November 11, 1982. Bonnie has another daughter, Tanya Quinn Bowermeister, born August 22, 1995.

The last child was Rocky Lane Brandon, born March 20, 1959. He is the father of five children, Jerry Lane, born July 6, 1977; Lee Garrett, born April 19, 1979; Colt Quinton, born January 24, 1983; Rachell Leigh-Ann, born July 12, 1984; and Autumn Grace, born August 29, 1995.

Mattie Lee Maxey, a sister-in-law, said of Brandon, "He was mighty good to me. We had our little disagreements, but we'd get over them. He was a good friend."

Rocky said that the children knew if they had a

problem at school, they had one with Quinton when they got home. He said, "I remember I was always in trouble at the Zwolle Intermediate School. The principal, Samuel Cross, always gave me a choice of taking a few licks or calling Daddy. I always took the licks, but somehow Daddy always knew about it when I got home. Mr. Cross was a man Daddy liked and respected."

Continuing, Rocky said, "Mother and Daddy taught us well. Daddy said it one time and that was it. He would walk into the house, take off his gun and put it on the dining table. No kid ever touched it. You knew not to bother his guns."

Rocky said when his brother, Jerry, was playing basketball at Louisiana Tech in Ruston, "We never missed a game the whole four years he was there." He said during hunting season, he, Jerry, his father, and his father's brothers would hunt in Hurricane Valley.

"We learned at an early age you couldn't hide anything from him," Rocky remembered. "He would find out. One time I was riding around in Mama's car and backed into the gym door at school. It did some damage to the door, but not much to the bumper. The next day, Daddy went to school to investigate. Three days later, I saw him come home and look at the bumper on Mama's car. He came in and said, 'You ran into that gym door?' I just replied, 'Yes sir, I did.'"

Mrs. Brandon added, "If something happened, he didn't let up. He'd get to the bottom of it."

Rocky said that the things he learned from his daddy were: to respect the law, to love America, to stand at attention and put your hand over your heart when the Star Spangled Banner is played, never to disrespect a law enforcement officer, and to always respect young children, and old folks.

Mrs. Brandon said that church has always been important to their family. "Quinton could not always go because he had to work so much," she said. "But the children and I always went."

Chapter 55

The Zwolle He Saw Tamed

"I wouldn't be afraid to arrest any of them,
even if I didn't have my gun."
—Quinton Brandon

Happily, Quinton Brandon lived long enough to see Zwolle tamed to a certain extent and basked in the glory of being the lawman who tamed her. It gave him a good feeling in his later years of law enforcement to be able to take things easy and not have to worry about what might happen next. He had put in his time; in fact more than his time. He had performed his duty; he had gone above and beyond the call of duty.

"The job isn't half that much now," Brandon told the *Baton Rouge Morning Advocate* in 1978. "It's a joke to what it used to be. When I used to make sixty-five to seventy arrests a week working by myself, we may make seventy to eighty a month and that's with three men working. My men and I are all deputy sheriffs and most of our work is outside of town now."

Brandon told *The Shreveport Journal* on August 8, 1978, "The people of Zwolle respect law and order. In the early days they didn't. I think now we are one of the quietest towns in the South."

He continued, "Most of Zwolle's law enforcement problems now are a few burglaries, some fights in the suburbs, and weekend drunks from nearby Toledo Bend." He added, "The lake brought some good people and the lake and legalization of liquor brought some undesirable ones."

An article sent out over the wire by Associated Press in 1978 stated, "Happily, the raucousness of earlier days in Zwolle have slowed with Brandon's will and ability to fight it. There are few arrests to make these days, and Brandon said suspects today aren't nearly as unpleasant as they used to be."

In an article in the June 7, 1973, *Sabine Index* Brandon was praised for not only doing a good job in law enforcement, but his financial records also look good as well.

The article stated, "The auditor recently told him his was the only police department in the state that pays for itself. Last fiscal year, the town collected $24,135.50 in fines and the expenses of the marshal's office ran between $16,000 and $17,000. Besides himself, the department has one full-time deputy, Wayne Ebarb, and two part-time, Glen Ebarb and Brad Falcon."

The article continued, "Brandon praised the citizens of Zwolle. 'We have a good bunch of people living here,' he said. 'They have been most cooperative and have always helped me down through the years. They want law enforcement and that is what I have always given them.' "

In a *Shreveport Times* article March 30, 1978, Brandon said the town's "...three-man police force rarely goes into combat these days and when the battle cry does go out it's to quell a half-hearted guerrilla attack by weekend drunks."

In an interview with *The Shreveport Times* published April 4, 1974, Brandon praised his deputies, Wayne Ebarb, Glen Ebarb, and Falcon, calling them, "the best police department in Louisiana." He added, "They have a job to do and they do it."

"Zwolle is a nice town now," Brandon said in the interview. "Sure, we have some mean people but most of them respect the law. Most of our people are good people. I would not be afraid to arrest any of them, even if I didn't have a gun."

Chapter 56

A Nephew Remembers
Uncle Quinton

"All my life, Quinton was there for me."
—-Dr. George D. Brandon

Dr. George Douglas Brandon owns and operates Brandon Veterinary Clinic in Leesville these days. He's a native son of Zwolle, his parents being Mr. and Mrs. Victor Brandon, but one of his favorite topics is his Uncle Quinton.

"The first recollection I have of my uncle is when I was about five-years-old," he said. "I remember him standing on our front porch talking to my dad and another uncle and I vividly recall seeing his knuckles bruised and swollen. He had been enforcing the law as a state trooper in Leesville."

"My next memory is Christmas the same year," Dr. Brandon related. "Much to the chagrin of my mother, he carried me to spend the holiday with his family. I remember the double toy pistols and holsters he gave me and Lorene had a bicycle under the tree. He carried me to Troop H at least once."

Continuing, Dr. Brandon stated, "I don't recall it, but my uncle told me the story several times in later years of how we became so close. He came to my house, picked me up to hold me, and I started crying. He promptly carried me to the barn, and when he brought me back, we were good buddies and remained that way."

"Another story he liked to tell was that my affection for him was contested by my grandfather, Webb Brandon," he continued. "When Jerry was born, Grandpa told me in confidence now that Quinton had his own boy, I could be his. Gleefully, Quinton said I came back with the statement, 'That old boy wouldn't be any good.' "

"Over the years, our relationship grew and matured into mutual love and respect," Dr. Brandon related. "Jerry and I were close as brothers and spent a lot of time with each other. Uncle Quinton gave me my first driving lesson on a country road. Jerry had his lesson right before me and went from ditch to ditch. Being older, I held the truck fairly close to the center of the road, and I remember him telling Jerry, 'Now that's how to do it.' "

Continuing, Dr. Brandon said, "Quinton loved to squirrel hunt, especially with a good dog, and my dad always had the best. We made a lot of memorable hunts together. One hunt I remember is where he, Jerry, and I were competing in finding the squirrels after the dog treed them. I found the first squirrel; without a word I raised my gun to shoot and was immediately tackled by Jerry. The squirrel moved during the commotion, and Quinton shot it and proceeded to have a good laugh on us."

"All my life Quinton was there for me," he related. "When I graduated from Louisiana State University in Baton Rouge, Louisiana, he was there. At Auburn University, he somehow managed to detour by there on a business trip to spend the night. But it was not just for me; Quinton was there for all his family, friends, and even strangers. Over the years, I have met several people who have asked my relationship with him. Most of these had been passing through Zwolle, had trouble, and had been befriended, and assisted by him. When you didn't do right, he was the first to criticize, but also the first to lend a helping hand."

"Quinton deplored the use of alcohol, and the ill effects of its consumption," Dr. Brandon said. "As marshal he waged an active campaign against the illegal sale of alcohol. As a young student at Zwolle, I remember he was asked to give the students a talk on the evils of alcohol, and I recall him stating he deplored it so much he wouldn't even wash his feet in it. That afternoon I went home from school with Jerry, and as most kids do after school, we went to the refrigerator first, and there was a bottle of whiskey. We looked at each other and couldn't wait to confront him with the fact that he had it. When we did, he sheepishly explained to us that someone had given it to him as a gift, and he didn't want to hurt their feelings by refusing it. In all the years I was around him, I never knew him to ever drink any form of alcohol."

Until about 1977, he recalled there was not a veterinarian in Sabine Parish and Quinton had a knack for "doctoring" animals and was frequently called upon to medicate downer cows, castrate animals, or help determine illness. "He was pretty good too," he stated.

Another story Dr. Brandon told: "He was once called upon to attend a cow, recumbent, and emaciated, that couldn't stand. The owner, a nephew, had asked him to give the cow an injection of an antibiotic. Quinton surveyed the situation and truthfully told the owner that the cow didn't need medication, but what it did need came in fifty pound sacks at the local feed store."

Dr. Brandon was there when his uncle was called upon to geld a stallion. He would apply ropes around the neck and hind legs and cast the animal; thus performing the surgery without the benefit of anesthesia. This did incur some risk to the animal and did not always go smoothly.

Dr. Brandon concluded by saying, "Quinton watched me geld a horse one day and the calming effect a tranquilizer had on the horse before he was put down. He immediately prevailed upon me to get him a bottle of that and it worked beautifully for him. However, one day he was called upon to castrate a bull and had complications. The tranquilizer I gave him sedates horses, but it anesthetizes cattle. When he gave the dosage to the bull, instead of relaxing, it went to sleep. Later, he laughingly told me he thought he had killed the bull because it slept for three days.

Chapter 57

He Was A Lawman's Lawman

"They will remember him as one of the most dedicated officers I've ever known. He was for doing the right thing. He didn't back down from the criminal element."
—*Marvin Melton, Mansfield law officer*

No one knows a lawman better than do the fellow officers whom he worked with through the years. This is certainly true of Quinton Brandon. Of those law officers interviewed about Brandon, none had anything but praise for him. He was described as dedicated, honest, hard working, loyal, trustworthy, there in time of need, a man you could count on, and a man who was brave.

Here is what a large sampling of law enforcement officers had to say about Brandon:

GUFFEY LYNN PATTISON, Sabine Parish sheriff: "Quinton was firm, but fair. He was a good law enforcement officer. He was always there. You didn't have to worry about him. The people in Zwolle respected him. He was there when times were tough and it took a tough man to stay. He was there when times were bad. He had to prove himself and he did.

"I think Quinton was one of the best in his time. What stood out with me was his voice. It alone would intimidate anybody. His voice carried out over everyone else. People listened when he talked. He came up when law enforcement was tough. You didn't have a backup then. One man had to carry it all."

FRANKIE HOWARD, Vernon Parish sheriff: "I thought he was a unique person. He was the Old West type police officer. He had a unique way of enforcing the law: in his own way. He had zero tolerance. When he told people to move out, they better move out. A lot of the things he did then, he couldn't get by with now. He was tough, but he treated people fair.

"I thought he was a professional in the way he went about his work. He was very dedicated to the job. He was more dedicated than most law enforcement officers are today. He got very little pay and he had very little to work with in the way of equipment, but I thought he did an outstanding job. The people respected him."

JAMES NAPIER, retired state trooper from Zwolle: "When I was in Viet Nam, the sweetest sound was that of a phantom jet coming over with napalm to get you out of your trouble. The sweetest sound when a law enforcement officer was in trouble was the voice of Quinton Brandon.

"Quinton was one of a kind. I don't know of any other like him. He couldn't get away with it now. Just his presence at a crime scene was a calming effect on everybody. He was one of a kind. He was a dinosaur. There won't be any more like him."

WAYNE EBARB, former Zwolle chief of police: "He was the best man for the job at the time. He couldn't do it now. He was rough and tough and fair. He had a good sense of what was right and wrong. Many times I've seen a person spend the night in jail and he would turn them loose the next morning."

W. F. JETER, JR., former deputy marshal for Zwolle: "He didn't have any fear. If I'd have to go somewhere that was dangerous, he is the one I would pick to go with me."

ALFICE BRUMLEY, former Sabine Parish sheriff: "I think he was fair. He was tough; tough enough to do his job. The people respected him. He would tend to business. Even after his stroke, he continued to police. He had a love for law enforcement.

"You could always count on him. You could find him drinking coffee. He was very visible. Or you would see his car parked in town. Many times, he'd just walk the streets and visit people. He was a man who strongly believed in law enforcement. He did his job twenty-four hours a day. Many times, he enforced the law alone."

MARVIN MELTON, former deputy sheriff and state trooper, Mansfield: "I was always impressed with him as a man who enforced the law. But I also found him to be a man with feelings. He was pretty strong. He didn't back down from a situation. There are none like him left in this country."

DON ENGLISH, Mansfield chief of police: "He had a gruff voice and we didn't have to be told who it was when he got on 39.5 and sounded off, 'Z-1 is on the air.' It sounded like that voice was coming from South Louisiana. When Quinton started, I was a pretty young boy. I compared his type of law enforcement to that of our late Sheriff Roy Webb. They were good friends and both were strong law enforcement men."

RALPH SHELTON, former DeSoto deputy sheriff: "As a law enforcement officer he was tops. He was trying as best he could. He believed in living right and doing right. He was a real capable man. I found him to be a prince of a man and a real outstanding law enforcement officer."

JIMMY RAY PLEASANT, former Sabine deputy sheriff: "He was one of the best old rascals I've ever met. He was a good man. If you were right, he was with you. If you were wrong, he would enforce the law. He took his job seriously."

LEE RAYMOND ISGITT, retired state trooper, Many: "Quinton was a mighty good policeman. Probably no one else could have handled it other than him. He had the respect of the people. If Quinton picked someone up and he was innocent, he would do everything he could to get him turned loose. There were no Miranda rights warning back then, but Quinton's was 'Let's go.'

"If Quinton told you, 'Let's go,' you had better go. The people of Zwolle supported him. He had a good reputation. He could put a fellow in jail one day and drink coffee with him the next day. There was nothing personal with him."

HUGH BENNETT, DeSoto Parish sheriff: "I first met him in 1956. He and my dad, Hugh Bennett, Sr., were real good friends. Quinton was a fine guy. He was not afraid of anything walking, that I know of. You could count on him; anytime, anywhere."

Chapter 58

Assessment

"Mr. Brandon and I had a deep personal relationship. We both lost our eldest sons in separate accidents at about the same time. We were unable to comfort one another, but we both realized the grief the other was going through."
- - - Retired Deputy Sheriff Bill Leslie

During and after a person's life, one will continually be assessed, especially if a public servant. Brandon was no exception. During his lifetime, his work was constantly being looked over and so has it been since he is gone.

The Shreveport Times, in its March 27, 1972, issue, stated, "When Brandon does die, a bit of history and legend will pass on."

He had cleaned up the town; he had a lot to be proud of when it came to his career. He had built a strong, solid, clean, good reputation as a lawman.

Brandon had been the youngest marshal to serve in Sabine Parish, and he had served Zwolle longer than any other law enforcement officer. He had served under five different sheriffs, T. M. Phillips, Harold Sandel, George R. Cook, Guffey Lynn Pattison and Alfice Brumley.

Here is how Brandon's career has been assessed by some of those who knew him.

PETE ABINGTON, Many: "He was a very proud guy. In his eyes, he seldom did wrong. He loved being marshal. He came along at a time when no one else could fill that job. He could survive on the low pay. His demure character was certainly conducive to being a law officer. People feared him, but they liked him. He was known as a man who could put the hammer on you. He commanded a lot of respect and obedience of the law. Zwolle got a real bang for their bucks."

GLENWOOD BULLARD, Zwolle: "Quinton would never shoot unless it was absolutely necessary. He'd rather try to settle a dispute by fist fighting."

JAMES COTTON, Many: "He was western style. He made a believer out of Zwolle."

BILL LESLIE, retired Sabine deputy: "For all his tough beliefs, he had a big heart and was always helpful to the needy regardless of race, creed, or color. His public service and law enforcement were two different things. Despite his methods, he was good at both. Not all people condoned his methods, but they could never find another to take his place."

JAMES McCOMIC, retired Sabine deputy: "Quinton was a red-blooded American. He was always making statements about the flag. He took his job seriously. He went down the middle and let the chips fall where they may. He loved the people of Zwolle, and he loved to help people. But he also loved to enforce the law. He was real witty. It was a joy to work with him."

DR. RICHARD J. OOSTA, Many: "He was always on the job. He was very assertive. He was very fair. When he said something, it was law. He didn't equivocate at all. When it was time to go to jail, it was time."

JOHN PATTON, Zwolle: "As a law enforcement officer, he was very fair. If you were a relative or a best friend and broke the law, you paid the price."

JOHN HENRY PROCELL, Zwolle: "Take him all the way around, Quinton was one of the best that's ever been in Zwolle. He worked by himself, many long hard hours. He furnished his own automobile. It wasn't like it is today where you work eight hours. It was nothing to see him still working at eleven and twelve o'clock at night. And he didn't make much money. Yes, he was a good one."

MURRAY SEPULVADO, Zwolle: "Quinton made his own law and made it work. Nobody knew what the law was back when he started. He was one of a kind. He was a friend. He had to have a good backbone or he couldn't have taken it."

JOHN S. PICKETT, JR., retired district judge, Many: "He was gung-ho on law and order. In court, he was never hesitant. He never stumbled. He would take on anybody, anytime. If you wanted to fist fight, he'd do that too."

RAYMOND WALRAVEN, Zwolle: "We worked together when I was mayor. He was always there. He did an excellent job as marshal. I always thought he had control of the town. He didn't put up with anything. But if you got in trouble, call him, and he'd be there to help."

Chapter 59

A Word From His Friends

"He would have wanted to be remembered
as a man who loved his country, family, town
and community and wanted the best for everyone."
—Mrs. Nannie Brandon

DR. GEORGE D. BRANDON: "His son, Jerry, ran into a train once in Zwolle. When Quinton got to the scene and found out Jerry was not injured; he took his Stetson off, twisted it up into an unrecognizable ball, stomped it and asked Jerry, 'Son, couldn't you find something bigger than a damn train to hit?'"

SAMUEL D. CROSS, former educator and public servant: "He was an outstanding marshal. He was brave and honest. He was respected by all and dedicated. He saw that the ordinances of Zwolle were enforced. Mr. Brandon was a strict lawman, but when a Zwolle citizen needed help, he was always there. On numerous occasions, he called me out after midnight to go with him and help someone in trouble."

JOHN PATTON, retired educator: "I first met Mr. Brandon when I came to Zwolle in the early 1950's. Since I was a young teacher, he told me he wanted to offer his assistance. When I went off to basketball games, he helped me haul the children. That was before the day of buses, when he used his own vehicle. I always loved to sit down and talk to him. I respected him and what he had to say. He was truly a walking tall example."

BOB KEY, who is married to Patricia Brown, the daughter of the late Mr. and Mrs. Max Brown of Zwolle: "Quinton was so clever when it came to rounding up people. He decided the bootleggers were getting out of hand. He sent twenty-one of them word to report to his office at noon on a certain day. He didn't tell them why. At the appointed date, twenty showed up. The other called in to say he had a flat and would be a little late. That's powerful."

MARTHA ANN MALMAY, Quinton's niece: "After the stroke, Quinton continued working for the city and he came upon a drunk one day. He told him he was under arrest and the drunk started running. Quinton started after him, but fell down and couldn't get up. The drunk felt sorry for him and went back, asking, 'Sir, can I help you?' Quinton looked up at him with that cold, angry stare and said, 'Boy, you help me up from here and you are gonna be the one who needs help.' The boy said he turned around and just started running again."

HOWARD BRANDON, Quinton's brother: "One time Earl Long came to Zwolle to campaign. He got on the back of a flatbed truck and was talking to the crowd. He had a big glass that looked like it was filled with water and as he talked to the crowd he would drink from it. One of the men who worked with Long kept filling up the glass and Quinton noticed that Long was sure drinking a lot of water.

"Finally Quinton slipped up to the back of the truck and sat down and when he got the chance he smelled the liquid in the glass. Just as he thought, it was whiskey, not water. He got Long's attention and told him he needed to talk to him. Long stopped his speech and as they walked away from the crowd, Quinton told him, 'Mr. Long, there is a law against drinking in this town and I've been appointed to make sure the laws are enforced. Now you're drunk and if you don't leave now, I'm going to have to arrest you.'

"Long told him, 'Do you know who you're talking to? This crowd came to see me and I'm not going anywhere.' Quinton got in Long's face and told him, 'I don't care who you are. You're drunk and you're gonna leave my town or you're going to jail. You've got five minutes to make up your mind which it's gonna be.'

"Long went back to the truck and told his men to get ready to leave. He had some very unkind words to say about Quinton at that time, but in later years they became friends. When Long was running for governor later, he came to one of Quinton's rodeos and made a speech, but this time he didn't have his glass with him.

"Quinton and Dr. Lloyd Murdock were very much alike in temperament and they locked horns pretty often. One such issue was that Dr. Murdock believed a person with a drinking problem needed to be rehabilitated and treated, not thrown in jail.

"One of Dr. Murdock's patients in a neighboring town 'fell off the wagon' and went on a drinking binge. The patient's wife came to Dr. Murdock's office in tears begging him to get her husband back in a rehabilitation center. Dr. Murdock told her to put her husband on the bus to Zwolle the next day and he would have someone take him to the rehab center.

"The next day, Dr. Murdock had a man meet the bus, but the patient had gotten there ahead of him and was no where to be found. He went back and told Dr. Murdock, who left the clinic and went to the bus station fearing the patient might have passed out on the bus or some other misfortune.

"The people at the bus station told him his patient had staggered off the bus and started down the street when Quinton pulled up in his patrol car and took him to jail.

"Dr. Murdock was furious and went storming to the jail demanding his patient. Quinton told him, 'Your patient ain't sick, he's drunk and he's staying here 'til he sobers up.' They say Dr. Murdock and Quinton yelled insults and curses at each other until both were too exhausted to say another word. Dr. Murdock left without this patient."

KENNETH EDWARDS of Alexandria: "Harden Lewis, a past major with the Rapides sheriff's office, told of a trip to Zwolle some years back. He went to a dance and was met at the door by Quinton. He eyed Harden over once and then demanded in a no nonsense tone, 'You got a gun on you, boy?' The answer was, 'No, sir.'

"'Have you got a pocket knife on you?' Quinton asked and again Lewis said, 'No.'

"With that answer, Quinton dug in his pocket and put something in Harden's hand. When the surprised Harden looked down, he saw in his hand a large unopened pocketknife. 'You'll need that if you're going in there,' Quinton told him with a smile."

NOLAN FARMER: "In May, 1955, my wife was having a baby at the Sabine Clinic. The doctor said that she needed blood. I ran to find Quinton. We walked back to the clinic together and he asked everyone we passed what type blood they had and to come with him if they had the right type. When we got to the clinic, Quinton was the first in line to give blood. It was a favor I won't forget as long as I live."

DR. RICHARD J. OOSTA, former Zwolle physician and Sabine Parish coroner: "Quinton got mad at me one time. Curtis Bush, who worked at the Sabine Clinic at the same time I did, was having trouble with boys stealing some things around his house. I had a five shot .38 pistol that I had brought home from the Korean War and I let him borrow it. About thirty minutes later, Quinton came with my pistol and he was mad. He had stopped Curtis and found a six pack of beer and my pistol in his truck. He gave me a good chewing out about it.

"Quinton had a man in jail one time who was hurt and needed sewing up. He called me and I went down, and the man was really belligerent. Quinton handcuffed him to a table so I could sew him up.

"I was traveling down Highway 171 one night, very late. I passed where Dr. J. Lane Sauls lived at the time and something told me there was something on the side of the road. I turned around, went back and there was this old drunk lying there. I called Quinton; he came out and put him in jail.

"Quinton called me one night to ride with him. We went out in the country, and there were two families that lived across the road from each other. They were kinfolks, but they were shooting across the road at each other with shotguns, rifles, and pistols. It was like the Hatfield and McCoy feud. Quinton didn't do anything. He just wanted me to see it.

"One time Quinton was in the quarters in Zwolle. He had gone to arrest a man. The man stuck a shotgun barrel out the door. Quinton just walked up on the porch, took the shotgun away from the man, and arrested him.

"If Quinton got a call about a stray dog, he would put the dog in the trunk of his car and go to the dump. He would open the trunk and if the dog could get away before Quinton got his gun, loaded it and shot, it was home free. I guess you could say he gave the dog a free and unbiased trial, but he was a crack shot."

JOE PAT SEPULVADO of Zwolle: "When I worked for Quinton for about two years, no one on the force liked to go into the quarters to arrest a suspect, because there was always trouble. Quinton had already had his stroke during that time and was not in good physical condition. If he were around, he would always go make the arrest with us. We would drive up to the house and he would holler from the patrol car, 'Come on out' and he would call the person's name, 'You are under arrest and you know better than to cause me any trouble.' The person would just come out and get in the back seat of the car. I never once saw anyone give him any trouble. He was that well respected, even though they knew he was not physically able to apprehend them."

NOEL TORRES, Zwolle school bus driver: "I loved and respected him. He was a good man and a fair man. When I was in high school and some of us were spinning wheels or drag racing, he would take us to his office and talk to us. He was like a Daddy. When he got through he would say, 'I don't want to see you here again.'

"One time Noble Marshal Willis Webb caught some of us watching a drag race from the side of the road. He didn't catch the racers, but he charged the spectators with blocking the highway and took us to

Zwolle. Mr. Brandon lectured us and told us to respect our parents. Then he tore up the tickets. He told us he was only going to do that one time; the next time the charges would stand. He wanted kids to straighten up and do right.

"On time Mr. Brandon took my husband, Kenneth, home because he had been showing out in Zwolle. He gave Kenneth's car keys to Mrs. Torres and told him to go to bed and quit worrying his mother. He told Mrs. Torres to give the keys back to Kenneth the next day.

"Quinton was strong and stern, but he wanted to teach you a lesson. He took time with people. That's why he could handle the town by himself. He cared for people and loved them."

Chapter 60

His Friends Remember

"What meant so much to Quinton over the years, were some of the boys who grew up in Zwolle, would leave and then come back and tell him how much he had done that helped them grow up and mature and become good citizens."
—*Mrs. Nannie Brandon*

DONNA SMITH AMMONS of Many: "I was put to the test the first time I met Mr. Brandon. I guess I passed with flying colors, because I proved to the gruff-voiced chief that I was willing to do what had to be done to complete a task. Late one night in the early 1970's I got a call from the sheriff's office. They needed a photographer at a crime scene. I had only worked at *The Sabine Index* for less than a year and was eager to prove myself. I rushed to the sheriff's office and they had a deputy there to take me onto a darkened country road where a man had been shot and killed.

"By the time I had accessed the scene, my eyes were as big as saucers. Deputies were all around conducting their investigation and trying to secure the scene. In the midst of all the activity lay a bare-chested dead man. 'Come here,' the gruff-voiced chief said, nodding to me. I stepped forward. 'I need some pictures,' he said, indicating the body on the ground. I began snapping away.

" 'I need some close up shots of the bullet hole,' he barked. I swallowed hard, took a deep breath, and knelt beside the body. Click, click, click went the shutter on the camera. Thump, thump, thump went my heart.

"When I stood up, I looked back at Chief Brandon. He was smiling. I had proven to him that I wasn't afraid or intimidated. After that we were friends. He always provided the information I needed for stories and he always had a kind word for me wherever we met. He was a colorful character and a man I respected.

"Years later, his daughter Becky and I were talking and I related the story to her. She confirmed he was testing me. 'He wanted to see what you were made of, Donna,' she said. I'll never forget that night or Quinton Brandon."

GLENWOOD BULLARD, Zwolle: "Quinton was well known everywhere. One time when I was in high school, he had a new police car, a 1966 Chevy Impala, with two doors, a four-speed transmission—a real sports car. All the kids were excited. I asked him about it one day and he replied, 'I'm gonna let my hair grow long, get me a pair of fancy sun glasses, and blend right in.'"

MRS. EDITH J. PALMER of Zwolle: "I was raised in Zwolle and my daddy, Ed Jones, had been marshal for a brief time in the 1930's. There was a rule that nice girls from nice families didn't wear shorts in Zwolle. I had graduated from high school and was going to Northwestern in Natchitoches. On a return trip home, I stopped at Frank Oakerson's station and I had my short shorts on. Mr. Brandon came over and told me to go home and get some clothes on. I was afraid of him, by reputation, of course. My daddy came home after work that night and he already knew I had been in downtown Zwolle with my short shorts. The point is, Mr. Brandon knew what was going on. He knew what the young people were doing. He knew what was going on in the quarters. He kept up with it all."

Mrs. Palmer continued with another story: "The day Bill (her late husband) had his accident, I was in Dallas, Texas with Scott, who was there for college testing. It was about 9:00 a.m. and the phone rang. It was Quinton, who said, 'You need to come home. Bill was in a bad accident.' I said, 'What happened?' He started crying. Quinton was real tender hearted. He said, 'You need to come home immediately.' We hung up and immediately the phone rang again. It was Quinton. He said, 'We're moving Bill to Shreveport; meet us up there.' He went and got my mother and Melissa out of school and stayed with them in Shreveport until I got there."

ROBERT DAVIDSON, DeSoto sheriff's investigator: "When I went to work for District Attorney James Lynn Davis as an investigator, it took about a year before Quinton trusted me, but after that he would do anything for me. He knew everything there was to know about Zwolle and the people who lived around there. If I needed to question someone up there, I'd call him and he would have him or her in his office when I wanted them there. That man had the total respect of the people. When he talked, they listened."

RUBY LEONE EBARB, Rosevine, Texas: "I grew up in Zwolle. Mr. Brandon was a very good man. He stood by his badge and the law. I never knew anything bad about him. My sister, Gertrude Leone Mullin lives in Utica, New York, and she and I thank the Lord we had an officer like him and that is from the heart."

MARGUERITE B. FERGUSON, Zwolle: In a letter in the April 19, 1979, issue of *The Index*, she wrote: "Many times citizens make derogatory remarks about our public servants, especially the police. We do not take the time to give them a pat on the back or tell them when a job is well done. Several days ago I was involved in an unfortunate incident in which I had to call the Zwolle police. These men did a superb job and traced every available clue. They went beyond the call of duty. I appreciate the diligent work of the Zwolle police."

Chapter 61

More Stories

*"Then he'd always tell me I'm going to heaven,
and that's worth a dollar to me."*
—Quinton Brandon

In a story in the June 7, 1973 issue of *The Sabine Index*, Brandon brought up the matter of Frank (Dummy) Rivers, who was sixty-four, a mute, practically blind, whom he termed "a child of the town."

"Every month he borrows a dollar from me," Brandon said. "When he gets his check, he always comes and tries to pay me back. He knows I won't take it. Then he always tells me I'm going to heaven and that's worth a dollar to me."

Mayor Roger Lopez told a story related to him by Allen Rivers. Lopez said, "Allen and his father were doing some construction work at the city hall. In order to reach the jail, you had to go through the courtroom. He and his father heard some racket in the courtroom and went in.

Lopez continued, "Glen Ebarb, a deputy, and a man were squared off. The black man had been arrested and as Glen was approaching the jail, he jerked loose and picked up a broom. He raised the broom to use as a weapon and when Glen put his hand on his pistol, he would lower the broom. It was sort of a stand off. The man was saying he was coming out and Glen was refusing to move and let him out."

Concluding the story, Lopez said, "About that time, Mr. Brandon came walking up and with his gruff voice said, 'What in the hell is going on in here?' The black man dropped his broom and started sweeping the floor. Mr. Brandon walked over, caught him by the arm, and walked him back to the jail and locked him up."

James Napier of Zwolle said one time there was a prisoner who escaped from the jail in Zwolle. Napier said, "Quinton was chasing him and caught him in Converse. I was right behind him in my state police car. When I got there, Quinton was whipping him with his lead slapper."

"How dare you escape from my jail," Napier said Brandon admonished the prisoner. "Quinton took it very personal. He didn't think anybody ought to escape from his jail."

Sheriff Guffey Lynn Pattison remembered how Brandon loved a good prank. The sheriff related: "One night Jimmy Ray Pleasant and I slipped up to the police station in Zwolle and took Wayne Ebarb's patrol car and hid it. We then called the dispatcher at the sheriff's office in Many and reported some kind of disturbance in Zwolle. We hid and watched as Wayne came running out of the station only to find his patrol car gone.

"Sometime later, Jimmy Ray and I were in Zwolle and Quinton made an attempt to catch us and pay us back for what we had done. I ran, but he caught Jimmy Ray. He took him back to the 'calaboose' and locked him up. It was hot summer time and not only did he jail him, Quinton turned on the heater. He kept him there about an hour. When Jimmy Ray come out, he had his shirt off and was wringing wet with sweat."

Pleasant said he recalled the event well and added, "Quinton brought me a hamburger while he had me locked up. I was hungry and wanted it. It looked good, but the problem was he put it on the floor in the hallway just out of my reach."

Another story Lopez told happened in the Blue Lake area. Said Lopez, "Leonard (Monk) Sepulvado was in a bar and got into a fight. He went home and got a gun to go back to the bar. His wife, Lucille Sepulvado, started fighting him, trying to keep him from getting the gun and going back. In the fight, he accidentally shot her. She fell to the floor and he thought she was dead. The children ran out of the house."

Lopez continued, "Sepulvado told me this story himself on the way back from Shreveport. He barricaded himself in the house because he felt like the officers were going to kill him. The sheriff's deputies were there and he refused to come out. It was a stand off. Marshal Brandon found out about the situation and went out there."

"Mr. Brandon went up to the picket fence and hollered to Monk that he was coming in to get him," Lopez said. "Monk said he raised the gun up twice to shoot Mr. Brandon. Deputy Truitt Walden had walked off to the side. He was talking to Monk. Mr. Brandon's only words were, 'I'm coming in to get you.' He walked up, kicked the door down and went in and got him. Monk said he raised the gun up to shoot, but he knew Mr. Brandon would not shoot him, but he might pistol-whip him. He feared he might be shot by the sheriff's deputies."

Napier said that one time he, Wayne Ebarb, and Glen Ebarb were at city hall. He told this story, "Quinton stayed with us and two couples came in. They had been in a round and they came in for Quinton to settle the dispute. One of the men said the word, 'damn.' Quinton made a fist and hit the desk and looked the man in the face. 'What did you say?' he asked. 'Sir?' was the reply. Quinton then said, "I want you to know this is a damn police station and we'll not have any of the damn cussing in here."

Lopez said one Sunday Brandon had been deer hunting. A man, who had either been on drugs or drinking, was involved in a dispute with his family. He fired a shotgun off and the family ran out of the house. Then he barricaded himself in."

"The Zwolle deputies tried to talk him out and he wouldn't come out," Lopez said. "Mr. Brandon came in from deer hunting and found out what was going on. He went to the house, kicked the door down, went in and brought the man out. It turned out he had an empty shotgun."

Napier pointed out Brandon never minced words. "He had a unique voice when he came in over the radio," Napier said. "Quinton had an old tube type 39.5 band radio and when he keyed the mike you could hear it all over the state. He radioed me to go on the east side of Zwolle and pick up a man. I replied, 'Okay, papaw, I'll take care of it.'"

"Quinton replied, 'Watch the son of a b——, he carries a knife in his back pocket,'" Napier related. "I arrested the man, checked his back pocket, and fortunately this time found no knife."

Chapter 62

More Stories They Tell

"Guff, I thought you done got you one."
—Brandon to Sheriff Pattison

MAYOR LOPEZ: "My father had a store in Zwolle where I worked a couple of years. This happened years ago. One day a black man, Leo Cook, came by and we were talking about Mr. Brandon. There was a two story building in Sabine Quarters, the bottom floor was a cafe and the upstairs had rooms they rented out and the blacks would go up there and gamble, shoot dice, and what have you. Leo had worked until noon one day and had gone to the cafe and ordered himself a hamburger. While he was waiting, he saw a black man in a U.S. Navy uniform. Some of those in the cafe said that he had been popping off about how bad he was, and what all he had been through.

"Shortly, they heard noise outside and when they went to look, they saw Mr. Brandon and the sailor in a tussle. They fell to the ground and were rolling around, and Mr. Brandon called for some help. Nobody would assist. Some were scared of Mr. Brandon, and some were scared of the sailor. They all sat back and watched.

"Finally Mr. Brandon got the sailor handcuffed and put him in the patrol car and left. Leo said he went upstairs to shoot dice and gamble. After an hour and a half, he got ready to leave and when he came out, Mr. Brandon was parked there in his patrol car.

"He called Leo over to the car. He opened the door and told him to get in. Mr. Brandon took Leo to jail and locked him up. The next day, Sunday, Mayor H. M. Burkhalter came down and Quinton took him through the jail and told him what each person was charged with. When they came to his cell, Leo asked, 'Mr. Brandon, what am I charged with?' The reply, "I'm charging you with drunk driving. I'm going to teach you folks to help me the next time I holler at one of you."

SHERIFF GUFFEY LYNN PATTISON: "Quinton called me over one time to help him arrest a guy who had gotten out of the army and had mental problems. He'd run every time an officer tried to arrest him. We went to the house and found him on the bed. We didn't put the handcuffs on him and I saw him eyeing the door. He took off running and I was right behind him.

"Quinton stayed on the porch. As I ran behind the man, Quinton pulled his gun and fired in the air. By that time, the man had reached the fence and was trying to climb it. I pulled my gun and fired into the air. The man fell to the ground as if he had been shot.

"Quinton and I just stopped. We knew we hadn't shot him, but we couldn't figure out what had happened. I went up to the man and saw his eyes blink and knew he was all right. I told Quinton he was okay. Quinton remarked, 'Guff, he always called me Guff, I thought for a minute you had done got you one.'"

SABINE DEPUTY, retired, who asked to remain anonymous: "This old boy had killed a fellow and his trial had ended in Many. The judge had given him life without the benefit of parole. After the sentencing, some of the law officers were standing outside the courtroom near the elevator. They brought the prisoner out by us and he glared at Quinton, who looked at him and said, "George, I'll be dead when you come back to Zwolle, but so will you."

Chapter 63

The Brandon Form of Justice

"Due Process was a foreign language to
Quinton Brandon."
—-Don Burkett, Sabine-DeSoto DA

You won't find out much about the police work those old timers did," R. V. Bolton of Leesville, a friend of Quinton Brandon and a retired state trooper said. "They had to do things in an unorthodox manner, things a policeman wouldn't be able to do now. Subsequently, they had a code of silence about the cases worked and how they accomplished their work."

In a nutshell, that tells the story. You will not find out the entire story, but you can learn bits and pieces. Here are some.

"He interpreted the laws to see that justice was done," Natchitoches Attorney Jack O. Brittain said of Brandon. Brittain represented an insurance company in suits, which were filed against Brandon. "I thought a lot of him as an individual. His idea in the way he operated was to create a better community."

Brittain continued, "He was a good law officer, but he was tough. He didn't take anything off anyone. He was brave. He was a quick thinker and a take-charge kind of man. He was a fatherly type to criminals. He would treat them tough enough to see they learned a lesson, but he wouldn't kill their spirit. He toned whatever he did with mercy."

Mayor Roger Lopez said that some people accused Brandon of getting kickbacks. Said Lopez, "I don't believe he did, if you will look at his life style."

Continuing, Lopez stated, "Quinton told a story of stopping a guy for bootlegging one time. He always asked for their driver's license first. Quinton said when the guy brought out the license, he had a roll of bills in his wallet. He told Quinton, 'If you don't look in the back of my truck, this is all yours.' Quinton said to him, 'Follow me to jail.' And he booked him."

Another time, Lopez said when he was on the town council he would patrol with Brandon at night. "He told me when he was patrolling alone and would stop a car and it would be someone he didn't know, the first thing he would do was ask for the driver's license. He would put the license in his pocket. His thinking was that if the occupant of the car shot him, they wouldn't think to get out and get the driver's license. He would have proof on him of who shot him."

"I saw him take his slap jack one time, throw a boy between his legs, and whip him," Pete McCormick recalled.

Many Chief of Police Dean Lambert pointed out, "Quinton, of course, was a take charge type of guy. He never would flinch from dispersing swift justice. He would not let small technicalities get in his way. That was something to be dealt with later, if ever. Sometime in Zwolle the legal process was not enough to keep someone from acting up, but the legal system and Quinton usually were."

Lambert continued, "I'm not sure if Quinton could have policed the years before his era or after his time, but I do know, he was the man for the time he was there. Through his strict law enforcement, Quinton brought Zwolle to a position that made it possible for the good citizens to control their own destiny."

Bob Key said that just because a criminal left Brandon's jurisdiction didn't mean it was over. "Quinton would go after them," Key said. "He would chase them to Texas or anywhere else. He had the reputation that if you were in trouble with Quinton Brandon, you were in trouble."

Former Sabine Sheriff Alfice Brumley said Brandon deserved the title, "The Man Who Tamed Zwolle," because of "...the type of policing he did." Brumley continued, "He controlled the town. All you had to do was call on him and he took care of it. He was a one man operation for a long time."

Wayne Ebarb said, "Back in those days, Quinton could dispense justice. He and George Cook were a lot alike in how they did policing. In the latter years there were some lawsuits against him."

Paul Maxey said, "He was fair. He didn't favor anyone. My younger brother was rowdy. Quinton put him in jail many times. Big, little or whatever, he would tie into any man. He would try to manhandle them, if he had to."

Howard Brandon, Quinton's brother, said at some point in the lawman's career that he arrested his own brother, Bob, his cousin, Stan, and his own son, Jerry.

In an interview with Richard Munson published in the *Morning Advocate* on March 26, 1978, Brandon showed the enlarged knuckles on his right hand and said he switched to fighting with open hands after he broke his fists while trying to convince a fighter he was under arrest.

Brandon stated, "I've had to use a lot of force other than my fists at times. A lot of times I was forced to use the gun. I carry a .357 heavy-duty magnum and use it as a club when I have to. I never carried a blackjack. One man was coming at me with a knife and when I hit him with the gun, it went off and hit him in the neck. But he wasn't seriously injured."

The lawman said he once had a gunfight with another man but the man escaped in the dark after three or four shots was fired. On another occasion, while he was helping sheriff's deputies arrest a man wanted for armed robbery in Dallas, Texas, he wounded the wanted man. "I shot that man in the right arm, but I had to," he stated. "I shot a shotgun out of his right hand."

The article continued, "Things have changed a lot since the old days. 'Most of our arrests are for drunk driving on weekends and people don't resist much anymore,' he said. 'I remember one occasion when the state police were chasing a car and asked me

Brandon through the Years

SABINE INDEX PHOTO

July 1967

SABINE INDEX PHOTO

August 1981

SABINE INDEX PHOTO

March 1972

MRS. NANNIE BRANDON PHOTO

November 1984

SABINE INDEX PHOTO

March 1974

BARBARA CLARY PHOTO

Circa 1990

to set up a roadblock. When I got the car stopped, there were five men in it and they all piled out, spoiling for a fight. I had five of them to fight, but I had things under control when the state police got there.' "

Concluding the story, Brandon said, "I didn't get a lick put on me in that one. When I saw what I was in for, I used this magnum as a club and when I'd hit one, he'd go down and stay down. You don't see much action like that now."

Robert Davidson said in 1978 he was in Zwolle and Brandon was questioning a boy about some case. "I don't remember the details," Davidson related, "but Quinton couldn't get a confession out of him. He took the boy back to the bathroom and put his head in the commode and flushed it. He did that a time or two and bobbed the boy's head in and out of the commode. It didn't take but three or four minutes and Quinton had his confession."

"Another time I remember is when Quinton had a boy who was involved in a burglary," Davidson said. "He couldn't get a confession out of the boy, so he took the boy to his mother. Quinton told the Mother all about it and the woman said, 'Let me talk to him a minute.' She came back a few minutes later and the boy told Quinton all about it."

Frank Eason, who managed Peoples Furniture in Many, remembered the help he got from Brandon. Eason told, "I had delivered a load of furniture to a family in Zwolle. We didn't get a down payment and couldn't find the people at home to get the furniture back."

Eason continued, "I called Quinton about it. He said to come up and bring my truck and he would get the furniture. We got to the house and there was no one at home and the door was locked. I asked Quinton what we were gonna do."

The story ends, with Eason saying, "Quinton didn't answer. He just flat kicked that door down and we flat got that furniture."

Sabine-DeSoto District Attorney Don Burkett said he remembered a story at the time when he was in high school at Stanley. He related, "Our basketball team was playing Zwolle one night. Some of the boys from Stanley had been watching TV and the newest thing was protesters who would lie down in front of the law officers. That was around 1969-1970."

Burkett finished the story, "Stanley was getting its regular rooking by the local Zwolle basketball referees and some of the boys who were in the stands decided to protest. Some of the boys had come over from Northwestern to see Stanley play. The boys were taunting someone. Quinton decided to go in the stands and arrest them. Well, they laid down. The last I saw of them, Quinton was dragging them out the door by the feet."

Sheriff Pattison recalled, "I walked into the city hall one day and heard a commotion in Quinton's office. He had a fellow bent over the desk, his pants dropped and arms outstretched and he was whipping him with a four-inch gun belt. Brandon's nephew, Dr. George D. Brandon of Leesville, had a like story, saying, "He reportedly used an old pistol belt on recalcitrant individuals to bring them into line."

Dr. Brandon also has other stories: "He reportedly cured fainting prisoners by cranking up the fire truck and turning the hose on them. After this was done a few times, the incidence of fainting dropped drastically." Another story: "Quinton once hid under a porch on a stakeout. This woman came out on the porch and urinated and, as he told it, it ran through the cracks onto his face."

Another time, the nephew said, "Quinton once broke into a house where all eleven people were involved in illegal gambling. Since the patrol car couldn't hold them all, he marched them down the street to jail." Dr. Brandon also remembered, "When force had to be used, his favorite was to hit the individual under the jaw with the palm of his hand."

Concluding, Dr. Brandon related, "He once

stopped a suspect for possession and sale of alcohol. After a thorough search and finding nothing, he followed the car for a short time. Stopping it a second time, he opened the hood and found bottles of whiskey taped inside to the motor and frame."

Rocky Brandon said a lot of men have told him about his father arresting them "...and talking to them in that voice, but with concern and how much they appreciated him straightening them out." He continued, "Dad always could do more with his lectures than others could do with punishment. I always hated for him to talk because he would make you feel awful. He was a good investigator because he'd make you tell him the truth."

Rocky recalled that once David Peacock was in jail on Christmas day. "Daddy brought him home to eat dinner with us because he couldn't stand for him to be in jail," he remembered. "After dinner, he went back to jail, but until he died, he never forgot that."

Another time, Rocky related, "Daddy had Jerry and Stanley Brandon put in jail once for fighting. He was always stricter with us than others because he never wanted it said he showed favoritism. A trooper picked them up and called Dad wanting to know what to do and Dad said, 'Put them in jail.' When Jerry got out of jail, he awoke me, and told me what happened. I was ten or twelve at the time. I was told never to allow anyone to badmouth Dad without kicking their ass, or Jerry would kick mine. No one ever did in my presence. One time the fight started because someone cussed Daddy and Jerry said he would gladly do the same thing over. Jerry and Daddy were a lot closer than Daddy and me, but I respected him and was always proud to say I was his son."

"I ran into Joe (Bud) Greer and he told me a story about being arrested for fighting when he was younger," Rocky continued. "Daddy came into the jail and asked Bud if he was hungry. Bud's smart reply was, 'Hell no, I don't want none of your damn hamburgers with mustard all over them.' Bud was thinking his grandfather would come and get him out of jail. Daddy politely left the cell that day and came back two days later. Daddy asked Bud if he was hungry and he gladly said that he wanted a hamburger no matter how much mustard it had on it. Many times I was with Daddy while he got hamburgers for prisoners. He always let them get cold and hard. One day I asked why and he told me he didn't want any man to say he came to the Zwolle jail to get a meal."

In an interview published in the September 6, 1979, *Sabine Index*, Brandon said he'd seen a lot of changes in law enforcement over the years. "Back in the early days a man was tried on his guilt or innocence," he said. "Nowadays a person is tried on technicalities. Our court procedure has changed. Now we have to think about the suspect's rights and forget about the victim's rights."

He concluded, "Every time the Supreme Court hands down a ruling, it's against law enforcement. There have been more changes in court rulings than in law enforcement."

Chapter 64

The Legend

"He was a good servant of the people."
—Mrs. Nannie Brandon

A lawman like Quinton Brandon would have to become a sort of folk hero and a legend, even in his own time. And nothing can create a legend any better than the stories those who knew him tell. Here is a sampling.

RALPH SHELTON, Mansfield: "I got shot in May, 1957. DeSoto Deputy James W. Gamble got killed. We were on Highway 171, a mile south of Kickapoo, when we observed a car with the right front wheel off the road and it was on high center and the other wheel was just spinning. It had no license plate and we figured someone had just bought a new car and was going to turn around and got in trouble. We stopped to help.

"When we got out, all shooting broke loose. The two men who did it were arrested. One was sentenced to life and was out of prison in six years. The other got out of jail here and was later put in a Texas prison where a ranger shot him for trying to run away. When our incident happened, Quinton came to help us. He worked with us about ten days, while at the same time he took care of his office back in Zwolle. I'll never forget him for that."

ROBERT DAVIDSON: "In April, 1973, I was working undercover in Leesville. In fact, it was my birthday, April 13, and I was on my way back to Mansfield. I had been speeding and didn't realize it. Trooper Lee Raymond Isgitt had radioed Quinton and he had a roadblock set up at the railroad crossing on Highway 171.

"I stopped and Quinton came from behind his

patrol car with a sawed-off shotgun and he pumped a load into it. He told me to raise my hands and get out of the car. I told him I had a seat belt on and a pistol on the floorboard. He got the pistol and I told him I was a law officer. He asked to see my identification. I told him it was in the trunk. When he opened the trunk, the first thing he found was a fully automatic carbine.

"When he found out who I was, he gave my guns back, but he wrote me two tickets. He told me nobody speeded through Zwolle and got away with it. I had to end up paying the speeding ticket."

MARVIN MELTON, probation officer in Mansfield and former state trooper and DeSoto deputy: "I first met him in 1956. I went down to do some undercover work for Quinton on the purchase of illegal alcohol. I remember he told me about a shootout he got into with a fellow. Quinton had confronted this man, who pulled out an automatic pistol. Quinton hit the ground rolling and ended up shooting the man. He didn't kill him, but he did get his man."

JACK BRITTAIN, Natchitoches Attorney: "I remember one story about Quinton arresting a drunk. Quinton had him half in the patrol car and half out when the drunk grabbed Quinton's gun. Thinking quickly, Quinton just slammed the car door on the man's head. Sounds like police brutality, but it wasn't. It was an act that may have saved Quinton's life."

PETE ABINGTON, chairman of the board, Peoples State Bank in Many: "When I was younger, we'd hang around Zwolle. We all liked his daughter, Lorene. In a subtle way, Quinton let us know about his jail. If you saw it, you sure didn't want to spend a night in it. It wasn't a Holiday Inn. He'd get the word back to you. It was only a clean-cut young man like Calvin Jones who could end up marrying Lorene with Quinton being happy about it."

ALFICE BRUMLEY: "I recall one time Quinton and I were running a search warrant for bootleg whiskey. We found it under a chicken house. He always reminded me of a big boss with that loud voice. You knew what he said was right and with the force behind it, you knew he meant it. Yes, he was the last of an era. I made many arrests with him. He knew the people and knew them well. He knew the criminal element. He knew his people totally."

W. F. JETER, JR.: "This happened down at the old Frank Gandy place. We got a call that a deputy had let a prisoner run away. Sheriff George Cook brought in his bloodhounds. We loaded Quinton's horse and headed down that way. I was driving the truck and when we got there, this man had a shotgun and had it drawn and pointed our way. Quinton got his horse out of the trailer and just rode up there and shot the shotgun out of the man's hand. I kidded him that I thought it was just a lucky shot. But, Quinton was a good shot."

WAYNE EBARB: "One time they were having the threat of a riot at the Apollo Apartments in Many. They called us. When something rough came up, they'd always call Quinton. He knew he was being used. Lots of other officers were scared, but they'd call us and we'd go. He always said if we needed them, they'd come help us. Anyway, when we got to Many, Quinton took charge. We arrested a few and that put an end to the riot."

"Another time, he arrested a boy on drug charges. The boy had on dirty clothes; he had long hair and a beard, and needed a bath. Quinton found out that he had a baby at home. He felt sorry for him. Quinton gave him a good lecture and told him, 'I'm going to try to help you.' He then told the boy he better get some clean clothes, cut his hair, shave his beard off, and take a bath."

JAMES NAPIER of Zwolle: "I tried to help the sheriff's office and city police departments as I could during my work. One time I heard a call from Zwolle. It was from J. O. Kimbrell and he reported a black male was drunk. Quinton was not in town, so I answered the call. It was my first day on duty.

"I found Monk Richardson. He's a living example that a person who can survive on hamburgers three times a day. He was always turning himself in when he was drunk. He'd go to jail and they'd lock him up. He just stayed too long at J. O.'s that day.

"I told him he was under arrest. He looked at me, cocked his head and said, 'You can't arrest me.'

"I told him, 'I'm a state trooper and I can and will arrest you.' He replied, 'The only man who can arrest me is Quinton Brandon.' As state troopers, we were taught to put handcuffs on anybody we arrested. I had to tussle to get them on him."

"He told me, 'Mr. Brandon never put those on me.' I replied, 'I'm gonna put them on you.' His answer, 'I'm gonna tell Mr. Brandon on you.'

"I brought him to Many and locked him up. When Quinton heard about it, he came and got him out. He chewed me out. We called Quinton Papaw. I said to him, 'Papaw, I didn't know you didn't want me to arrest him.'

"Quinton finished the conversation by saying, 'You know that Monk stays in Zwolle.' "

MILTON McFERRIN: "Somebody started shooting at Quinton on the corner where Hoyt Maxey had a grocery store. When the shooting started, Quinton was on the corner and he went for a concrete water fountain for protection. I don't think he saw the other person well enough to recognize him, but he did have his suspicions." Maxey's son, Guy Wayne of Zwolle, stated, "Quinton showed me the place in the fountain where the bullet hit."

"Quinton went a lot with the Sabine Parish deputies when they had to go to Ward five," McFerrin said. "Somebody had taken possession of a house and wouldn't allow anybody in. The sheriff's department was there when Quinton arrived. This character was ready to shoot. He had his gun pulled. Quinton went right on in. He told the man, 'You don't want to shoot me,' as he took the gun away from him."

Chapter 65

The Legacy

"And when you go
To that better home, some day;
The only thing you'll take
Is what you gave away."
—Fallen Leaves

Without doubt, Quinton Brandon had lived long enough to see his mission of cleaning up the town of Zwolle accomplished. He had enjoyed talking about it, but more than that, he had enjoyed hearing others talk about it.

His name was known far and wide. A lot of folks didn't know him personally, but they knew him by reputation.

He had given the best years of his life to law enforcement. Folks who knew him remembered that first of all, he was always fair to everyone regardless of race, creed, or color. He was always firm, always said what he meant, and always meant what he said. One might fool around with some law enforcement officers, but one did not mess with Brandon.

So, his biggest legacy is the law and order he brought to Zwolle. And in the beginning, Brandon said that he had to fight every day just to stay there. He had been shot at, beat up, and knocked down, but he endured. His hard work and persistence made it easier for all law enforcement officers who followed him.

Speaking to Shreveport Journal reporter Gary Hines in 1978, Brandon said, "I hope my legacy to Zwolle will be one of equal treatment for everyone. We have the same law enforcement for everyone. When I first took over here, a black man couldn't walk through this town at night. That's been eliminated."

A second legacy Brandon left Zwolle was the

work he did on the Zwolle Cemetery. For twenty-five years he cared for and improved it. When he started, it was a jungle. Today, his work lives on at the Zwolle Cemetery.

Another legacy is the good deeds he had done for people all his life. Being born a country boy, Brandon learned early on the importance of being a good neighbor. Sometime city folks do not learn that lesson. But Brandon learned it and he never forgot it.

The writers of this book heard many stories of Brandon's goodness, many times to people he didn't even know. Stories abound of his buying groceries for needy folks, of his filling up a car with gasoline so somebody could be taken to the charity hospital in Shreveport, and of his locking someone in jail for the person's own good and then turning them loose the next day. And the stories go on and on.

Then a small part of his legacy is the love of the rodeos and the goat barbecues and the fond memories of these that he left with many of his friends. They still talk about those events with relish.

A very big legacy he left were the many warm friendships he developed over many years. People still talk about him with dignity, respect, love, and honor. He had many, many friends over a wide area.

Another important legacy, which was near and dear to his heart, was his love for America. He loved the flag and wanted it honored. He had fought in World War II and he knew first-hand the importance of freedom. He wanted everyone to know about and love this great country and to appreciate the freedoms all enjoy and sometime take for granted.

And last, but certainly not least, was the legacy he left his family. He was always known to look out for and take care of any matters his brothers and sisters and their families needed. He looked out for his mother and father until their deaths.

In his immediate family he always talked about how proud he was of his wife and their five children. He said that he was proud to have been able to send

318

three of his five children through college. He said that the other two could have had a college education had they chosen. From him, the children learned the value of honesty, the value of hard work, and the value of being true to one's self.

Brandon is gone, but his legacy lives on.

Chapter 66

The Legend Continues to Walk Tall

"And sometimes at night,
When the cold wind mourns
In a long black veil
She cries 'ore my bones."
—Lefty Frizzell Song

Close your eyes and you can hear the sound of steps coming toward you on the sidewalks of Zwolle. It is the dark of night. Look down and the street light shines on a pair of brown cowboy boots deliberately, confidently making those steps. Your eyes move upward and you see he is wearing the uniform of a law officer. You notice that four inch gun belt around his waist with the big black holster hanging on his right hip. In that holster hangs a .357 Smith and Wesson magnum. It is big; it is battle-scared; and it is impressive.

As he keeps coming toward you, on his chest you see an American flag sewn on his freshly starched and ironed shirt. He has always been proud of his country, his community, and his family. He is also proud of himself, but he tries not to let it show. On the other side of his chest proudly shines a badge. That badge means everything to him. Through the years he has lived for that badge, always; and at times, he has almost died for it.

Now you see his face. It is tough and weathered and scarred from the battles he has fought through the years. The lines in his face show he has done a lot of hard living. You look at his eyes. They are stern and cold, and hard. They are intimidating. It seems as if they could look a hole straight through you.

You look at his hands and they look swollen and out of shape from all the fights and scrapes he has had to be in for so many years.

You look at the face again. It is stern; it is solemn; it tells you this is a no nonsense kind of man. On his head sits that brown Stetson hat. He never went anywhere without it. He thought a good lawman always wore his hat. In his left hand he carries a neatly whittled hickory club. Guffey Lynn Pattison made that for him many years ago, when everyone was comparing him to the Walking Tall Sheriff, Buford Pusser of McNary County, Tennessee. He never used the club on anybody, but he carried it with him sometime.

He liked the attention folks paid him, although he didn't show it too much. He was just that kind of man. He just did not like to show his true feelings. Maybe that was right; maybe that was wrong, but anyway, that was the way he was.

As he comes closer, you hear him speak. It is that rough, gruff voice that has put fear in so many criminals for so many years. Some women thought of it as being sexy; the criminals never did.

He passes you and turns on another street. The sound of those boot steps fade gently into the warm summer night, but you know he is out there somewhere, walking the streets of Zwolle, making one more round. The wind blows gently across your face as you open your eyes and tears slowly run down your cheeks. You know that Quinton Brandon is gone, but you also know that the legacy and legend are still walking tall in Zwolle.

I'm A Policeman

(NOTE: Mrs. Quinton Brandon said the following was one of her late husband's favorites. The author of the piece is unknown.)

"Washington, Lincoln, Kennedy,
These Great Men have gone before me.
Their life's work is recorded in time,
But you'll never hear of the one that's mine.
I'm a Policeman, I have no name.
My work is measured by honor or shame.
Right or wrong, whatever I do,
I'm judged now, by people like you...
If I save a life, it's because I should.
If I make a mistake, then I'm no good.
You make mistakes, then why can't I?
Because if I do, someone could die...
If you break our law, in a "minor way,"
And believe me, you do, day after day,
And I take action and call you down,
Then you call me "Pig," all over Town.
But if I don't act, and look the other way,
Then just listen, to what they'll say.
Then I'm no good, a worthless bum.
This is how I'm judged by some...
Remember this and don't forget,
While I'm still breathing and walking yet,
I'll do my job, and do it well,
While you live you "Heaven" and I my "Hell"...
I've been spit at and stoned by my brothers.
Been laughed at, called "Pig" by others.
They don't understand what I'm trying to do,
Trying to keep order that's demanded by you...
Come along on patrol and help me some night.
You'll see that things aren't so sunny and bright.
There's a lot to be done and a lot to see,
So, put out your hand and come with me...
Help me to take a child in my arms,
A child that you say I'm to keep from harm.
Try not to listen, as he cries his last.
Hit by a drunk or one going too fast...
Or come along to Charlie Smith's,
His wife will whimper a lot of "ifs"

She'll tell you that Charlie had nothing to hide,
As you look at the mess of his suicide...
Headquarters calls, there's a domestic fight,
We'll turn our collar and make things right.
On this job you're Doctor, Friend and Confessor,
If you knew what's expected, you'd be a Professor.
I love my country...I always shall.
Don't sell her short, with me around, Pal.
Because deep down inside I've a great feeling of pride,
For this Great Land...I don't want a free ride...
So, if you're in trouble, no matter when or where,
Just give me a call and I'll be there,
Because you pay my salary, I hear it everyday.
But I don't hear from people that want to swap pay.
"Pig," stands for Prestige, Intelligence and Guts;
Got to have all three, no ifs, ands, or buts.
You like to hear this...You're anti-cop,
But think of all you have that I haven't got.
Want my job? Do you have dedication?
Some think it's one big happy vacation.
Ask my kids when they saw me last.
They remember their Dad, somewhere in the past...
Ask my wife what she thinks of this.
The part of life that we'll have to miss,
Because others come first, and then there's her,
But she's proud of me; I'm a Policeman...Sir.
This is all I ask from you,
Respect for my uniform, brown, green, or blue.
It's not the suit, or the man that's in it,
It's what we, as a people, want to "win it"
So when you see me...look over...say "Hi,"
Then listen close, you'll hear me sigh,
For, your small greeting has paid me well,
You've given "thanks" for my moments of hell...
Prestige, Intelligence, Guts...You say the word.
Washington, Lincoln, Kennedy have all been heard.
You'll hear from me, when you err,
That's because, I'm a policeman...Sir.

Note to the Reader

"Challenged and strengthened by the personal tribulations and tragedies of the Great Depression and World War II, we have been blessed as a nation, by a certain unusual caliber of individuals that rose to collective and unprecedented greatness.

"We are forever in their debt and can but hope that others shall be able to arise to the occasion as they pass from our midst."

- - - M. D. Morris

In the 1940's, a handful of Louisiana State Policemen comprising Troop H, worked out of Leesville, Louisiana. They had no office, but did their paper work out of their homes, a vacant boxcar, or wherever they could. Recognizing a need, the Morris family, donated land for an office. The troopers gathered material from various sources, and built their own office. This building still stands today, and currently houses the Vernon Parish Chamber of Commerce.

It was to this troop headquarters that a newly commissioned state trooper, Quinton Brandon, was first assigned. Born into a large family with meager means, reared during the economic challenges of the Great Depression, a veteran of the most devastating war Americans ever fought, he was thankful for the opportunity to have the job. He was to stay in law enforcement for the rest of his working life, and along the course of this career, he established himself as a principled man, bound by duty to uphold the law at any cost, but never forgetting his humble beginning, and empathy for others.

Quinton Brandon was to his family as all others, a husband, father, brother, uncle, or grandfather. We loved him, and received love in return. While proud of his fearless devotion to the law, his memory as all of these relationships, and what they meant to us individually and as a family, will always be foremost in our conscious thoughts. As a family, we will quietly and with dignity, remember him for all he was to us. We rejoice, that long ago, he publicly confessed his sins to our Creator, and is at rest with Him today, and our fervent prayer is to join him in eternity, as our Lord wills.

Mr. Robert Gentry, a respected journalist and publisher, of his own accord, has chosen to write this book, without solicitation from anyone. He and his co-author and Quinton's niece Patricia Brandon Martinez have carefully and meticulously researched official documents, newspaper articles, and conducted interviews in order to be historically accurate. Not all things in this work reflect favorably on my uncle, however, he was human, and had his failings as we all do. To insist on a whitewash, or to portray this man as anything more or less than he was would be an injustice to generations of readers yet to come, and compromise the integrity of the authors, a non-option.

As a family, we are grateful to Mr. Gentry, for his unswerving support to Quinton Brandon through the years, and we are grateful to he and Mrs. Martinez for their interest in preserving the legacy of one of many individuals who arose to the occasion when the need was there. It is a story that needs telling.

Dr. George D. Brandon
Leesville, Louisiana
January 22, 1999

Index

An Index of Pictures